JOURNAL FOR THE STUDY OF THE OLD TESTAMENT
SUPPLEMENT SERIES
196

Sheffield Academic Press

Corporate Responsibility in the Hebrew Bible

Joel S. Kaminsky

Journal for the Study of the Old Testament
Supplement Series 196

Copyright © 1995 Sheffield Academic Press

Published by
Sheffield Academic Press Ltd
Mansion House
19 Kingfield Road
Sheffield, S11 9AS
England

Typeset by Sheffield Academic Press
and
Printed on acid-free paper in Great Britain
by Bookcraft
Midsomer Norton, Somerset

British Library Cataloguing in Publication Data

A catalogue record for this book is available
from the British Library

ISBN 1-85075-547-7

CONTENTS

ACKNOWLEDGMENTS

I would like to take time to thank some of those people who were instrumental in helping me bring this book to completion. This project began as a dissertation under the guidance of Professor Jon D. Levenson. I cannot begin to express my gratitude to him. He has been instrumental in my intellectual growth and has been of immense help by reading and commenting on numerous drafts of this project. I am also very indebted to Professor John J. Collins who gave me a great deal of practical advice, and much of his personal time to read and reread a project which was not initiated under his tutelage. Professor Arthur Droge and the late Professor Gösta Ahlström participated in my intellectual development and provided many critical suggestions as this book took shape. Additionally, I wish to thank Gabriel Danzig, Terence Fretheim, Toni Schlesinger and Greg Spinner who assisted me by reading various portions of the manuscript and by taking the time to talk over certain ideas; my students who over the years provided a sounding board for my ideas, especially Louie Bernstein and Adam Phillips; James Hanson, Muriel Kolinsky and Gary Stansell who assisted me in the task of proofreading and solving grammatical problems; and the staff at Sheffield Academic Press for being so helpful, with special thanks to my Desk Editor Steve Barganski. All of the above improved this book in some way and saved me from many errors. Any errors or deficiencies that remain in this book are solely my fault. Finally, as a small token of my gratitude and love for them, I wish to dedicate this book to my mother and father, Charlotte and Elliott Kaminsky.

Author's Note: I have devocalized all occurrences of the Tetragrammaton throughout this manuscript in accord with Jewish practice.

ABBREVIATIONS

AB	Anchor Bible
AnBib	Analecta biblica
ANET	J.B. Pritchard (ed.), *Ancient Near Eastern Texts*
ARM	Archives royales de Mari
ASTI	*Annual of the Swedish Theological Institute*
BA	*Biblical Archaeologist*
BASOR	*Bulletin of the American Schools of Oriental Research*
Bib	*Biblica*
BJS	Brown Judaic Studies
BZ	*Biblische Zeitschrift*
BZAW	Beihefte zur *ZAW*
CBQ	*Catholic Biblical Quarterly*
ConBOT	Coniectanea biblica, Old Testament
CTM	*Concordia Theological Monthly*
EncJud	*Encyclopaedia Judaica*
GKC	*Gesenius' Hebrew Grammar*, ed. E. Kautzsch, trans. A.E. Cowley
HAT	Handbuch zum Alten Testament
HSM	Harvard Semitic Monographs
HTR	*Harvard Theological Review*
HUCA	*Hebrew Union College Annual*
ICC	International Critical Commentary
Int	*Interpretation*
JANESCU	*Journal of the Ancient Near Eastern Society of Columbia University*
JAOS	*Journal of the American Oriental Society*
JBL	*Journal of Biblical Literature*
JJS	*Journal of Jewish Studies*
JPSV	*Jewish Publication Society Version*
JR	*Journal of Religion*
JSOT	*Journal for the Study of the Old Testament*
JSOTSup	*Journal for the Study of the Old Testament*, Supplement Series
JTS	*Journal of Theological Studies*
NCB	New Century Bible
OBO	Orbis biblicus et orientalis
OTL	Old Testament Library
OTS	*Oudtestamentische Studiën*
PEQ	*Palestine Exploration Quarterly*
SBFLA	*Studii biblici franciscani liber annuus*

SBLDS	SBL Dissertation Series
SBLMS	SBL Monograph Series
SBT	Studies in Biblical Theology
SJLA	Studies in Judaism in Late Antiquity
SJT	*Scottish Journal of Theology*
TDOT	G.J. Botterweck and H. Ringgren (eds.), *Theological Dictionary of the Old Testament*
TS	*Theological Studies*
TynBul	*Tyndale Bulletin*
UF	*Ugarit-Forschungen*
UUÅ	Uppsala universitetsårsskrift
VT	*Vetus Testamentum*
ZAW	*Zeitschrift für die alttestamentliche Wissenschaft*
ZTK	*Zeitschrift für Theologie und Kirche*

INTRODUCTION

> Rabbi Simeon bar Yohai taught: There is a story about men who were sitting on a ship, one of them lifted up a borer and began boring a hole beneath his seat. His companions said to him: 'What are you sitting and doing?' He replied to them: 'What concern is it of yours, am I not drilling under my seat?' They said to him: 'But the water will come up and flood the ship for all of us'.[1]

This story reflects upon an important and often misunderstood dimension of Israelite religion. I call this dimension corporate responsibility, by which I mean the way in which the community as a whole is liable for the actions committed by its individual members. Corporate responsibility is an important concept because it is a fundamental theological principal in ancient Israel that God relates not just to autonomous Israelites, but to the nation as a whole. Inasmuch as God relates to the community as a whole, he holds each member of the nation to some level of responsibility for the errors of any other member of that community. Not only is one responsibile for one's own proper behavior, but one must also actively prevent others from sinning.

Scholarship over the past century has frequently interposed a series of modern biases into discussions surrounding the relationship between the individual and the community in ancient Israel and thus has rarely examined these ideas from a neutral standpoint. There has been a recurring tendency to prefer ethical elements in ancient Israelite thought over more ritualistic ways of thinking, which has led to a characterization of ritualistic ideas as either primitive holdovers that were eventually superseded or as late priestly tendencies that signal the death knell of the true spiritual religion of ancient Israel. Thus instances of corporate punishment, which often occur in contexts that involve ritual violations (Josh. 7 and 2 Sam. 24), are usually regarded by scholars as theologically troubling, and consequently they are treated as aberrations and exceptions that do not reflect the higher aspects of Israel's religion. There has also

---

1.   *Lev. R.* 4.6.

been an equally problematic tendency to exaggerate the importance of certain late texts that give a greater emphasis to the place of individuals in their relationship to God. These texts have frequently been seen to signal a radical shift toward a new individualism that rejected the older corporate ways of thinking. Both the tendency to marginalize the importance of corporate ideas and the movement to highlight texts that appear to emphasize the individual probably stem from a common modern bias that individualistic ideas are superior to more community based conceptions of identity. It has been assumed that a theology of divine retribution that is more individualistic is superior to one that is more corporate in nature. This has led scholars to read Israelite religious ideas in an anachronistic fashion that highlights those ideas that fore-shadow various contemporary ideas and plays down those ideas that are currently out of theological fashion. This has resulted in giving us an unbalanced and inaccurate view of a set of ideas that are central to any proper understanding of ancient Israelite theology.

This study is intended to investigate the ways in which the various misunderstandings surrounding the notion of divine retribution occurred and to provide a corrective by evoking a clearer and more accurate picture of the ways in which the individual and the community were related together in ancient Israel, especially in regard to divine retribution. I will argue the following theses:

1. The tendency to view corporate ideas as rare, marginal or exceptional is in fact mistaken. Ancient Israel considered it quite normal for divine and sometimes even human punishment to be corporate in nature. Corporate ideas of retribution are not confined to a few unusual cases; rather, a corporate understanding of punishment pervades the major theological systems found in the Hebrew Bible.

2. In order to show just how central corporate ideas are, I will demonstrate that Deuteronomy and the deuteronomistic history employ corporate notions of reward and punishment in their portrayal of Israel's history. It will be argued that this has occurred because the notion of covenant, which occupies a central role in both Deuteronomy and the deuteronomistic history, maintains a corporate understanding of reward and punishment.

3. One should in no way be surprised that the larger theological systems in which the notion of covenant plays such an important role conceive of punishment as corporate in nature. After all, these larger theological constructs were partially built upon, and continued to

maintain, certain ancient religious conceptions that are strongly corporate in nature. Although these ancient religious ideas may have undergone some development once they were placed in a larger covenantal framework, they still remained substantially intact and thus continued to exert a powerful influence over Israelite conceptions of reward and punishment throughout the biblical period.

4. Certain late biblical texts did challenge some of the theological implications that flow from the notion of corporate punishment and proposed other conceptions of how divine retribution functions. Because these texts focus more strongly upon the individual, they have often been misinterpreted as signaling the rise of a new individualism in ancient Israel. There are two flaws in this position. (a) Although these later biblical texts do focus more upon the individual, it is fallacious to make an evolutionary argument that presumes that texts that highlight the individual are always later than those that focus upon the corporate whole. One should note that many of the most highly developed corporate ideas are from the later biblical period. (b) Although one should clearly acknowledge the concern with the fate of the individual that these texts espouse, a contextual reading of these texts suggests that they are primarily interested in the individual as a member of the larger corporate whole.

5. Only after having clarified the various ideas implicit in the Israelite understanding of the relationship between the individual and the community in relation to divine retribution, in a way that evokes the internal logic of Israelite thought without any modern value judgments, will I then place these ideas into juxtaposition with contemporary preferences. It is at this point that I will explore whether Israel's theological ideas of divine retribution are better, worse or simply different from our own. Here I intend to argue that the modern bias that grades texts that are more individualistic as theologically superior to those that are more corporate is highly dubious. This is true not only because this bias interferes with making an accurate assessment of Israelite ideas, but because there are compelling reasons to argue that the ideas underpinning the corporate approach are as theologically perceptive, if not more so, than the individualistic ethic that informs much of biblical theology. In no way am I interested in fostering a return to the norms by which ancient Israel lived. But I do intend to argue that ancient Israel's fundamental insight into the fact that we are all our 'brother's keeper' could provide a corrective to many of our current philosophical

and political tendencies that inform us only of our rights as individuals, but rarely of our responsibilities as members of larger communities.

This task will be accomplished in the following way:

1. A brief examination of the history of scholarship in this area. Special attention will be paid to the ways in which there has been a tendency to characterize corporate ideas as rare, marginal and primitive (Chapter 1).

2. A demonstration of the frequency, centrality and persistence of the notion of corporate punishment in ancient Israelite theology. To facilitate the argument, the discussion will focus on Deuteronomy and the deuteronomistic history. Special attention will be paid to the connection between corporate ideas and the covenantal theology of both Deuteronomy and the deuteronomistic history (Chapter 2).

3. Exploration of the connection between the covenantal notions of corporate thinking found in Deuteronomy and the deuteronomistic history and ancient religious ideas such as the wrath of God, holiness and bloodguilt (Chapters 3–5).

4. Investigation of texts that focus upon the individual and thus have often been interpreted as advocating a new individualism. Special attention will be paid to the ways in which covenantal ideas began to qualify corporate ideas and push Israelite theology toward a conception of divine punishment that took greater account of the place of the individual, but still maintained a strong corporate focus as well (Chapters 6–7).

5. Theological reflections on corporate as opposed to more individualistic conceptions of divine retribution. Here I will argue that not only have certain modern biases distorted Israelite theology, but these modern assumptions are not necessariliy ethically or theologically superior to the various assumptions that undergird Israelite notions of corporate punishment (Chapter 8).

Part I

Chapter 1

A BRIEF SURVEY OF THE HISTORY OF SCHOLARSHIP

For nearly a century now there has been a series of debates about exactly how one should explain certain corporate features of Israelite religion and culture. There are numerous instances in the Hebrew Bible in which God acts in a way that offends modern sensibilities. For example, it is well known that God may punish other apparently innocent family members for the crimes of a single individual (Josh. 7 and 2 Sam. 21). The first extensive scholarly discussion of the rationale behind these cases was put forward by H. Wheeler Robinson who, as early as 1911, began to use the term 'corporate personality' as a conceptual key to elucidate these disturbing cases.[1] Although he never completely defines the term corporate personality, one can gain a fairly clear idea of the concept from the following statement:

> The larger or smaller group was accepted without question as a unity; legal prescription was replaced by the fact or fiction of the blood-tie, usually traced back to a common ancestor. The whole group, including its past, present, and future members, might function as a single individual through any one of those members conceived as representative of it. Because it was not confined to the living, but included the dead and the unborn, the group could be conceived as living forever.[2]

Robinson drew many of his ideas from contemporary scholars in related areas and particularly from the field of anthropology. He relied very

---

1. H.W. Robinson, *The Christian Doctrine of Man* (Edinburgh: T. & T. Clark, 1911), p. 8.

2. H.W. Robinson, 'The Hebrew Conception of Corporate Personality', in *Corporate Personality in Ancient Israel* (Philadelphia: Fortress Press, rev. edn, 1980), pp. 25-26. This article was orginally published in P. Volz, F. Stummer and J. Hempel (eds.), *Werden und Wesen des Alten Testaments: Vorträge gehalten auf der Internationalen Tagung alttestamentlicher Forscher zu Göttingen vom 4.-10. September 1935* (BZAW, 66; Berlin: Töpelmann, 1936), pp. 49-62.

heavily on Durkheim and Levy-Bruhl, who employ the notion of 'primitive psychology' in their attempts to explain totemism among so-called 'primitive' peoples. It is often asserted by these anthropologists that tribes with a totemic religion inhabit a very different psychic reality from the one in which modern humans live. This primitive mind-set is described by terms such as 'synthetic thinking' or 'psychical unity', implying an inability of individuals to separate themselves totally from nature, and especially of their inability to differentiate themselves from other members of their clan and from the totemic species that represent their clan. As evidence for the existence of such a psychology, Durkheim quotes a field report in which the anthropologist is showing a native a photograph of himself. Upon observing it, the native says, 'that one' referring to the photograph, 'is the same as me; so is a kangaroo' (the totemic symbol of his clan).[3] Quite similar is a quote of Levy-Bruhl's actually cited by Robinson in his article on corporate personality. 'Things, beings, and phenomena can be incomprehensible for us, at once themselves and something other than themselves.'[4] Often this totemic psychology is called 'pre-logical' and it is considered to be a type of mystical union with reality as a whole. It is clear that Robinson never suggests that ancient Israelite religion was totemistic in any way. But, it is equally clear that he fully believes that ancient Israel, especially in the earlier period, exhibited a very similar or perhaps even the same psychology, which these anthropologists believed they had found among 'primitive' tribes.

Over the course of the next several decades Robinson and many other scholars who utilized his ideas[5] (or ideas that, although developed independently, were in fact quite similar to his)[6] began to apply these notions as a type of cure-all that was invoked to solve a host of interpretive problems in the Hebrew Bible. In turn, as with any theory that

3.   E. Durkheim, *The Elementary Forms of Religious Life* (trans. J. Swain; New York: The Free Press, 1915), p. 157.

4.   Robinson, 'Corporate Personality', p. 31.

5.   A.R. Johnson, *The One and the Many in the Israelite Conception of God* (Cardiff: University of Wales Press Board, 2nd edn, 1961), and *The Vitality of the Individual in the Thought of Ancient Israel* (Cardiff: University of Wales Press Board, 1949); D.S. Russell, *The Method and Message of Jewish Apocalyptic 200 BC–AD 100* (Philadelphia: Fortress Press, 1964), p. 138.

6.   J. Pedersen, *Israel: Its Life and Culture* (4 vols.; London: Oxford University Press, 1926, 1940); A. Causse, *Du groupe ethnique à la communauté religieuse: Le problem sociologique de la religion d'Israël* (Paris: Alcan, 1937).

becomes overextended, the critics began to disassemble it piece by piece and eventually consigned it to the scrap-heap of scholarly ideas. The criticisms levelled at the notion of corporate personality fall under four basic rubrics. (1) This theory creates a false dichotomy between the idea of the individual and the idea of the group and leaves one with the impression that Israelite society had little awareness of the individual until the later biblical period (Mendenhall).[7] (2) The various cases that are discussed under the rubric of corporate personality are sometimes better explained by different ideas such as bloodguilt, ancient conceptions of property rights, and violation of holiness taboos (Daube and Porter).[8] (3) The concept of corporate personality grew out of certain anthropological ideas that are now recognized to be fallacious (Evans-Pritchard, Rogerson, Snaith, Smith).[9] (4) Robinson used the term in an imprecise

7.   G.E. Mendenhall, 'The Relation of the Individual to Political Society in Ancient Israel', in J.M. Meyers (ed.), *Biblical Studies in Memory of H.C. Alleman* (Locust Valley, NY: J.J. Augustin, 1960), pp. 89-108. Mendenhall astutely noted that scholars who claim that the concept of the individual only arose in the later part of Israelite history overlook the fact that the pre-monarchic era is described as a time when 'every man did as he saw fit' (Judg. 21.25). Furthermore these same scholars who advocate a sudden revolution in individualism in the time of Ezekiel understand the exilic text of Isa. 53 as an archetypical example of corporate personality.

8.   Daube argues that it should be recognized that scholars have created a confusion by using a single rubric to explain two distinct but related ideas. The first concept, which he calls communal responsibility, refers to cases in which individuals can suffer or be rewarded because they are inseparable from the larger groups to which they belong. The second idea, which he labels ruler punishment, includes cases in which individuals may suffer punishment because their owner or ruler is being punished. In such cases people may be suffering, but it is questionable to call such suffering a punishment because the punishment is wholly directed at their owner or ruler. Daube also notes that it is not always absolutely clear whether a case involves a question of communal responsibility or ruler punishment and that certain cases involve both types of ideas. D. Daube, *Studies in Biblical Law* (Cambridge: Cambridge University Press, 1947), pp. 154-89. J.R. Porter, 'The Legal Aspects of the Concept of "Corporate Personality" in the Old Testament', *VT* 15 (1965), pp. 361-80. Porter discusses many of the cases raised by Robinson as instances of corporate personality and argues that although corporate personality plays a role in some of these cases, many of them are better explained by reference to other ideas such as ancient conceptions of sin, holiness and bloodguilt. It should be noted that neither Porter nor Daube argue for the complete elimination of the idea of corporate personality. Both scholars call for the idea of corporate responsibility to be applied more carefully and the need to recognize that specific cases can be explained by other factors.

9.   E.E. Evans-Pritchard, *Nuer Religion* (New York: Oxford University Press,

way and thus employed different senses of the term to solve different types of problems. In doing so he emptied the term of any clear meaning and thus of any usefulness (Rogerson).[10]

The critiques levelled at the idea of corporate personality are quite powerful and in fact the idea of corporate personality as conceived and used by Robinson is rarely invoked by scholars today. But there are difficulties inherent within some of these critiques, as well as in the way in which Rogerson, who makes the strongest critique, overextends some of the earlier critiques. Rogerson claims that Porter has sucessfully explained every case he discussed by ideas other than corporate personality. Only after Porter has shown how useless the term corporate personality is, can Rogerson mount an argument for the complete elimination of the term from biblical scholarship. The difficulty is that Porter grants the fact that the notion of corporate personality is useful in certain cases, although he limits the implications of the idea by arguing that these cases are of an exceptional stature and fall outside the normal purview of Israelite law.[11] Not only does Rogerson overlook the place that Porter grants to the idea of corporate personality, but there are difficulties with Porter's analysis itself. Many of the notions that Porter employs to solve some of the difficult narratives he discusses may not be

1956), pp. 123-43; J.W. Rogerson, 'The Hebrew Conception of Corporate Personality: A Re-Examination', *JTS* NS 21 (April 1970), pp. 1-16; J.Z. Smith, *Map is not Territory* (SJLA, 23; Leiden: Brill, 1978), pp. 265-88; and N.H. Snaith, review of A.R. Johnson, *The One and the Many in the Israelite Conception of God*, *JTS* 44 (1943), pp. 81-84.

10. Rogerson is really the first scholar to call for the complete dismissal of the term corporate personality. According to Rogerson, Robinson vacillates not simply between two definitions of corporate personality, one implying a type of psychical unity and one implying a type of corporate responsibility, but Robinson also uses the idea of corporate responsibility in an ambiguous manner. Sometimes he means a person might be liable for the action of his community or part of that community because he was not recognized as an individual with individual rights. At other times he means that an individual, though not directly involved, might suffer the consequences generated by the misdeeds of his community. The first definition of corporate responsibility is tied to the idea of a psychical unity; the second one is not. Robinson exploits this ambiguity within the terminology to explain how Ezekiel's individualism could be synthesized with the concept of corporate personality. Rogerson, 'Hebrew Conception', pp. 6-7.

11. Porter, 'Legal Aspects', pp. 363-67. Porter recognizes that the fact that all Israel suffers in both Josh. 7 and 1 Sam. 14 is best explained by the idea of corporate personality or group-soul.

alternatives to a type of corporate thinking, but various aspects of a common way of corporate thinking. Porter's critique of Robinson has not eliminated the notion of corporateness by providing other alternate explanations that are non-corporate; rather, his argument has begun to reveal some of the factors that participate in cases that are clearly corporate in nature.

Additional problems with Porter's analysis are his portrayal of cases that involve corporate elements as unusual and primitive and his attempt to draw a hard line between legal cases that are totally individualized and these other strange cases that are infected with a religious bias.

> The Hebrew, it may be suggested, realized as well as we do that, if a particular person commits a crime, he is responsible for it, in a way that even those closest to him, his wife or his son, really cannot be. But his basic recognition was qualified, *as far as the operation of the law was concerned*, not so much by ideas of 'corporate personality', as by the notion that a man can possess persons in much the same way that he possesses property and by *early religious beliefs* about the contagious nature of blood, holiness, sin and uncleanness. That we do not share these concepts no doubt makes our recognition of individual justice more equitable than it often could be in practice in Old Testament times.[12]

By attributing the corporate elements in these cases to early religious beliefs and by separating these cases from the legal domain, Porter creates a false dichotomy and leaves one with the sense that there is a sharp contrast between the legal sphere in which individualism reigns supreme and the religious sphere in which certain older corporate ideas seem to persist. It is clear that Porter is on the right track when he suggests that notions such as holiness, sin and bloodguilt are operating in the cases that are corporate in nature. What is problematic is his assumption that these ideas are early holdovers that are unconnected to more normative legal trends in ancient Israel.

Porter is being anachronistic both in his tendency to draw a sharp distinction between secular and religious law,[13] and in his subtle preference for describing the former as more equitable than the latter. In Porter this anachronistic gloss seems to be produced from a pervasive modernist bias that views the sequence of historical periods as progressing toward

---

12. Porter, 'Legal Aspects', pp. 379-80, emphases mine.
13. Porter, 'Legal Aspects', pp. 362-67. This sharp dichotomy between legal and religious ideas is all too convenient and not sustained by the data. See further discussion in Chapter 4 on Josh. 7.

more refined stages of civilization. It should be noted that a secularized evolutionism is sometimes compounded by a specifically Christian supersessionism. In this Christian version the content of the Hebrew Bible is evaluated through the lens of the New Testament. Therein, the Hebrew Bible is seen as an imperfect expression of ideas that reached fruition in the New Testament period. Thus certain scholars have characterized the religion and morality of the Hebrew Bible as inferior to that of the New Testament.

> In the New Testament, the actual point where God and man meet is the human heart. The decisive question is, 'What must I do to be saved?' The salvation here meant is the salvation of the individual soul, and it is a supramundane, heavenly salvation. Compared with this, the Old Testament is on a lower level, for in its pages religion deals in the first instance with national life, although it was out of this national religion that the higher religion of the individual gradually arose.[14]

Apart from the fact that it is questionable that early Christianity was a religion that focused on the individual as an individual, rather than as part of a community (1 Cor. 12.12),[15] it is methodologically unsound to read Israelite religion as an imperfect expression of either Christian thought and/or modernist tendencies to emphasize the individual. Although one may eventually compare and critically evaluate various theological systems, this can only be done after one has attempted to investigate each system from a more neutral standpoint. To do otherwise is to bias the investigation from the starting point.

---

14. H. Gunkel, 'What is left of the Old Testament', in *What Remains of the Old Testament* (trans. A.K. Dallas; New York: Macmillan, 1928), p. 42. This article was originally published in *Die Deutsche Rundschau* 41 (1914). It should be noted that the tendency to characterize the Hebrew Bible as inferior to the New Testament still occurs. Note the comment made in a recent book that applies René Girard's ideas to the Hebrew Bible and the New Testament. Uncomfortable with the conflicting views of God and violence in the Hebrew Bible, we are told not to worry because 'a real center can be found only when all the writings are interpreted anew in the light of the fate of Jesus'. R. Schwager, *Must there be Scapegoats?* (trans. M. Assad; San Francisco: Harper & Row, 1987), p. 135.

15. For a recent corrective to this tendency, see W. Meeks, *The Moral World of the First Christians* (Philadelphia: Westminster Press, 1986); E.E. Ellis, 'Biblical Interpretation in the New Testament Church', in M.J. Mulder (ed.), *Mikra* (Assen: Van Gorcum, 1988), pp. 717-20. I object to Ellis's attempt to understand the origin of certain christological ideas as flowing primarily from the notion of corporate personality.

Furthermore, it is precisely such biases, modernist and occasionally supersessionist, that have time and again led scholars to overemphasize the importance of various passages that stress the individual and to devalue corporate notions. This oversimplified view, that places Israelite ideas in an evolutionary framework moving from early, regressive, corporate conceptions toward later, progressive, individualistic ideas, creates an inaccurate portrait of Israelite religion. As will be argued in depth, there is extensive evidence that corporate ideas remained integral to Israelite thought.

This is not to say that one should revert to Robinson's romantic reading of Israelite religion, nor to imply that Porter and Rogerson have not substantially advanced the discussion of this topic. Their critique of Robinson's theory remains trenchant, but it is overstated to argue that all of Robinson's insights were fundamentally incorrect. His insight that corporate ways of thinking constitute part of the Israelite *Weltanschauung* is still fruitful. Furthermore, his attempt, flawed though it may be, to understand the internal logic of these ideas on their own terms should again be tried, but within a more critical and nuanced reading. To that end this project intends a new and more comprehensive evaluation of the cases that involve corporate ideas.

In this regard, there are other related debates within biblical scholarship that must be integrated into our discussion. One such debate is centered around a theory propounded by Klaus Koch in an article he wrote in 1955.[16] Koch had studied the literature on divine retribution and soon began to notice something unusual. Almost every biblical scholar and theologian had simply assumed that the Hebrew Bible had a clear and understandable doctrine of divine retribution. According to Koch, this untested presupposition leads to the failure on the part of modern scholarship to explore in a systematic manner the biblical view of reward and punishment. Koch uses a form-critical method and categorizes texts according to their *Sitz im Leben* in order to attain a more accurate picture than a chronological survey can provide. He begins his examination with Proverbs 25–29 because it has so often been claimed that retribution is one of the central themes that runs

---

16. Klaus Koch, 'Gibt es ein Vergeltungsdogma im Alten Testament?', *ZTK* 52 (1955), pp. 1-42, partially translated (by T.H. Trapp) and reprinted as 'Is there a Doctrine of Retribution in the Old Testament?', in J.L. Crenshaw (ed.), *Theodicy in the Old Testament* (Philadelphia: Fortress Press, 1983), pp. 57-87.

through ancient Israelite wisdom.[17] Even a cursory reading of Proverbs 25–29 quickly reveals that, although many sayings found here imply a belief that goodness proceeds from righteous actions and evil flows from wicked deeds, it is questionable what role, juridical or otherwise, God plays within this process.

> To speak here about a 'retributional belief' is clearly a case of misunderstanding, since an essential part of the concept of retribution is that a *judicial process* must take place.[18]

Koch finds little evidence of a legal process in which reward and punishment are distributed by God on the basis of a pre-established set of norms or a legal code. Koch points out that only one citation within this section of Proverbs mentions YHWH in connection with the consequences of an action performed by a person. This is Prov. 25.21-22 in which it is stated that 'YHWH will ישׁלם you if you feed and give drink to your enemy'. This word is often rendered as 'reward' in many translations of the Bible. But there is little reason to assume that this rendering is the correct one. Rather, the root שׁלם means 'be complete' and its *piel* should be translated as 'make complete'. It is possible that the meaning of 'to reward' could have developed over time but other verses in this section of Proverbs speak against this translation. Furthermore, in many legal passages throughout the Hebrew Bible this word carries the sense of 'to provide reimbursement for' or 'to restore to completeness' any damaged property. It is not used to describe the act of a judge. In this verse YHWH merely completes an action that was already set in motion by a human being or, to use Koch's terminology, he acts like a 'midwife'.[19] Other examples from the remainder of the book of Proverbs are also examined by Koch. Most interesting for our investigation is his discussion of two other etymological points. The first is the *hiphil* use of the root רשׁע in Prov. 12.2, which shows that ancient Hebrew has the ability to represent the idea that the consequences of an action and YHWH's response are merged into a single word. Secondly, he discusses the *hiphil* of the root שׁוב in Prov. 24.12b. Koch sees this verse as a key to all the passages which he has discussed. He does not think that punishment, reward or requital accurately describes the action

---

17. Koch, 'Doctrine of Retribution', p. 58.
18. Koch, 'Doctrine of Retribution', pp. 58-59, emphasis is his.
19. Koch, 'Doctrine of Retribution', p. 61.

of YHWH in this verse. Rather, it means that YHWH turns or returns the consequences of the action back upon the person who initiated it. Koch acknowledges that the passage indicates that a person can temporarily escape the consequences of his action until the time that YHWH retrieves it and places it back on the person to whom it belongs. But he emphatically rejects the idea that one can find the notion of divine retribution in the book of Proverbs.

> What we do find repeated time and time again is a construct which describes human actions which have a built-in consequence. Part of this construct includes a conviction that YHWH pays close attention to the connection between actions and destiny, and hurries it along, and 'completes' it when necessary.[20]

Koch also extends his discussion to numerous other areas of the Hebrew Bible and claims that the data support the following conclusions:

1.   Divine retribution does not exist in the Hebrew Bible.
2.   What does occur is a type of reflex arc between actions and consequences. Good actions and evil actions are repaid in kind.
3.   This reflex arc between actions and consequences has an almost material quality to it.
4.   This idea of a process in which actions and consequences are bound together is underlined by the language used in the Hebrew Bible. The action and the consequences that follow from it are described with the same word.
5.   God has some relationship to this process, but it is not a juridical relationship.
6.   God's relationship to this process is not always described in the same way in all portions of the Hebrew Bible.
7.   This idea is criticized in some of the later literature within the Hebrew Bible, but it is never replaced by a newer, different or superior idea.

Koch's theory has provoked a good deal of criticism, but it should be noted that no one has completely rejected his theory. In general, his theory is viewed as insightful, but overstated. The major criticisms that have been levelled against Kochs ideas are:

---

20. Koch, 'Doctrine of Retribution', p. 64.

1. Koch's analyses of certain words in biblical Hebrew are questionable at best. He tends to limit the meaning of a particular word in a given context to its original root meaning.[21]

2. Koch's use of the term *Vergeltungsdogma* in and of itself has certain inherent difficulties.[22] He never really fully defines what he means by retribution but seems to limit it to the legal idea of a judge who metes out punishment on the basis of a preexistent norm. One must question whether this is the only possible or even the best possible understanding of retribution.

3. Koch reads the text in too literal a fashion. He fails to notice that often the Hebrew Bible uses literary techniques or rhetorical devices that are not meant to be taken literally.[23]

4. Koch fails to explain the way in which his theory about actions and consequences fits into the larger picture of the religion of ancient Israel. Is it possible that a religion that gives YHWH such an active role in the creation of the world and in the unfolding of world history relegated YHWH to the peripheral station that he holds in Koch's theory?[24]

---

21. This critique is made most powerfully by James Barr: 'The etymology of a word is not a statement about its meaning but about its history; it is only as a historical statement that it can be responsibly asserted, and it is quite wrong to suppose that the etymology of a word is necessarily a guide either to its 'proper' meaning in a later period or to its actual meaning in that period'. J. Barr, *The Semantics of Biblical Language* (Oxford: Oxford University Press, 1961; repr.; London: SCM Press, 1987), p. 109. A similar critique of Koch's tendency to ignore the fact that older formulaic language may be employed in later contexts and thus that the older language may have to be read in terms of the new contexts rather than limited to its original meaning, can be found in H.G. Reventlow, 'Sein Blut komme über sein Haupt', *VT* 10 (1960), pp. 311-27.

22. J.G. Gammie, 'The Theology of Retribution in the Book of Deuteronomy', *CBQ* 32 (1970), p. 3. The idea is cited by Gammie but was made first by E. Pax, 'Studien zum Vergeltungsproblem der Psalmen', *SBFLA* 11 (1960), pp. 56-112.

23. P.D. Miller, *Sin and Judgement in the Prophets* (SBLMS; Chico, CA: Scholars Press, 1982), pp. 121-39; A. Thiselton, 'The Supposed Power of Words in Biblical Writings', *JTS* NS 25 (October 1974), pp. 283-99; J. Barton, 'Natural Law and Poetic Justice in the Old Testament', *JTS* NS 30 (April 1979), pp. 1-14.

24. Thus Miller suggests that the *lex talion* and the idea of covenant are often the motivating factors behind the Hebrew Bible's tendency to connect actions and consequences. Miller, *Sin and Judgement*, pp. 121-39. A similar hypothesis is advanced by Barton who argues that 'texts which speak of poetic justice may probably be seen as making appeal to the idea of natural law'. Barton, 'Natural Law', p. 14.

One of the most interesting points to be noted about Koch's theory and the debate it has provoked is the great similarity between this and the debate over the idea of corporate personality. Koch pursued his study of this topic only after reading K. Fahlgren's study on צדקה;[25] Fahlgren's monograph has an extended discussion of various biblical Hebrew words that carry double meanings. These include: רע, meaning an evil person as well as one who experiences the consequences of evil; רשע, which in the *hiphil* stem can mean either to become guilty or pronounce someone guilty; חטאת, meaning both sin and disaster; עון, meaning both trespass and misfortune, and several other words. Fahlgren claims that these words that carry double meanings reveal that at some point in Israel's past people were unable to distinguish between the cause and the effect of an action because the ancient Israelites viewed both the cause and effect of an action as the same entity. Fahlgren labels this type of mind-set a 'synthetic view of life'.[26] Koch accepts Fahlgren's thesis,[27] but criticizes Fahlgren for not drawing the conclusions to which his investigation led. Fahlgren argued that the synthetic view of life only applied to individual lives, but that the community as a whole was judged by YHWH. Koch not only extends the lexical arguments that Fahlgren made but applies the theory of a synthetic view of life to all domains of Israelite thinking about reward and punishment.

It is precisely at this point that the connections to the debate over the validity of the concept of corporate personality come clearly into view. A.R. Johnson, who frequently resorts to the concept of corporate personality, makes use of the term 'synthetic thinking' in his description of the Israelite mind-set.[28] Johnson also claims that biblical Hebrew reveals a type of thinking that cannot distinguish between realities such as cause

25. K. Fahlgren, *Ṣedaka, nahestehende und entgegengesetzte Begriffe im Alten Testament* (Uppsala: Almqvist & Wiksell, 1932). Cited in Koch, 'Doctrine of Retribution', n. 40.

26. Koch, 'Doctrine of Retribution', pp. 75-76.

27. It should be pointed out that Koch notes that one could object to this type of analysis because we also have such double meanings in our modern languages. He cites as examples the way we use words such as good and bad to describe health or weather or the way that a word like wicked can describe a cold. But he dismisses this objection on the grounds that in biblical Hebrew the most important theological terms carry these double meanings rather than certain common idioms. Koch, 'Doctrine of Retribution', p. 86 n. 51.

28. Johnson, *Vitality*, p. 7.

and effect. Johnson, of course, makes a much larger claim based upon the notion of corporate personality, about the general inability of ancient Israelites to distinguish between the individual and the group. Although neither Fahlgren nor Koch advocates the concept of corporate personality, Fahlgren's usage of the term 'synthetic view of life' is quite akin to Johnson's term 'synthetic thinking'. It is clear that there are strong lines of continuity between Johnson's argument, Fahlgren's and Koch's. All of these theories are constructed upon anthropological ideas that are now viewed as dubious.[29] But this is not the only connection. The fact remains that Koch's thesis resembles the theory of corporate personality in that it points toward certain specific ways in which Israelite thought differs from modern Western thought.

The arguments surrounding Koch's theory about the way in which divine retribution operates in the Hebrew Bible and the arguments surrounding the concept of corporate personality reveal a hermeneutical tension within the field of biblical scholarship. There are two polar positions within biblical scholarship about the nature of Israelite thought. One position asserts that Israelite thought has little if any resemblance to our way of thought. The proponents of this line of thinking are those who argue for concepts such as a 'synthetic view of life' or 'synthetic thinking'. The other position claims that basically our manner of thinking is identical with that of ancient Israel. Proponents of the latter position argue that metaphorical language or various stylistic or lexical patterns are being over-interpreted and thus are being misused to prove the existence of thought patterns that only exist in the mind of the critic and not in the mind of the ancient Israelites who produced the text of the Hebrew Bible. We have before us a rift that runs down the middle of biblical scholarship: Is the world of the ancient Israelites really foreign and other, or is it fundamentally the same as the world that we currently inhabit, but its descriptive language differs from our descriptive language?[30]

I agree with those critics who reject psychological notions such as synthetic thinking and who point out that many of the philological

---

29. See n. 9 above for bibliography on this subject.

30. For an interesting discussion of this question, see J.W. Rogerson, 'The Old Testament View of Nature: Some Preliminary Questions', *OTS* 20 (1977), pp. 67-84. For a more general essay about how anthropologists deal with this recurrring methodological problem, see S. Lukes, 'Some Problems about Rationality', in B. Wilson (ed.), *Rationality* (Oxford: Basil Blackwell, 1974), pp. 194-213.

arguments that are adduced in support of such notions are quite weak.[31] It seems clear that Koch has in fact overstated his case and that his bid to remove God from the nexus between sin and punishment has ultimately failed. But one must still ask whether there are aspects of Koch's theory and even of the notion of corporate personality that remain intact and which could be helpful in illuminating some of the specific problems with which this project is grappling. Indeed, Koch's insightful investigation into this topic has revealed that there is a very old notion of retribution, which is almost magical in its mode of operation, that lurks behind certain formulae in the Hebrew Bible. The evidence for this assertion comes not only from the Hebrew Bible, which often describes actions as creating an almost physical residue that can affect one at a later time, but also from our awareness that many of the concepts and practices found in ancient Israel were borrowed from other earlier and contemporary religions that were pervaded by magical thinking. The difficulty is in determining exactly how such ideas operate once they are appropriated by ancient Israelite thinkers and set within the larger theological constructs of the Hebrew Bible. The question turns on how one understands both the language employed and the more general theological contexts in which these ritual ideas are now set. Are these words and practices more metaphorical or do they still retain much of their original magical content? To reach a proper understanding of how these religious ideas functioned in ancient Israel one must examine both the language employed and the more general theological contexts in which these ritual ideas are now set. Thus there is the necessity of analyzing the concepts of wrath, holiness and bloodguilt in the Hebrew Bible.

More recent scholarship has again brought various aspects of this problem to the surface. Both Paul Joyce and Gordon Matties have engaged this topic insofar as it impinged on their respective investigations into certain problems in the book of Ezekiel.[32] Each of them has forcefully rejected an evolutionary model that suggests a steady progression from earlier corporate ideas toward later individualistic ones. Both scholars

31. For a critique of a similar tendency to use a strict philological approach in order to demonstrate that ancient Greeks thought in fundamentally different ways and had no awareness of individual consciousness or personality see B. Knox, 'The Oldest Dead White European Males', *The New Republic* (25 May 1992), pp. 27-35.

32. P. Joyce, *Divine Initiative and Human Response in Ezekiel* (JSOTSup, 51; Sheffield: JSOT Press, 1989), pp. 79-87 and G. Matties, *Ezekiel 18 and the Rhetoric of Moral Discourse* (SBLDS, 126; Atlanta: Scholars Press, 1990), pp. 113-58.

acknowledge that corporate and individualistic ideas continue to be produced in the later biblical period, although they offer different explanations of how one might make sense of texts that appear to affirm these two very different sets of ideas.[33] These scholars have focused much of their attention on the book of Ezekiel, and more specifically on the conflict between the apparent stress upon the individual in passages such as Ezekiel 18 as compared with other parts of Ezekiel that seem to advocate a more corporate perspective. Although both scholars do give a history of scholarship, and Joyce in particular does explore the problem in a fuller and more general fashion, neither of them has systematically gone back through the various cases discussed by Robinson, Daube and Porter.[34] The close relationship between Koch's ideas and Robinson's ideas also seems to have gone unnoticed.[35] A more accurate understanding of the various instances of corporate punishment will only be attained after one re-analyzes these cases in the light of the above-discussed debates. A more comprehensive review of these cases and of the history of scholarship surrounding them will not only reveal that various corporate ideas are linked together, but that certain biases found within the history of scholarship developed from larger cultural presuppositions which continue to persist. By addressing not only the individual elements that operate in specific cases, but also the way in which these individual elements evolved into and participate in a larger system of thought, we hope to reach a more sympathetic and accurate understanding of the way in which corporate ideas functioned in ancient Israel. Only after reaching a fuller understanding of the origin and development of the corporate ideas found in the Hebrew Bible will we turn to the questions discussed by Joyce and Matties about the apparent conflict between these corporate notions and certain alternative theological views that are more individualistic.

33. Both these authors' ideas will be discussed in much greater detail in Chapter 7 below.

34. Not only does Joyce discuss this in *Divine Initiative*, pp. 79-87, but also in 'The Individual and the Community', in J. Rogerson (ed.), *Beginning Old Testament Study* (Philadelphia: Westminster Press, 1982), pp. 75-89.

35. In particular Joyce sees the various alternate explanations given by Daube, Porter and Koch as basically unrelated to each other or to any larger set of ideas. He understands Koch's ideas of the infectious power of sin as not at all related to issues of responsibility. I intend to argue that the infectious power of sin and the notion of responsibility are part and parcel of a single interconnected set of ideas. Joyce, *Divine Initiative*, pp. 80-83.

Chapter 2

CORPORATE IDEAS:
THEIR FREQUENCY, CENTRALITY AND PERSISTENCE

The primary task of this chapter is to demonstrate that corporate ideas are common, central and persistent in the Hebrew Bible. I have compiled an extensive but not exhaustive list of various instances of corporate punishment in the Pentateuch and the deuteronomistic history (see Appendix). Although this chart defies simple typological analysis, there are certain basic types of corporate punishment:

1. God may inflict a corporate punishment on a given group of people either because (a) an individual within that group errs (Josh. 7; 2 Kgs 5.27), (b) several individuals within that group err (Num. 16; 1 Sam. 2.31), (c) because the ruler of that group errs (2 Sam. 24; 2 Kgs 21.11), (d) or because earlier leaders or ancestors erred (Gen. 9.20-27).
2. The nation as a whole may execute a corporate punishment against a particular group. Often this is ordered by God (Deut. 13.13-18; Josh. 7).
3. Rulers often eliminate all their rivals in a corporate style. This may be associated with a divine oracle calling for the complete destruction of the last ruler's offspring (1 Kgs 15.29; 16.11).

There are cases which straddle these categories and I am particularly interested in those cases that are complex and thus involve a series of factors that interact with each other in a dynamic fashion. In order to facilitate our exploration of the various factors that operate in different corporate cases and to demonstrate the centrality and persistence of corporate ideas in ancient Israelite theology, it will be necessary to examine certain select texts more closely. I have chosen to concentrate on texts that occur within Deuteronomy and the deuteronomistic history, and will bring in other texts only when they help illuminate the issue under discussion. This chapter will focus mainly on three passages in 2 Kings that attribute Judah's exile to Manasseh's sins and thus advocate some type of corporate thinking. The reasons for choosing these texts are: (1) there is strong evidence that these texts that deal with Manasseh were rewritten after the exile in an attempt to explain why God exiled Judah even after Josiah's reform efforts; (2) there is also strong evidence that indicates that an earlier edition of the deuteronomistic history utilized the figure of Jeroboam in a similar fashion to explain the exile of the North; (3) if it can be shown that this tendency to blame earlier monarchs and earlier generations for the respective exiles of the North and South is a theological maneuver that is pervaded by corporate ideas, I will have demonstrated not only the importance of such ideas but also the way in which they continued to persist even after the exile of Judah.

The first text discusses the reign of Manasseh in an extensive manner.

> Manasseh was twelve years old when he began to reign, and he reigned fifty-five years in Jerusalem; his mother's name was Hephzibah. 2 And he did evil in the sight of the Lord, after the manner of the abominable practices of the nations that the Lord had dispossessed before the Israelites. 3 He rebuilt the bamoth that Hezekiah his father had destroyed; and he erected altars[1] to Baal and made an Asherah just as King Ahab of Israel had done. He prostrated himself to all the host of heaven and served them. 4 He built altars in the house of the Lord, the place about which the Lord said, 'I will set my name in Jerusalem'. 5 He built altars to all the host of heaven in the two courtyards[2] of the house of the Lord. 6 He caused his son[3] to pass through fire,[4] he practiced soothsaying and divination, he

---

1. LXX reads the singular here and in the next verse.

2. The notion of two courtyards may be a retrojection of the architecture of the second temple back into the first or it may be a reference to the new court added by Jehoshaphat if one grants the accuracy of 2 Chron. 20.5.

3. LXX and 2 Chron. 33.6 read the plural here.

4. There is a debate about whether this is a form of child sacrifice or a type of ritual of dedication to a god. Some of the debate hinges on whether there is a distinction between passages such as Deut. 12.31 and 2 Kgs 17.31 which use the root שׂרף and passages like 2 Kgs 16.3 and this text which use the *hiphil* form of the root עבר. For more on this dispute, see J. Day, *Molech: A God of Human Sacrifice in the Old Testament* (University of Cambridge Oriental Publications, 41; Cambridge: Cambridge University Press, 1989), pp. 15-28; G. Heider, *The Cult of Molech* (JSOTSup, 43; Sheffield: JSOT Press, 1985), pp. 232-73; J.D. Levenson, *The Death and Resurrection of the Beloved Son* (New Haven: Yale University Press, 1993), pp. 3-24. M. Smith, 'A Note on Burning Babies', *JAOS* 95 (1975), pp. 477-79; M. Weinfeld,

performed necromancy and seances;[5] he did many things that were displeasing to the Lord thus angering him.[6] 7 And he set a sculpted image of Asherah that he made in the house about which the Lord had said to David and to Solomon his son, 'In this house and in Jerusalem which I have chosen from all the tribes of Israel I will set my name. 8 And I will not again cause the feet of Israel to wander from the land which I gave to their ancestors, if only they will be cautious to execute all that I command them—all the Torah which my servant Moses commanded them'. 9 But they did not obey and Manasseh led them astray to do more evil than the nations that the Lord had destroyed before the Israelites. 10 Thus the Lord spoke by means of his servant the prophets: 11 'Because Manasseh king of Judah has done all of these abominations—evil greater than the Amorites who lived before his time—and he has caused Judah to sin with his idols, 12 therefore, thus says the Lord God of Israel: I am going to bring evil upon Jerusalem and Judah and the ears of everyone who hears of it[7] will tingle. 13 I will spread the measuring line[8] of Samaria and the level the house of Ahab over Jerusalem and I will wipe Jerusalem clean as one wipes a dish, wiping it and turning it[9] upside down. 14 I will forsake the remnant of my possession and I will give them over into the power of their enemies. They will be plunder and booty for all their enemies 15 because they have acted wickedly in my sight and they have angered me from the day that their fathers came out of Egypt until today.'

16 Moreover, Manasseh spilled so much innocent blood he filled Jerusalem from one end to the other with it. This is separate from the sin of causing Judah to do evil in the sight of the Lord.

17 The rest of the events of Manasseh's reign and all that he did, and the sin that he committed, are indeed recorded in the book of the Chronicles of the Kings of Judah. 18 Manasseh slept with his ancestors and he was buried in the garden of his palace, that is the garden of Uzza;[6] Amon his son ruled in his stead (2 Kgs 21.1-18).

'The Worship of Molech and of the Queen of Heaven and its Background', *UF* 4 (1972), pp. 133-54.

5.   The terms וידעני and אוב regularly occur together and appear to indicate some type of communication with the dead, most likely through the use of a ritual pit. For a more extensive discussion, see H.A. Hoffner, Jr, 'Second Millennium Antecedents to the Hebrew Term '*ÔB*', *JBL* 86 (December 1967), pp. 385-401.

6.   Adding the third masculine singular pronominal suffix following several Hebrew manuscripts, the Greek, Syriac, Targum, Vulgate and 2 Chron. 33.6. This may be an instance of haplography in that the next word begins with a ו.

7.   Reading שמעה with the *qere* following certain Hebrew manuscripts and the versions instead of the plural with the singular suffix like the *kethib* שמעיו.

8.   Repointing the קָו of the MT to קָו.

9.   Reading the infinitive absolutes מָחֹה וְהָפֹךְ instead of מָחָה וְהָפַךְ found in the text.

10.   Gray makes the interesting suggestion that the Garden or enclosure of Uzza is

The second passage is also about Manasseh's reign, although it occurs in ch. 23 as an appendix to the end of Josiah's reign. This text informs its readers that in spite of the great works of righteousness wrought by Josiah, Judah was still to be exiled and Jerusalem destroyed because of the abominable deeds performed during Manasseh's reign.

> Yet the Lord did not turn away from his great anger that he had directed against Judah because of all the things that Manasseh did to enrage him. The Lord said, 'Judah too, I will remove from my sight just as I banished Israel; and I will disown Jerusalem, the city that I chose, and the house where I said my name would be' (2 Kgs 23.26-27).

The third text is the annalistic report from Jehoiakim's reign which attributes the punishments that followed Jehoiakim's rebellion against Nebuchadnezzar to Manasseh's sins.

> 36 Jehoiakim was twenty-five years old when he began to reign and he was king in Jerusalem for eleven years; his mother's name was Zebudah[11] daughter of Padaiah from Rumah. 37 He did evil in the sight of the Lord just as all his ancestors had done. 24.1 In his days Nebuchadnezzar of Babylon came up, and Jehoiakim was his vassal for three years; then he turned and revolted against him. 2 The Lord sent Chaldean, Aramean, Moabite, and Ammonite raiding squads against him; he sent them against Judah to destroy it, in accordance with the word of the Lord that he spoke by means of his servants the prophets. 3 Indeed, the word of[12] the Lord was against Judah to remove [them][13] from his presence because of the sins of Manasseh, according to all that he had done, 4 and also the innocent blood that he spilled, for he had filled Jerusalem with innocent blood and the Lord was not willing to forgive. 5 The other events of Jehoiakim's reign and all that he did are indeed recorded in the Book of the Chronicles of the Kings of Judah. 6 Jehoiakim slept with his ancestors and Jehoiachin ruled in his stead (2 Kgs 23.36–24.6).

Each of these texts has been the subject of much scholarly discussion. In particular scholars have focused on these passages in an attempt to clarify the redactional history of the books of Kings. Recent scholarship

---

a sacred site of Attar-Melech, the Venus-star, which is called Uzza in Arabic. It is also possible that it refers to Uzziah directly or to an area he built. J. Gray, *I & II Kings* (OTL; Philadelphia: Westminster Press, 1963), pp. 646-47.

11. Following the *qere*.

12. It is possible that one should read anger, אף, following the LXX θυμόν and also following v. 20.

13. LXX reads αὐτόν here, thus making one suspect that the third masculine singular suffix fell out of the MT.

has built upon the work of Martin Noth who made the argument that 'Dtr. is wholly responsible for the coherence of this complex of material and hence for the unity of the whole history in Joshua–Kings'.[14] The term deuteronomistic history, that is the books between Joshua and 2 Kings, is now a commonplace in discussions about the Hebrew Bible. While more recent scholarship has generally accepted the literary unity of Joshua–2 Kings, it has become increasingly critical of Noth's arguments about the author and date of the composition. Noth argues the following:

> Hence the history was probably the independent project of a man whom the historical catastrophes he witnessed had inspired with curiosity about the meaning of what had happened, and who tried to answer this question in a comprehensive and self-contained historical account, using those traditions concerning the history of his people to which he had access.[15]

Noth thus maintained that a single person composed the deuteronomistic history and that he composed it during the exile.[16] Much of recent scholarship has mounted a rather convincing case for the argument that the deuteronomistic history was originally promulgated before the exile, most likely during Josiah's reign, and was subsequently redacted at least one more time during the exilic period.[17] Such a hypothesis helps

14. M. Noth, *The Deuteronomistic History* (JSOTSup, 15; Sheffield: JSOT Press, 1981), p. 10.

15. Noth, *Deuteronomistic History*, p. 99.

16. Noth does acknowledge that this unified history has received later supplementation.

17. Exactly how many editions of the deuteronomistic history there were and the contents of each edition are still a matter of considerable debate. Much of the current literature argues that there were either two or three redactions, but many different hypotheses have been put forward about the dating and contents of these various redactional layers. For the purposes of this project, it is not necessary to enter into this complex set of issues because the argument I am making is not contingent on the final outcome of this larger debate. For more on the redactional questions surrounding Deuteronomy and the deuteronomistic history, see the discussions in the following books: F.M. Cross, *Canaanite Myth and Hebrew Epic* (Cambridge, MA: Harvard University Press, 1973), pp. 219-89; R.E. Friedman, *The Exile and Biblical Narrative* (HSM, 22; Chico, CA: Scholars Press, 1981), pp. 1-43; *idem*, 'From Egypt to Egypt: Dtr 1 and Dtr 2', in B. Halpern and J.D. Levenson (eds.), *Traditions in Transformation* (Winona Lake, IN: Eisenbrauns, 1981), pp. 167-92; *idem*, *Who Wrote the Bible?* (New York: Summit, 1987), pp. 101-35; B. Halpern, *The First Historians* (San Francisco: Harper & Row, 1988); G.N. Knoppers, *Two Nations Under God: The Deuteronomistic History of Solomon and the Dual Monarchies* (2 vols.; HSM, 52-53; Atlanta: Scholars Press, 1993, 1994); J.D. Levenson, 'Who

account for shifts in perpective that occur within the deuteronomistic history and especially within the last few chapters of the book of 2 Kings.

Although the number of editions and the parameters of each edition remain contested, there is a growing consensus that much of the first and all of the second and third passages that we are examining in this chapter belong to an exilic redaction of the deuteronomistic history.[18] For example, in speaking about 2 Kgs 23.26-27, Cross informs us that this passage 'is evidently from the hand of an Exilic editor'.[19]

2 Kgs 21.1-18 is seen by most commentators to contain a good deal of exilic material that accumulated around what originally was a rather short annalistic notice about Manasseh's reign and his eventual death. Nelson, a proponent of Cross's position, who supports a double redaction theory, offers a concise and balanced reconstruction of the relationship between the earlier and later material in this passage:

> In other words, it seems most likely that the exilic editor found before him 1-3b and 16-18, with the annalistic notices 4a, 6a, and perhaps 7a, floating somewhere in between. In his revision of the history, he expanded Manasseh's sins and sermonized upon them in 3c-15, utilizing in the process some fragments of the historian's comments upon the evil of the king, which probably consisted of quoted annalisic notices.[20]

2 Kgs 23.36–24.6 in all likelihood comes entirely from an exilic hand, although it may contain annalistic information that was penned at an

---

Inserted the Book of the Torah?', *HTR* 68 (July 1975), pp. 203-33; *idem*, 'From Temple to Synagogue: 1 Kings 8', in Halpern and Levenson (eds.), *Traditions in Transformation*, pp. 143-66; *idem*, 'The Last Four Verses in Kings', *JBL* 103 (September 1984), pp. 353-61; R.D. Nelson, *The Double Redaction of the Deuteronomistic History* (JSOTSup, 18; Sheffield: JSOT Press, 1981); M. Noth, *Deuteronomistic History*; M.A. O'Brien, *The Deuteronomistic History Hypothesis: A Reassassment* (OBO, 92; Göttingen: Vandenhoeck & Ruprecht, 1989); I.W. Provan, *Hezekiah and the Books of Kings* (BZAW, 172; Berlin: de Gruyter, 1988); C.R. Seitz, *Theology in Conflict* (BZAW, 176; Berlin: de Gruyter, 1989), pp. 164-200; M. Weinfeld, *Deuteronomy and the Deuteronomic School* (Oxford: Clarendon Press, 1972). I take up some aspects of this difficult problem in Chapter 5.

18. Provan, who argues that the Josianic addition of the deuteronomistic history ended with 2 Kgs 19.37, attributes all of the passages that we are examining in this chapter to the hand of an exilic editor. Provan, *Hezekiah*, pp. 117-31 and 144-55.

19. Cross, *Canaanite Myth*, p. 286.

20. Nelson, *The Double Redaction*, p. 67. Also see O'Brien, *Deuteronomistic History*, pp. 227-34.

earlier time. Our interest in this passage centers on vv. 2-4 which likely contain the fulfillment of the prophecy spoken in 2 Kgs 21.10-15. This is clear from a quick comparison of the language found in 2 Kgs 21.10, 14 with 24.2.

21.10 וידבר יהוה ביד־עבדיו הנביאים לאמר:
14 ונטשתי את שארית נחלתי ונתתים ביד איביהם
והיו לבז ולמשסה לכל־איביהם:

24.2 וישלח יהוה בו את־גדודי כשדים ואת־גדודי ארם
ואת גדודי מואב ואת גדודי בני־עמון וישלחם ביהודה להאבידו
כדבר יהוה אשר דבר ביד עבדיו הנביאים:

It seems highly probable that the bands of raiding parties in 24.2 are seen as a fulfillment of the prophecy noted in 21.14 in which the Judahites will be plunder in the hands of their enemies. It should also be noted that 2 Kgs 21.10 and 24.2 use almost identical language in describing 'the word of the Lord that he spoke by means of his servants the prophets'. The fact that no specific prophet is named is in itself an indicator 'that the attribution of Judah's demise to the unforgivable sins of Manasseh is tacked on and not integral to the original structure of the history'.[21]

The very fact that these passages place the blame for the exile on Manasseh points to the probability that they are part of a secondary redaction that occurred during the exile and thus that they are later than much of the other material found in the deuteronomistic history. In the pre-exilic edition of the deuteronomistic history it is probable that Manasseh was no more than a foil against whom one could measure the achievements of Josiah.[22] This is nicely explicated by Friedman who attributes all of the first eight and a half verses in 2 Kings 21 to Dtr 1.

> The first seven verses of the chapter describe the crimes of Manasseh in terms which relate to the activities of Josiah, i.e., the writer names the wrongs which Josiah set right. Manasseh rebuilds the *bāmôt*, Josiah smashes them. Manasseh sets up an Asherah, Josiah burns it. Manasseh sets altars 'to all the host of heaven' in the Temple precincts, Josiah smashes them.[23]

---

21. Cross, *Cannanite Myth*, p. 286.

22. Although Provan would argue that Josiah had no function in the pre-exilic edition of the deuteronomistic history, he would agree that the portrayal of Manasseh as the cause of the exile is an exilic motif.

23. Friedman, *Exile*, pp. 10-11. Also see O'Brien, *Deuteronomistic History*, p. 43.

Nevertheless, one should keep in mind that although an exilic editor may have penned the passages that attribute the exile to Manasseh, he did not really invent a new theological motif; rather, he extended certain corporate theological ideas that were already present in the earlier edition of the deuteronomistic history. One can see by the way in which Dtr 1 describes the history of the Northern kingdom, that he was not afraid to invoke notions of retribution that are strongly corporate in orientation. The refrain heard time and again throughout the deuteronomistic historian's report of the Northern kingdom and its eventual demise, is that each king either followed in, or failed to turn away from, the evil ways of Jeroboam (1 Kgs 15.30, 34; 16.2, 19, 31; 22.53; 2 Kgs 3.3; 10.29, 31; 13.2, 6, 11; 14.24; 15.9, 18, 24, 28; 17.21-22). In fact, it seems likely that the role that Manasseh plays in Dtr 2 is modeled on the role played by Jeroboam in Dtr 1.

Before proceeding with an in-depth theological analysis of the various corporate ideas employed by Dtr 2 in his explanation for the exile of Judah, and the way in which each rationale builds upon earlier models already employed by Dtr 1, let us review what has so far been argued.

1. The exilic stratum of the deuteronomistic history employs the figure of Manasseh, and his sinful behavior, as a major rationale in its explanation of why God caused Judah to be exiled.
2. The exilic editor of the deuteronomistic history is invoking an idea that is quite common within the earlier, Josianic edition of the deuteronomistic history.

The Sins of Manasseh and Corporate Responsibility

The texts that attribute the exile to Manasseh contain two different, but interrelated aspects of corporate punishment:

1. They imply that the king is representative of the whole nation, and thus if he errs the nation as a whole might suffer for his misdeed. I refer to this phenomenon in which sin spreads horizontally across a generation as intra-generational retribution.
2. They place the blame for the fall of Judah upon the deeds of those who lived in earlier generations, especially upon Manasseh and his generation. I refer to this phenomenon in which sin spreads vertically across numerous generations as trans- or inter-generational retribution.

Although I will discuss each of these aspects of corporate thinking separately, one should not imagine that they are unrelated. In fact, it will be shown that these different modes of corporate thinking often occur together in such a fashion that they are not always easy to separate from each other and that, furthermore, they belong to a common set of theological ideas.

While there is strong evidence within these passages for the notion that the whole nation can suffer for the misbehavior of the king, this evidence is not completely unambiguous. On the one hand, 2 Kings 21 uses singular verbs that refer only to Manasseh in vv. 1-7 and 16-18. On the other hand, the language in vv. 8-15 becomes more generalized and appears to fluctuate in terms of who receives the brunt of the blame for the exile.[24] Verses 9-11 places most, if not all, of the blame on Manasseh who not only sinned but led the populace of Judah astray, while v. 15 places the blame upon the many generations of sinful Judahites who have continually aroused God's wrath. One cannot but wonder whether v. 15 is from a different redactional layer from vv. 9-11. Perhaps there is an internal theological dispute about who ultimately is responsible for the exile—the king, the people, or both. This is precisely what O'Brien suggests.

> Whereas 2 Kgs 21.11-14, with its accusation in v. 11 and announcement of disaster in vv. 12-14, clearly form a unit, there is evidence in favor of v. 15 as a later addition. It introduces a further accusation after the announcement of disaster in vv. 12-14, and shifts the blame from Manasseh (v. 11) to the people. The focus on the people associates this verse with the addition in 2 Kgs 21.8-9 and the later nomistic stage of redaction. One may provisionally conclude therefore that the nomistic additions in 2 Kgs 21.8-9, 15 are later than the post-DTR redaction of 2 Kgs 21.1-7 and the prophecy associated with it in vv. 10-14.[25]

It is clear that not only here, but also in several other places within the last few chapters of 2 Kings, there is a tension between those materials that place the blame for the exile most heavily on Manasseh (2 Kgs 23.26;

24. Here I disagree with certain proponents of the Cross school, such as Friedman who argues that throughout 8b-15 'the center of attention becomes the people instead of the king'. Friedman, 'From Egypt to Egypt', p. 177. Friedman fails to notice that there are internal tensions within 8b-15 about who is primarily responsible for the exile. Failure to account for these tensions shows a certain weakness in the two-stage redaction theory and may in fact provide additional support for a three-stage redaction theory. I discuss this at length further below.

25. O'Brien, *Deuteronomistic History*, pp. 233-34.

24.3-4) and those that indict the populace at large (2 Kgs 22.17; 24.20). This tension is one of the focal points of the current debate between those who advocate either two or three major redactions of the deuteronomistic history. O'Brien has noticed this tension and views it as evidence of redactional activity that supports his larger hypothesis about the three major redactional layers in the deuteronomistic history. If O'Brien's hypothesis proved true it would bolster my hypothesis for the existence of texts that speak about the transference of sins between a ruler and his population because it would prove that there was a distinct stratum in which Manasseh alone was blamed for Judah's downfall. Unfortunately, the evidence for the existence of such a stratum is rather tenuous. Although O'Brien's triple redaction theory does recognize and account for certain textual nuances that the advocates of the double redaction theory tend to gloss over, it is plagued by many of the same difficulties that cast doubt on the double redaction theory. A verse-by-verse redactional reconstruction is inherently difficult to sustain because of the sheer circularity of any such argument. This type of argument presupposes that each redactional layer is totally self-consistent, thereby enabling the critic to distill out each stage of redaction from the conglomerate by careful analysis. But the parameters of each stratum are predetermined by the nature of the passages that one assigns to a particular redactional level. It is true that specific terminology can be helpful in isolating a redactional stratum, but such a method presumes a consistency of language within each stratum. It is precisely this rigidity that leads O'Brien to the dubious conclusion that 2 Kgs 23.26-27 is from the same level of redaction as 2 Kgs 21.10-14, but must be by a different redactor because the terminology is not precisely identical.[26]

David Damrosch eloquently points out that this method has severe limitations.

> It is not impossible that some of the tensions in the material result from two editions of the overall history, but the arguments for two (or three) editions often lack literary depth; they assume a remarkable purity in the sources used by the first edition, a univocality of theme that is more plausible in simple chronicle writing than in developed historiography.[27]

Theological tensions within a passage are not always a sure sign of different redactors or of different redactional strata, but may be

---

26. O'Brien, *Deuteronomistic History*, p. 268.

27. D. Damrosch, *The Narrrative Covenant* (San Francisco: Harper & Row, 1987), p. 179.

attributable to the editorial technique of a single redactor who combined various types of material together. There is solid evidence that the deuteronomistic historian has structured his history by punctuating it with annalistic excerpts from the Book of the Chronicles of the Kings of Judah and the Book of the Chronicles of the Kings of Israel (1 Kgs 14.19, 29; 15.7, 23, 31; 16.5, 14, 20, 27 etc.).[28] Obviously these annalistic sources are exclusively interested in the person of the king. Building on these annalistic sources, the deuteronomistic historian, in similar annalistic form, evaluates each monarch on the basis of his cultic behavior. One could argue that the same redactor who focused on the cultic behavior of each king also penned the passages that place the blame upon the populace as a whole. After all, the populace bears some responsibility in that they both requested a monarch (Deut. 17.14; 1 Sam. 8.5) and followed the evil ways of certain corrupt monarchs.

It is even possible that passages such as 2 Kgs 23.26 and 24.2-3 that focus on Manasseh do so simply because they are short references intended to remind the reader of the prophecy in ch. 21 which announces the coming punishment because of Manasseh's and his generation's sins. The exclusive preoccupation of these passages with Manasseh may be an accidental effect caused by their terse form. One should note that the language of 24.2b-3 is very reminiscent of 17.22-23a in which God removed the people of Israel from his presence because they walked in all the sins of Jeroboam.

17.22 וילכו בני ישׂראל בכל־חטאות ירבעם אשר עשה לא־סרו ממנה:
23 עד אשר־הסיר יהוה את־ישׂראל מעל פניו
כאשר דבר ביד כל־עבדיו הנביאים

24.2b כדבר יהוה אשר דבר ביד עבדיו הנביאים: 3 אך על־פי יהוה
היתה ביהודה להסיר מעל פניו בחטאת מנשה ככל אשר עשה:

The resemblance between these two passages is so striking it seems likely that the passage in 24.2b-3 is modelled on the earlier passage in ch. 17. If this is true, it raises doubts about whether the passage in ch. 24 intended to focus exclusively on Manasseh, or whether it is just shorthand for the longer formula found in ch. 17 which places a good deal of the blame on the monarch, but also recognizes the guilt of the populace who followed their leader's footsteps.

But even if O'Brien is wrong about his hypothesis that there is a

---

28. S.R. Bin-Nun, 'Formulas from Royal Records of Israel and of Judah', *VT* 18 (October 1968), pp. 414-32.

stratum that placed the blame upon Manasseh alone, there is still ample evidence to support the contention that these texts do advocate a type of intra-generational corporate punishment in which the actions of the king can have adverse effects upon the nation as a whole. In such a reading Manasseh is seen as the king who initially incited the populace to sin, but the populace remains at least partially responsible for their fate, inasmuch as they followed in Manasseh's footsteps. This theological maneuver in which a dynamic tension is set up between a particular monarch and the populace at large, has deep roots in the deuteronomistic history, which time and again tells us of the sin(s) that Jeroboam committed and caused Israel to commit (1 Kgs 14.16; 15.30; 2 Kgs 13.6; 17.18-23 etc.). Manasseh functions in Dtr 2 in a manner that is similar to the way Jeroboam functions in Dtr 1. Just as Dtr 1 recognizes that although Jeroboam led the populace astray, the fact that they followed his lead makes them somewhat culpable, so Dtr 2 places the blame primarily on Manasseh, but also recognizes that the populace bears some responsibility because they followed his lead.

It should be noted that there is other evidence to support my contention that the deuteronomistic historian subscribes to the notion that guilt can be transferred between an individual, especially a king, and the population at large. One such piece of evidence can be found in an alternate rationale for the exile that stresses the idea that each king who lived after Josiah's time also acted corruptly in God's sight, and that by doing so they brought disaster upon their respective populations (2 Kgs 23.31-36; 24.8-17).[29]

These passages not only reveal that the deuteronomistic historian employs the idea of intra-generational retribution in his attempt to explain the eventual downfall of both the North and the South, but additionally they provide support for the existence of another type of corporate thinking in which sins transfer across generations. This second type of corporate punishment can be seen in the above-discussed passages inasmuch as they advocate the idea that the sins of Manasseh and his generation are inherited by later generations who ultimately pay for this wicked behavior by being exiled. Here I disagree with Weinfeld who argues that one need not assume that Manasseh's sinful behavior transfers to later generations.

---

29. This motif is discussed in more detail below. Also Josh. 7, a text in which the sin of a single individual has adverse consequences upon the whole people, is discussed in Chapter 4.

> The Deuteronomist is careful to point out the role played by the principle
> of individual retribution. Thus the monarchs in whose reigns the dynasty
> was destroyed do not perish as a consequence of their fathers' sins but
> because they have adopted and propagated the evil ways of their fathers.
> We do not, indeed, hear of any king 'who did that which is just in the sight
> of the Lord' but was nevertheless destroyed in requital for the sins of his
> fathers.[30]

It is clear that Weinfeld is basing his argument on the notices concerning
the last four kings of Judah which all begin with the phrase 'he did evil
in the sight of the Lord' (2 Kgs 23.32, 37; 24.9, 19). Such an argument
runs into several difficulties. To begin with, Weinfeld highlights these
passages which contain an alternate explanation for the exile at the
expense of ignoring the language in the passages examined above, which
clearly place the blame for the exile of Judah upon Manasseh and his
generation. It should be noted that 2 Kgs 24.2-4, a passage that explicitly
informs the reader that God is sending various raiding parties to destroy
Judah because of Manasseh's sins, occurs in the middle of these four
citations that Weinfeld focuses upon. Thus, his argument fails to take
account of all of the evidence at hand. But even excluding this problem,
his reading of the alternate motif, as one in which individual retribution
is stressed, is itself questionable. The fact that this formula is repeated
over and over leaves one with the impression that the final punishment
is being imposed because of the continual obstinacy of Judah and its
kings over many generations, just as the end of the Northern Kingdom
is attributed to the continual failure of Israel and its kings to turn away
from the sins of Jeroboam (2 Kgs 13.2; 14.24; 15.9 etc.). The idea of
explaining the harshness of the coming punishment by demonstrating
that the people and their rulers had been obdurate over a long period of
time is an idea modeled upon Dtr 1's use of Jeroboam. Dtr 1 time and
again informs the reader about how Israel continued to act wickedly, and
in doing so they persistently angered God (1 Kgs 14.30; 15.15, 26 etc.).
This motif portrays Israel as continually provoking God's anger until it
reaches a critical point when this anger is poured out upon the generation
that is sent into exile.[31] Thus it is likely that when Dtr 2 uses the motif of
persistent obstinacy, he utilizes it not to separate the culpability of the
various generations, but to create a linkage between them. That this

---

30. Weinfeld, *Deuteronomy and the Deuteronomic School*, p. 319.
31. That God's anger can reach a point of no return is also implied in Ezek. 9.9-
10.

reading is correct can be demonstrated by looking at the content of the second half of each of these four verses which Weinfeld fails to mention. Here one is informed that each king who acted evilly imitated his ancestors or a specific predecessor (Jehoiakim is specified as the evil predecessor for both Jehoiachin and Zedekiah). This type of language implies that even though these later kings were certainly guilty of evil behavior, the punishment that falls on the generation that is exiled is a punishment for their sins and those of their ancestors who were also led astray by corrupt monarchs. It is even possible that the evil behavior of the ancestors noted in 2 Kgs 23.32 and 37 is an oblique reference to Manasseh. One should note that Amon who is Manasseh's son is said to have acted like Manasseh his father (2 Kgs 21.20). It is most probable that the formula that says Jehoahaz and Jehoiakim 'acted in accord with all that their fathers had done' occurs here because their actual father, Josiah, acted righteously.[32] Thus it could not say that each king acted like 'his father' and instead went for the less specific wording 'his fathers'. It should be noted that this specific formula only occurs elsewhere in 2 Kgs 15.9 which speaks of the reign of Zechariah the son of Jeroboam II:

> He acted corruptly in God's sight just as his ancestors did; he did not depart from the sins of Jeroboam the son of Nebat caused Israel to sin.

It is most probable that the two formulae in ch. 23 are based on this prototype, a prototype that makes mention of Jeroboam. This is significant for several reasons. One is that it is further proof of the way in which Dtr 2 is modeled on Dtr 1. But what is most significant is that it seems to indicate that Dtr 2 may have wished to create a chain of transmission that explained how this corruption reached from Zedekiah and Jehoiachin to Jehoiakim, from Jehoiakim and Jehoahaz to Manasseh, and from Manasseh back to Jeroboam, who was the first monarch to lead Israel astray by following the ways of the nations that God had dispossessed (2 Kgs 17.8). A connection between the sins of Judah initiated by Manasseh and those of Israel initiated by Jeroboam is implied in 2 Kgs 17.19, a passage that is clearly from an exilic stratum:

> Not even Judah kept the commandments of the Lord their God; rather they followed the statutes that Israel practiced.

---

32. This is probably the explanation behind Zedekiah's formula too inasmuch as Josiah is his father as well. For an interesting discussion of the formulae surrounding the last Judean kings, see Seitz, *Theology in Conflict*, pp. 189-98.

Even if one should contest the connections I have attempted to draw between these last regnal formulae and Manasseh and Jeroboam, it is difficult to contest that these formulae testify to the guilt of numerous generations and thus support my contention that the deuteronomistic history advocates the notion of trans-generational retribution. In fact, Weinfeld himself assents to this position:

> The conception that God only requites the sins of the fathers on the children only if the latter propagate the evil ways of their fathers is, in effect, the underlying view of the concept of retribution in the deuteronomic history.[33]

The difficulty is that Weinfeld inaccurately categorizes cases in which a guilty generation receives punishment for both their own and their ancestors' sins. The fact that the generation which received the punishment was sinful does not necessarily mean that the punishment follows the principle of individualized retribution. This is clearly a case of trans-generational corporate retribution in which the party who receives the punishment did act wickedly, but nevertheless received the punishment that had been building for several generations. Trans-generational retribution is a form of corporate retribution in which the guilt of a sinful generation and its consequent punishment are stored for a generation or more and then released against a later generation. It does not exclude the idea that the recipient may also be somewhat deserving of punishment.[34] Such an idea is rather common in the Hebrew Bible, especially in describing an event as disastrous as the exile.[3] Thus a text in Jeremiah, pervaded by deuteronomic language, advocates precisely this idea.

33. Weinfeld, *Deuteronomy and the Deuteronomic School*, p. 318.

34. Also it should be noted that I affirm Weinfeld's insight that a good king might temporarily postpone the coming punishment.

35. This notion, that a guilty generation may be punished for its own errors and for those that its predecessors committed, is strongly implied in several places in the Hebrew Bible. In Exod. 32.34 after the Golden Calf episode God says, 'in the day that I visit, I will visit their sin upon them'. The rabbis explicitly draw the connection between the destruction of the Jerusalem and the Golden Calf episode by noting that the root פקד is used in both Ezek. 9.1 and in Exod. 32.34. 'Until when did [the consequences of] the golden calf last?...They lasted until the destruction of the Temple; as it is stated, "Cause the visitations of the city to draw near, every man with his destroying weapon in his hand"; and it is also written, "Nevertheless in the day when I visit, I will visit their sin upon them"' (*Lam. R.* 2.3). While the rabbinic attempt to draw the explicit connection between the exile and the Golden Calf episode on the basis of the verb פקד may not stand up to modern scrutiny, their insight that

> When you announce all these words to this people they will say to you,
> 'Why has the Lord spoken all of this great evil against us? What is the
> iniquity and the sin that we committed against the Lord our God?' You
> will reply to them, 'Because your fathers abandoned me—declares the
> Lord—and followed after other gods and served them and worshiped
> them; they abandoned me and did not keep my instruction. And you have
> acted worse than your fathers, indeed each of you is going after the
> stubbornness of his own evil heart and not listening to me. Therefore I will
> hurl you out of this land to a land that neither you nor your fathers have
> known and there you will serve other gods day and night; for I will not be
> merciful to you' (Jer. 16.10-13).

Even Chronicles, a text that does not attribute the downfall of Judah
to Manasseh (2 Chron. 33.1-20) and, in fact, highlights the culpability of
Zedekiah and his generation for the exile (2 Chron. 36.11-14), lets it be
known that the exile of Judah came about because of the continual
disobedience of the Judean populace over many years.

> And the Lord the God of their fathers had regularly sent (word) to them
> through his messengers, because he had pity on his people and on his
> dwelling place. But they mocked the messengers of God and spurned his
> words and taunted his prophets until the Lord's wrath against his people
> became irreversible (2 Chron. 36.15-16).

Such a proposition, that the punishment of the exile is caused by sins
that are carried across several generations, is *a fortiori* true for the
books of Kings. It may be true, as Weinfeld asserts, that the ruler of the
generation that experiences exile did evil, but this does not exclude the
idea that this generation receives a punishment not only for its own
errors, but for the sins of earlier corrupt generations as well. In Kings
the exile of Israel and that of Judah are each tied to the misdeeds of a
specific earlier king: Jeroboam for Israel (2 Kgs 17.21-23), Manasseh for
Judah (2 Kgs 23.26-27). Dtr 1, which tells us how each Northern king
acted corruptly and thus carried on the sinful tradition inaugurated by
Jeroboam, does so to inform us that the exile was caused by a rebellion
inaugurated by Jeroboam and continued by the people and its leaders

the Hebrew Bible contains the idea that a guilty generation can inherit the guilt of its
ancestors is on the mark and is supported by other biblical passages (Lev. 26.39;
Jer. 3.25; 16.10-13; Ezek. 20.23). This idea might also help explain two verses in
Lam. 5 that appear to contradict each other. Lam 5.7 implies that the exile is due to the
sins of earlier generations and Lam. 5.16 is an admission of guilt by those who were
exiled. A possible explanation is to advocate that both are true in that the guilt of
earlier generations was visited upon those who were themselves guilty.

over numerous generations. In Dtr 1 Jeroboam's sin is a necessary but not a sufficient cause for the exile. The sufficient cause was that numerous later monarchs and their respective generations followed in his evil ways.

One can find this same notion of persistent obduracy in two places in Dtr 2. One is the fact that Dtr 2 informs the reader that each of the last four kings acted corruptly. The second (whether it is part of Dtr 2 or of a third nomistic redaction) attributes the exile to the sins of the whole populace over numerous generations (2 Kgs 21.15; 22.17; 24.20). This second motif explicitly draws the connection between the way in which persistent evil behavior on the part of the Judean population has provoked God to ever greater levels of anger, until it reaches a point at which it is inextinguishable. Each of these motifs implies that the guilt of earlier generations is visited upon the generation that is finally exiled.

Additionally, it should be noted that in certain passages in Dtr 2 the sin of Manasseh appears to carry more of a sense of sufficient cause (2 Kgs 23.26-27; 24.2-4). Although it is possible that these texts are less interested in blaming just Manasseh, but instead intended to highlight how Manasseh initiated a type of religious behavior that each of the last four kings followed, nevertheless, these passages imply that the exile was inevitable because Manasseh's behavior was so heinous.[36] This motif of the inevitability of punishment further reinforces my contention that the deuteronomistic historian utilized the notion of trans-generational retribution.

Before proceeding with the theological analysis of the various corporate ideas that we have been discussing, a brief summary is in order. To this point I have argued the following:

1. Dtr 2's use of Manasseh to explain the exile of Judah is basically an imitation of Dtr 1's use of Jeroboam to explain the fall of the North, with the exception that Dtr 2 may have innovated in his tendency to blame Manasseh as a sufficient, rather than just a necessary cause for the exile.

2. The ways in which Dtr 1 and Dtr 2 utilize Jeroboam and Manasseh in their respective attempts to explain the exiles of the North and South reveal that both historians subscribe to intra- as well as inter-generational ideas.

---

36. This notion of the inevitability of exile due to earlier sins of the ancestors is expanded upon in other biblical texts such as Ezek. 20.23.

3. That these corporate ideas are invoked in order to explain some of the theologically most significant events in Israelite history points to the centrality and importance of these corporate ideas.
4. The fact that both editions of the deuteronomistic history utilized such ideas demonstrates that not only were they employed in pre-exilic times, but that these corporate ideas continued to persist into the exilic period.

Theological Analysis

That corporate ideas play such a significant role within the general framework of the deuteronomistic history compels us to inquire about the deeper theological rationale behind these corporate ideas. Why does the king's cultic behavior affect the nation as a whole and why does the sin of ealier generations and the punishment that it entails transfer across numerous generations? The answer to these questions is very complicated because there are various levels on which one might pursue this issue. On the broadest level, one could answer that the deuteronomistic historian's theological framework is one that is pervaded by the concept of covenant and that one should seek the answer to these questions within the constellation of covenantal ideas found within the Hebrew Bible in general and specifically within the deuteronomistic history.

When one turns to the covenantal ideas within the deuteronomistic history, it immediately becomes clear that there are two major patterns of covenantal thought operating within this corpus of material. There is the high royal theology that speaks of God's relationship to David and his progeny (2 Sam. 7) and there is the more general covenantal notion of God's special relationship with his people Israel (Josh. 24). Levenson has usefully understood these two covenantal modes as theological constellations that he labels as Zion and Sinai respectively.[37] At the outset it should be noted that both covenants are essentially corporate inasmuch as they deal with the fate of the nation as a whole. This can easily be demonstrated for the Sinaitic theology espoused by the deuteronomic school. Thus the following passage from Deut. 29.9-14 tells us that the covenant applies horizontally to everyone in this present

---

37. J.D. Levenson, *Sinai and Zion* (New Voices in Biblical Studies; Minneapolis: Winston, 1985). Also see his article entitled 'The Davidic Covenant and its Modern Interpreters', *CBQ* 41 (1979), pp. 205-19.

generation (vv. 9-10) and also vertically to all those who are not yet born and thus not actually present at this ceremony (vv. 13-14):

> You who are all standing here before the Lord your God—your tribal leaders, your elders, your officials, all the men of Israel, your children, your wives, the stranger within your camp, from the woodcutter to the drawer of water—to enter into the covenant of the Lord your God and its curses, which the Lord your God is making with you today. In order that he may establish you today as his people and he as your God, just as he proclaimed to you and as he swore to your ancestors, Abraham, Isaac, and Jacob. Not with you alone am I making this covenant and its curses, but both with those who are standing here today before the Lord our God and with those who are not with us here today.

The royal theology, in its various manifestations, is also corporate because its ultimate purpose is to provide security for the nation as a whole.[38] Thus even the texts that speak of an eternal promise to David, and inform him that that he will always have a descendant on the throne, maintain that the true purpose of such a covenant is to provide stability for God's people, Israel.

> I will set a place for my people Israel, plant them that they may dwell in it and tremble no more. No longer shall evil men oppress them as in the past, from the time that I appointed judges over my people Israel. I will give you rest from all your enemies (2 Sam. 7.10-11a).[39]

The motif of God's giving rest to the Israelites is central to deuteronomic theology (Deut. 12.9-10; Josh. 1.13; 21.42; 22.4; 23.1; 1 Kgs 5.18; 8.56).[40] The dynastic promise to David is intertwined with the security of the nation as a whole. 'David and his line will usher in the "rest" the judges

38. There are several different types of royal theology found in the Hebrew Bible. 'Not all royal theology was Davidic, and not all Davidic theology was covenantal'. Levenson, 'The Davidic Covenant', p. 217

39. McCarter following Ewald, Driver and Wellhausen emends the text to read, 'I will give him rest from all his enemies'. Although this reading will strengthen my argument, there is no textual support for it. Furthermore, the thrust of the passage makes it clear that the purpose of dynastic security is national security not vice versa. P.K. McCarter, *II Samuel* (AB; New York: Doubleday, 1984), p. 193.

40. For more on the significance of this concept in deuteronomic writings as well as elsewhere in the Bible, see G. von Rad, 'There Remains Still a Rest for the People of God: An Investigation of a Biblical Conception', in *The Problem of the Hexateuch and other Essays* (trans. E.W. Trueman Dicken; Edinburgh: Oliver & Boyd, 1965), pp. 94-102.

could not achieve.'[41] The close connection between royal theology and the fulfillment of God's promises of security for the nation as a whole indicates the corporate thrust inherent in this type of theology.

What must still be explored is the theological rationale behind the specific types of intra- and trans-generational retribution found in the passages that attribute the fall of Judah to Manasseh and his generation. The fact that God made a covenant with David and his progeny (2 Sam. 7) helps clarify why a given monarch, or his descendants, might suffer when he errs (2 Sam. 7.14). Why the nation as a whole suffers for the sins of its king is more difficult to explain. It is possible to view the connection between the sin of the king and the punishment of the people as an instance of what Daube calls 'ruler punishment'.[42] By this Daube means the following:

> A sinner might be punished by being deprived of human 'property' (his men if he was a king, his son if he was a father, his wife if he was a husband) just as well as being deprived of any other goods.[43]

Daube invokes this idea to elucidate texts such as 2 Samuel 24 in which an errant king brings disaster on his subjects. He argues that the death of the seventy thousand Israelites does not necessarily indicate that they are guilty or are in fact being punished.

> It was he, not they, who was chastised for his arrogance by their decimation... His sin was not laid at his property's charge but it was damaged simply in order that he should be impoverished. But, then obviously, the mere fact that he was made poorer by a host of men instead of coins, sheep or slaves did not alter the direction of the vengeance: it was still he whom God meant to hit.[44]

In other words, the Israelites are all the property of the king and thus they may be hurt in order to punish the king. This idea may be useful in explaining certain instances of divine retribution and it fits in well with the theology advocated by 2 Sam. 7.14, which tells us that if a king errs God will 'chastise him with the rod of men and with the stripes of humankind'.[45] Unfortunately it is less useful in explaining the

---

41. McCarter, *II Samuel*, p. 219.
42. Daube, *Studies in Biblical Law*, pp. 160-86.
43. Daube, *Studies in Biblical Law*, p. 165.
44. Daube, *Studies in Biblical Law*, pp. 161-62
45. It should be noted that even Daube admits that it is not always easy to tell whether a given case is due to ruler punishment or due to communal responsibility. I

punishment in the three passages currently under examination. The complete dissolution of the Judean state is a punishment of such great proportion that it seems unlikely that a thinker as sophisticated as the deuteronomistic historian would view this *tremendous* national disaster as a punishment directed solely at the sins of an errant monarch.[46]

It is at this point that Levenson's discussion of the interaction between the Davidic covenant and the Sinaitic covenant becomes quite helpful for this investigation. The punishment of exile is actually one that originally belongs to the Sinaitic traditions in which blessing and curse are contingent upon one's obedience or disobedience to the legislation handed down by God. Exile is specifically listed among the punishments for covenantal disobedience in both Leviticus and Deuteronomy.

> I will scatter you among the nations and I will unsheath the sword against you. Your land will be a desolation and your cities a ruin (Lev. 26.33).

> And the Lord will scatter you among all the peoples, from one end of the earth to the other, and there you will worship other gods of wood and stone that neither you nor your ancestors have known (Deut. 4.27).

> And the Lord will scatter you among the peoples and only a few of you will remain among the nations to which the Lord will drive you (Deut. 28.64).

It seems that over time both the specific stipulations and the blessings and curses from the Sinaitic traditions began to pervade the royal theology, as can be seen from the way in which the Davidic covenantal theology became more conditionalized over time (1 Kgs 2.3-4; 8.25; 9.2-9; 2 Kgs 21.7-8; Ps. 132.11-12).[47] I say more conditionalized because

---

am not as confident as he is that 2 Sam. 24 is a clear-cut instance of ruler punishment. It may be that the people are punished not just as David's property but because they share a portion of the guilt, inasmuch as he acted as their proxy when he took the census.

46. Although the deuteronomistic historian subscribes to the ancient covenantal notion that any individual or group of individuals who sins may bring punishment on the whole nation (Josh. 7; 22.20), it is dubious to assert that he advocates the idea that God would impose a punishment as severe as the exile solely because Manasseh sinned.

47. There is an ongoing debate about whether the passages in Kings that conditionalize the promise of eternal dynasty to David are the work of Dtr 2, or whether these texts are the work of Dtr 1 who conceived of two different promises: one of conditional eternal dynasty over all Israel and one of unconditional eternal dynasty over Judah. See Friedman, *Exile*, pp. 10-13; Halpern, *Historians*, pp. 144-80; Levenson,

even the earlier forms of the Davidic royal theology include some stipulations and some type of punishment.[48] Thus 2 Sam. 7.14-16 and Ps. 89.20-37 tell us that if certain Davidids fail to act properly they will be punished, but the dynasty will endure eternally, while 1 Kgs 2.4, 8.25, 9.2-9, 2 Kgs 21.7-8 and Ps. 132.11-12 make eternal dynastic succession contingent upon obedience to the commandments of God.

> The subordination of the Davidic covenant to the Sinaitic in 1 Kgs 8.25, therefore, must be seen as a reinterpretation of the pristine Davidic covenant material, a reinterpretation that reflects the growing canonical status of the Sinaitic traditions that will become the Pentateuch. 1 Kgs 8.25 is the vengeance of Moses upon David, of the 'kingdom of priests' upon the hubris of the political state, for it resolves the clash between the two covenants in favor of the Mosaic one. The entitlement of the house of David is no longer indefeasible; it is contingent upon observance of the *mitsvot*.[49]

I would argue that it is precisely this further conditionalizing of the Davidic covenant caused by the growing influence of the Sinaitic covenant that elucidates the rationale behind Dtr 2's move to link the exile of Judah to Manasseh's sinful behavior. The exile of Judah could justifiably be attributed to Manasseh's behavior inasmuch as the Davidic dynasty's continuity became contingent upon the proper behavior of each monarch and also of each monarch's generation. That the monarch

'From Temple to Synagogue', p. 163, and 'The Last Four Verses in Kings', pp. 354-56. There are good arguments on both sides of this dilemma, and because of the circular nature of both arguments, it remain dubious that the debate will ever be resolved without new evidence.

48.   The terminology used of the two types of covenants is somewhat problematic. The Sinaitic covenant, which is compared to ancient Near Eastern suzerainty-vassal treaties, is described as conditional. The Davidic covenant which is compared to a type of covenantal grant is described as unconditional, at least in its earliest form. But as noted by Levenson 'this terminology is regrettable, since it can encourage the notion that the covenant with David is without stipulations, a covenant of grace rather than of law. In fact, however, the Davidid is still obligated and hence subject to punishment'. Levenson, 'Who Inserted the Book of the Torah?', p. 225. Levenson suggests the terms ancestral (Davidic) versus contemporary (Sinaitic) as well as mentioning Weinfeld's preference for obligatory and treaty (Sinaitic) versus promissory and grant (Davidic). M. Weinfeld, 'The Covenant of Grant in the Old Testament and in the Ancient Near East', *JAOS* 90 (1970), pp. 184-203. It seems that no single pair of terms can do full justice to the nuances of each type of covenant, and thus I have employed the more common terms, conditional and unconditional, but with qualification.

49.   Levenson, *Sinai*, p. 211.

was responsible for the behavior of his fellow citizens should not at all be surprising. The oldest strata of Israelite religion appear to affirm the idea that Israelites are corporately responsible for each other.[50] The Sinaitic covenantal traditions express this ancient notion by implying that every Israelite is responsible for preventing any other Israelite from sinning (Lev. 19.17), or failing this, he is responsible to identify the sinner and even participate in his punishment (Deut. 13.7-12).[51] Such corporate responsibility is *a fortiori* true of the reigning monarch who sat upon God's throne and thus became responsible for enforcing God's laws.[52] But just as the king was responsible for the sins of the general populace, the general populace also became implicated in the sins of the monarch. The king was no ordinary individual but was God's vicar on earth, the single most important mediator between the people and their God. If the king sinned, he endangered the welfare of the populace in two ways. First of all, this sin was done by the nation's representative before God and thus the monarch never truly acts only on his own behalf. Secondly, the king set the tone of official state worship and thus automatically implicated the people in any cultic sins that he committed because they were bound to follow his lead in cultic matters. That this in fact happened is proven by the numerous passages that tell us that not only did Jeroboam and Manasseh sin, but they also caused Israel or Judah to sin (1 Kgs 14.16; 15.30; 2 Kgs 3.3; 21.11, 16; 23.15 etc.). This does not mean that Jeroboam and Manasseh single-handedly brought down Israel and Judah respectively. But it does point to the existence of a type

50. This thesis will be substantiated in greater detail in the next three chapters.

51. I will explore this concept at much greater length in Chapter 4 below.

52. See G.W. Ahlström, *Royal Administration and National Religion in Ancient Palestine* (Studies in the History of the Ancient Near East, 1; Leiden: Brill, 1982), pp. 1-9. Ahlström notes that King Solomon built his palace-temple complex as a separate acropolis like other ancient Near Eastern monarchs. This meant that the king and his God shared the same living space and even the same throne (Ps. 45.7; 1 Chron. 28.5; 29.23; 2 Chron. 9.8) and 'therefore that the royal throne was divine'. Ahlström, *Royal Administration*, p. 6. The king played a very central role in ancient Israelite religion and was accorded much of the respect normally reserved only for the deity (Exod. 22.27). For more on the status and importance of the king in ancient Israel, see R. de Vaux, *Ancient Israel*. I. *Social Institutions* (New York: McGraw-Hill, 1965), pp. 110-14. The king also appears to have been responsible for the condition of the nation and especially for its fertility (Ps. 72). For more on the connection between the king and fertility, see A.S. Kapelrud, 'King and Fertility: A Discussion of II Sam. 21.1-14', *Norsk Teologisk Tidsskrift* 56 (1955), pp. 113-22.

of corporate thinking in which the king of a given generation, acting as that generation's representative before God, can implicate the general populace in his evil actions.

We must now proceed to examine the connection between the notion of covenant and the transference of punishment across generations. Trans-generational recompense is actually quite at home within both the Davidic and the Sinaitic traditions. The promise of dynastic continuance that God makes to David in 2 Samuel 7 carries within it the idea that merit can transfer across numerous generations (2 Kgs 8.19). Additionally, one could argue that the promise to the patriarchs, which itself is theologically intertwined with the royal theology,[53] functions as a reservoir of merit that remains in effect across numerous generations and is invoked in order to mitigate the punishment that Israel might have received (Exod. 32.13 and Deut. 9.5-8).[54] It seems equally clear that the deuteronomistic historian, building on Sinaitic covenantal ideas surrounding the transference of punishment across generations (Exod. 20.5), often utilizes this motif (1 Kgs 21.29; 2 Kgs 20.16-18). Thus it is not surprising that the deuteronomistic history contains various explanations for the exile of Judah that rely on the validity of the notion of trans-generational retribution. Whether it is blaming the exile on Manasseh and/or his generation, on the last four kings and/or their generations, or on the whole populace ever since they came out of Egypt, the deuteronomistic history is utilizing the idea of trans-generational retribution.

Conclusions

1. The texts examined in this chapter demonstrate that corporate notions of punishment are not only found in occasional narratives, but are in fact

53. Weinfeld, 'Covenant of Grant', and R.E. Clements, *Abraham and David* (SBT, Second Series, 5; Naperville, IL: Allenson, 1967).

54. The notion that the actions of the patriarchs can benefit later generations is developed extensively in rabbinic literature under the rubric of זכות אבות. Although it is clear that the merit of the patriarchs is not identical to the covenant with the patriarchs, the two notions are closely allied. For a fuller discussion of this idea in the rabbinic literature, see A. Marmorstein, *The Doctrine of Merits in Old Rabbinical Literature* (New York: Ktav, 1968 [1920]), pp. 3-188. This study was originally published in 1920; S. Schechter, *Aspects of Rabbinic Theology* (New York: Schocken Books, 1961 [1909]), pp. 170-98; E.E. Urbach, *The Sages* (trans. I. Abrahams; Cambridge, MA: Harvard University Press, 1987), pp. 483-511.

one of the major devices employed by both Dtr 1 and Dtr 2 in their respective attempts to elucidate the whole history of ancient Israel and Judah and their eventual exiles. Thus there is strong evidence for the prevalence, centrality and persistence of these corporate ideas within Israelite thought.

2. The prevalence, centrality and persistence of the corporate ideas becomes much more understandable once one realizes that these ideas flow out of the covenantal theology that is so important to the whole structure and ideology of the deuteronomistic history. This covenantal theology is ultimately based on a dynamic interaction between what were originally two distinct constellations of ideas: a Davidic royal theology and a Sinaitic theology. The Sinai covenant appears to have had the effect of making the promise of dynastic continuance contingent upon the king's religious behavior. Thus, if a king acts improperly, he might endanger both the continuance of his dynasty, as well as the continuance of the nation as an independent, political entity. The concept of trans-generational punishment is a notion firmly rooted in the Sinaitic as well as in the Davidic traditions, and thus it should come as no surprise that the deuteronomistic history informs us that the wicked behavior of earlier monarchs and earlier generations is a major cause of the exile of Israel and Judah from their lands.

Chapter 3

DIVINE WRATH AND CORPORATE PUNISHMENT

It is generally recognized that the covenantal theology produced by the various biblical authors is a comprehensive system of ideas that developed over a long period of time.[1] The deuteronomistic historian developed a highly sophisticated form of covenantal theology which utilized many ideas that were quite ancient. Where did the various notions of corporate guilt and punishment stem from in the period before these notions became part and parcel of the larger deuteronomistic covenantal framework?

I contend that the deuteronomistic historian's covenantal understanding of the concept of corporate guilt was strongly influenced by *earlier* conceptions of sin, bloodguilt, holiness and divine wrath. This is so not only because the deuteronomistic historian and the author of the book of Deuteronomy continued to use these early religious notions, but also because much, although by no means all, of the corporate thrust of covenantal theology developed out of these early religious notions.[2] If a reasonable case can be made for this hypothesis, it will not only clarify why corporate ideas are so prevalent throughout the biblical period, but it will also give us a greater understanding of corporate ways of thinking, and ultimately a greater sympathy for them.

In order to substantiate this claim more fully, I will explore the way in

---

1. For a summary of the major arguments surrounding this idea see E.W. Nicholson, *God and his People* (Oxford: Clarendon Press, 1986). Nicholson argues that these ideas really only begin to take shape in Hosea's time (late eighth century). Other scholars who subscribe to notions of an early league or tribal amphictyony would obviously argue that covenantal ideas began to develop at a much earlier period in Israelite history. For example, see G.E. Mendenhall, *The Tenth Generation* (Baltimore: The Johns Hopkins University Press, 1973), pp. 1-31.

2. It is important to recognize that other antecedents, such as the legal forms of treaty literature, which are addressed not only to vassals but to their nations as a whole, have also contributed to the strongly corporate character of Israelite covenantal theology.

which each of these concepts functions in the deuteronomistic history and demonstrate the ways in which these ideas are linked to the more sophisticated forms of covenantal theology. I will begin this procedure by focusing on the notion of divine wrath in both Deuteronomy and the deuteronomistic history.

The notion of divine wrath could easily be the focus of a monograph-length exposition, but such an exposition would take us too far afield from our current focus.[3] For the purposes of this project we only need to establish the following points:

1. Divine wrath is an important, persistent and prevalent motif within the book of Deuteronomy and the deuteronomistic history.
2. Divine wrath, within the Hebrew Bible in general, and within Deuteronomy and the deuteronomistic history in particular, is frequently portrayed as having the following qualities: (a) it can be set off accidentally or unintentionally; (b) it is sometimes stored up over a long period and then released in a disproportionate way upon the individual, or group, who happens to cause its release; (c) once it is set off either accidentally, or by the intentional error, it may spread indiscriminately to the larger surrounding population.
3. Although the theological framework of Deuteronomy and the deuteronomistic history has covenantalized the notion of divine wrath by linking it to both human sin and divine punishment, this development has not eliminated the more ancient ideas that are traditionally associated with this concept.

Divine anger or wrath is quite ubiquitous within the Hebrew Bible. In fact, 'words for anger are connected with God three times as often as

---

3.   For more extensive discussion, see the following works: W. Eichrodt, *Theology of the Old Testament* (trans. J.A. Baker; Philadelphia: Westminster Press, 1961), I, pp. 258-69; S. Erlandsson, 'The Wrath of YHWH', *TynBul* 23 (1972), pp. 111-16; J. Gray, 'The Wrath of God in Canaanite and Hebrew Literature', *Journal of the Manchester University Egyptian and Oriental Society* 25 (1947–53), pp. 9-19; H.M. Haney, *The Wrath of God in the Former Prophets* (New York: Vantage, 1960), pp. 11-75; A.J. Heschel, *The Prophets* (New York: Harper, 1962), II, pp. 59-86; F. Lindström, *God and the Origin of Evil* (ConBOT, 21; Lund: Gleerup, 1983); P. Volz, *Das Dämonische in YHWH* (Sammlung gemeinverständlicher Vorträge und Schriften aus dem Gebiet der Theologie und Religionsgeschichte, 110; Tübingen: Mohr [Paul Siebeck], 1924).

they are connected with man in the OT'.[4] The concept of divine wrath is also quite prevalent within Deuteronomy and the deuteronomistic history. Within this corpus one finds a variety of roots each employed across a wide spectrum of texts that speak about divine anger. These include אנף (Deut. 1.37; 4.21; 7.4; 9.20; 11.17; 13.18; 29.23, 26, 27; Josh. 7.1, 26; 23.16; 2 Sam. 6.7; 24.1; 2 Kgs 13.3; 23.26; 24.20, etc.); כעס (Deut. 4.25; 9.18; 32.16; 1 Kgs 14.9; 15.30; 16.2, 7, 13, 26, 33; 21.22; 22.54; 2 Kgs 17.17; 21.6, 15; 22.17; 23.19, 26); חרה (Deut. 7.4; 11.17; 13.18; 29.26; 31.17; Josh. 23.16; 2 Sam. 22.8; 2 Kgs 13.3; 23.26); קצף (Deut. 1.34; 9.7, 8, 19; Josh. 22.18, 20); חמה (Deut. 9.19; 29.27; 2 Kgs 22.13, 17).[5] This extensive list of citations reveals that the thinkers who worked within the deuteronomic tradition commonly employed the notion of divine wrath in their writings. Furthermore, as one might have already noted from the discussion in the previous chapter, the notion of divine wrath occurs quite frequently in texts that attempt to explain why God exiled Israel and Judah. Thus, the notion of divine wrath is not only invoked often in the deuteronomic corpus, but it is employed as a central theological concept that helps explain the greatest tragedy in ancient Israelite history.

The three primary elements that commonly occur in texts that describe divine wrath do not all occur in every text that speaks about God's anger. Different texts stress different facets of divine anger. But the three ideas I have chosen to highlight recur with great frequency across a wide spectrum of texts.

The notion that divine wrath can be set off unintentionally is nicely illustrated in a narrative about the attempted transference of the ark to Jerusalem.

> When they came to the threshing floor of Nodan,[6] Uzzah reached out to the ark of God and steadied it because the oxen had slipped.[4] The anger of the Lord flared up against Uzzah and God struck him down there because

4. E. Johnson, 'אנף', in *TDOT*, I, pp. 348-60.

5. This list is not exhaustive and also does not take note of the references in the book of Jeremiah that stem from this same school of thought.

6. There appears to be some discrepancy about the name here. 1 Chron. 13.9 has כידן and the LXX has Νωδαβ. Following McCarter's suggestion it seems easiest to explain the variants from an original נודן found in 4QSamᵃ. McCarter, *II Samuel*, p. 164.

7. It has been suggested that this should be emended to שָׁמְטוּ inasmuch as there is no other evidence that the *qal* stem of the verb could be used intransitively. Unfortunately, there is little textual evidence to support such an emendation. The LXX

he reached out his hand toward the ark[8] and he died there beside the ark of God. David became angry because the Lord had burst forth against Uzzah—that place is called[9] Peretz Uzzah to this day (2 Sam. 6.6-8).[10]

This particular narrative is one in which the punishment is so severe in relation to the error committed that it is difficult, if not impossible, to argue that such a punishment is equitable. Uzzah may have committed a breach of ritual conduct by touching the ark (Num. 4.15),[11] but the narrative portrays him in such sympathetic terms that one cannot help feeling that God had acted unfairly. Uzzah appears to be punished for preventing the ark from falling off the cart and smashing on to the ground below. This passage depicts the ark and the God who sat enthroned on its cherubim as somewhat enigmatic and fickle.[12] Thus

reads ὅτι περιέσπασεν αὐτὴν ὁ μόσχος. But it is unclear whether this is a translation of a superior Hebrew text. The LXX of this verse is quite a bit longer than the Masoretic text which may indicate that it was attempting to fill in a text that was terse and difficult to understand, rather than containing a superior version.

8.   Reading עַל־הֹשֵׁל as a remnant of אֲשֶׁר־שָׁלַח יָדוֹ עַל־הָאָרוֹן עַל with 1 Chron. 13.10 and 4QSam[a].

9.   I have opted to read it as an impersonal use of קְרָא on analogy to Exod. 17.7 and 2 Sam. 2.16. But it is possible to read it as an active use referring to David on analogy to 2 Sam. 5.9 or 2 Kgs 14.7.

10.   For more extensive discussion of 2 Sam. 6, see McCarter, *II Samuel*, pp. 161-84; J.R. Porter, 'The Interpretation of 2 Samuel VI and Psalm CXXXII', *JTS* NS 5 (1954), pp. 161-73; N.H. Tur-Sinai, 'The Ark of God at Beit Shemesh (1 Sam. VI) and Pereṣ 'Uzzah (2 Sam. VI; 1 Chron. XIII)', *VT* 1 (October 1951), pp. 275-86.

11.   I say 'may' because Num. 4.15 warns the Kohathites not to touch the sacred objects, but the overall gist of ch. 4 does not imply that Aaron and his sons were prohibited from touching these sacred items. Aaron and his sons, in fact, had to cover them all and when not covered they often touched many of these sacred items that the Kohathites are not allowed to touch (Num. 4.14). One gets the impression that Uzzah, who is Abinadav's son, is a direct descendant of Aaron and thus might have even been allowed to touch the sancta directly. One might argue that Uzzah's sin was not that he touched the ark, but that by stabilizing the ark he called into question God's ability to take care of himself. The idea that one might be punished for implying that God was not powerful can be seen in Num. 20.12. I argue below that this is a case of a holiness violation, but it is important to note that this argument is not watertight.

12.   Certain Jewish and Christian apologists would object to my claim that the Uzzah incident depicts God as fickle and enigmatic. Such a response is required by these apologists because they cannot accept that ancient Israelite religion would advocate the idea that God may have an amoral or capricious dimension. Heschel argues that 'there is no belief in divine arbitrariness, in an anger which consumes and afflicts without moral justification'. Heschel, *The Prophets*, p. 77. Eichrodt similarly states

David is afraid to bring it into Jerusalem (2 Sam. 6.9-10) and only does so when he hears that although dangerous, it is also beneficial (2 Sam. 6.11-12).

The notion of sin being stored up over numerous generations and finally being released in a disproportionate manner upon the sinner, or the generation, that finally pushes God beyond his limit, is one that was discussed at length in the previous chapter. The whole notion of trans-generational punishment presumes that God can and often does store up sin in this fashion. The clearest evidence for the existence of this principle can be found in the reaction to the respective Northern and Southern exiles. The deuteronomistic history portrays the generation that received such punishment as guilty, but it also stresses the notion that the punishment has been accumulating for a long period of time. Such sentiments occur in exilic texts that reflect on the fact that though punishment is warranted the suffering appears disproportionate, especially when compared to the evils committed by other nations (Lam. 5.7-8 and Hab. 2.12-17).

The idea that once wrath is released it has a tendency to spread beyond the guilty and consume anyone in its vicinity can be illustrated from Num. 17.6-15.[13]

> On the following day all the congregation of Israel complained against
> Moses and Aaron, saying, 'You have killed the people of the Lord'. When
> the congregation gathered against Moses and Aaron, they turned toward
> the Tent of Meeting; the cloud had covered it and the glory of the Lord

'that in the case of God there can never be any question of despotic caprice striking out in blind rage'. Eichrodt, *Theology*, p. 265. While I agree that in many instances of divine retribution, the Hebrew Bible does make a strong connection between God's punishment and the specific misdeeds of those who receive the punishment, I find it difficult to assent to the argument that there are no cases in the Hebrew Bible in which God's action is either completely inscrutable to those being punished, or is vastly out of proportion to the human error that released the punishment. Additionally, it should be noted that this is only one of several texts that speak about God as a dangerous power who is apt to strike out at those who are around him in a highly volatile manner (Lev. 10.1-7; 1 Sam. 6.19-7.2; 2 Sam. 24). The severity of God's reaction does not always match the deed that set it in motion; thus the language of divine dread and terror (Isa. 63.2-6).

13. On this passage and others that speak of the uncontrollable wrath of God, see J.D. Levenson, 'Cataclysm, Survival, and Regeneration in the Hebrew Bible', in D. Landes (ed.), *Confronting Omnicide: Jewish Reflections on Weapons of Mass Destruction* (Northvale, NJ: Jason Aronson, 1991), pp. 49-56.

appeared. Moses and Aaron went to the Tent of Meeting, and the Lord spoke to Moses, saying, 'Remove yourselves from this congregation that I may annhilate them at once'. They fell on their faces. Moses said to Aaron, 'Take the censer and put fire from the altar and incense on it; go quickly into the congregation and make atonement for them because the wrath (הקצף) has gone out from before the Lord; the plague has begun'. Aaron took it as Moses had commanded and he went into the midst of the congregation, and indeed the plague had begun among the people. He burned incense and made atonement for the people; he stood between the living and the dead and the plague was checked. Fourteen thousand seven hundred died in the plague aside from those who died in the Korah affair. Aaron then returned to Moses at the Tent of Meeting; the plague was over.[14]

In this particular narrative God's wrath is characterized as an almost independent entity; once set off by the complaint of the people it indiscriminately kills everyone in the area. Notice the wording in v. 11 which speaks of הקצף (the word 'wrath' with the definite article) as something that proceeds from God and moves through the camp leaving a plague among the people in its wake.

At this point one might object by noting that, even if these cases indicate that divine wrath sometimes exhibits these traits, it is far from clear that the concept of divine wrath, which is usually invoked within Deuteronomy and the deuteronomistic history, commonly exhibits these qualities. One might regard these cases as evidence that there was an earlier, primitive conception of divine wrath which was eventually displaced by a more sophisticated conception in which divine wrath is always an understandable and quite measured response to a specific error. The best way to clarify this matter is to look at the language employed in passages that are steeped in covenantal theology and also utilize the idea of divine wrath.

> Watch yourselves lest you forget the covenant of the Lord your God that he made with you, and you make any graven image of any likeness for yourselves, which the Lord your God prohibited to you. For the Lord your

---

14. One should note that the link between corporate ideas of punishment and divine wrath as expressed in a plague is also found in 2 Sam. 24, a narrative that is located within the deuteronomistic corpus. Clearly the narratives share a common set of assumptions about divine anger and ritual expiation. Both plagues are stopped by ritual means: Aaron offering incense in Num. 17.12 and David offering sacrifices in 2 Sam. 24.25. Also both narratives describe the plague with the word המגפה and they both use a *niphal* form of the root עצר to indicate that the plague was stopped (Num. 17.13, 15; 2 Sam. 24.25).

God is a consuming fire, a jealous God. When you have sons and grand-sons and you have become settled in the land, should you become corrupt and make any sculpted image and act wickedly in the sight of the Lord your God, thus angering him, I call heaven and earth to witness against you today that you will soon perish from the land that you are crossing the Jordan to possess; your days upon it will not be long because you will be utterly destroyed (Deut. 4.23-26).

And all the nations will ask, 'Why did the Lord do thus to this land? Why this mighty burning wrath?' They will be told, Because they abandoned the covenant of the Lord, the God of their fathers, that he made with them when he brought them out from the land of Egypt. They went and served other gods and worshipped them, gods whom they had not known and that he did not apportion to them. Thus the the anger of the Lord was against this land bringing upon it every curse written in this book. The Lord uprooted them from their land in anger, fury, and great wrath and threw them into another land, and so it is today (Deut. 29.23-27).

But they did not listen and they stiffened their necks like their fathers who did not have faith in the Lord their God. They rejected his statutes and his covenant that he made with their fathers, and the warnings he issued them. They went after worthless things and became worthless [acting] like the nations that were around them which the Lord had commanded them not to imitate. They abandoned all the commandments of the Lord their God; they made two molten calves for themselves and made an Asherah and they worshiped all the host of heaven and served Baal. They caused their sons and their daughters to pass through fire; they practiced divination and soothsaying, and sold themselves to do evil in the sight of the Lord thus angering him. The Lord became very angry at Israel and he turned them away from his presence; none remained but the tribe of Judah alone (2 Kgs 17.14-18).

Because they abandoned me and they burned incense to other gods and angered me with all their deeds my anger will burn against this place and not be quenched (2 Kgs 22.17).

Each of these passages speaks rather directly about the ability of Israel to misbehave and thus transgress God's covenant, and by doing so to stir up divine wrath. Once this divine wrath reaches a critical point, it is poured out upon the nation in the form of the covenantal curses that eventuate in the exile of the nation. What is not noticed immediately, but becomes clear upon further reflection, is the strength of the language used to describe the action of divine wrath. It is like a consuming fire that cannot be quenched (Deut. 4.24; 2 Kgs 22.17), or like a violent storm that uproots things and cast them into far away places (Deut. 29.27; Jer. 23.19-20). The Uzzah and Korah incidents reveal a time when such language accurately described the way in which ancient Israel conceived of divine wrath. In fact, it is highly probable that the powerful language that surrounds the concept of divine wrath in Deuteronomy and the deuteronomistic history is borrowed from these earlier conceptions. The question is, how has the covenantal framework which has utilized these notions changed them? In their current context should these expressions be read only as metaphors that appeal to the poetic imagination, or should this type of language be understood more literally?

Scholarly opinion is divided as to how the language of divine wrath should be understood. Certain scholars such as Baruch Levine[15] and Klaus Koch[16] read the language of sin, wrath and punishment in a very literalistic manner and thus tend to understand these phenomena as still steeped in a magical worldview. Other thinkers like John Barton[17] and Anthony Thiselton[18] view much of the language of the Hebrew Bible as a type of poetic rhetoric that is all too often overread and thus misunderstood.

Although I acknowledge that there are ways in which Israel's covenantal theology has transmuted certain earlier ideas that it absorbed, the evidence appears to favor those who do not read the language of divine wrath as merely metaphorical and who thus recognize that it reveals a religious understanding that is vastly different from that found in the modern West. Not only is this case in a few isolated narratives, but there is evidence to suggest that this conception of divine wrath is typical of Deuteronomy and the deuteronomistic history.[19] To argue this case successfully one must not, as Koch did, argue from the root meaning of specific words to the general theological propositions which they advocate. Rather, one must examine the larger theological systems and see the ways in which specific words function in this larger complex of ideas. What evidence is there that the notion of divine wrath commonly invoked in texts that speak of the exile has the same qualities that it had

15. B.A. Levine, *In the Presence of the Lord* (SJLA, 5; Leiden: Brill, 1974), pp. 67-91.

16. Koch, 'Doctrine of Retribution', pp. 57-87.

17. Barton, 'Natural Law', pp. 1-14.

18. Thiselton, 'The Supposed Power of Words', pp. 283-99.

19. Dennis J. McCarthy, 'The Wrath of YHWH and the Structural Unity of the Deuteronomistic History', in *Institution and Narrative* (AnBib, 108; Rome: Biblical Institute Press, 1985), pp. 341-52. Originally published in J.L. Crenshaw and J.T. Willis (eds.), *Essays in Old Testament Ethics. J.Philip Hyatt, In Memoriam* (New York: Ktav, 1974), pp. 97-110.

in the Uzzah and Korah incidents? To begin with, there is no inherent reason to differentiate the conception of divine wrath found in the Uzzah and Korah incidents from that found in other passages in Deuteronomy and the deuteronomistic history. Once one has proven that divine wrath has certain qualities as expressed by the Uzzah and Korah incidents, the burden of proof now rests upon those who wish to advocate that a substantial evolution in religious ideas has taken place in the later biblical period. But this is an argument *e silentio*. The best way to support the contention that the notion of divine wrath found throughout Deuteronomy and the deuteronomistic history is fundamentally the same as that found in Uzzah and Korah cases is to demonstrate that the religious worldview espoused by the Uzzah and Korah texts is an essential part of the covenantal theology found in Deuteronomy and the deuteronomistic history.

The Uzzah incident is bound up in the larger issue of holiness and the danger that one runs into if one comes into direct contact with it (Exod. 19.12, 24; 1 Sam. 6.19). Although this topic will be discussed at length in the following chapter, it is necessary at this point at least to broach it. Different sources within the Hebrew Bible have different understandings of the idea of holiness, yet they do share certain basic assumptions about this notion.[20] Holiness, and the consequences that flow from it, often operate in what could be termed an amoral universe (Lev. 10.1-7; 2 Sam. 6.6-8). It is precisely this idea that Rudolf Otto so profoundly elucidates in his now famous book.

> It is patent from many passages in the Old Testament that this wrath has no concern whatever with moral qualities. There is something very baffling in the way in which it is kindled and manifested. It is, as has been well said, 'like a hidden force of nature', like stored-up electricity, discharging itself upon anyone who comes too near.[21]

20. An excellent comparison of the differences between P and D can be found in M. Weinfeld, 'Pentateuch', in *EncJud*, see especially XIII, cols. 243-57. On the concept of holiness in the Hebrew Bible, see J.G. Gammie, *Holiness in Israel* (Overtures to Biblical Theology; Philadelphia: Fortress Press, 1989). For a survey of the ways in which the concept of holiness changed between the biblical and rabbinic periods, see Jacob Neusner, *The Idea of Purity in Ancient Judaism* (SJLA, 1; Leiden: Brill, 1973) and most recently, H. Eilberg-Schwartz, *The Savage in Judaism* (Bloomington: Indiana University Press, 1990). For an overview of holiness in general, see R. Otto, *The Idea of the Holy* (trans. J.W. Harvey; London: Oxford University Press, 1958).

21. Otto, *The Idea of the Holy*, p. 18. One may go even further and suggest that

Such a terrifying view of divine wrath is no doubt linked to concepts that are quite ancient. Thus, as early as the exodus narrative, one finds the conception of God as a dangerous power that can only be counteracted by certain ritual procedures, such as the act of circumcision performed by Zipporah for Moses (Exod. 4.24-26), the apotropaic lamb's blood that is smeared on the doorposts to protect the Israelites from the effects of the tenth plague (Exod. 12.1-13), or the incense offered by Aaron in his successful attempt to stay the divine plague (Num. 17.6-15).[22] That this is an important dimension of Israel's experience of the divine can be demonstrated by the fact that ancient Israel called its God by the epithet אל קנא (Exod. 20.5; 34.14; Deut. 4.24; 5.9; 6.15; אל קנוא in Josh. 24.19; Nah. 1.2).[23]

It is Barton's failure to recognize these ancient ideas and the fact that they continue to be used in the later biblical period that leads him to draw an oversimplified view of divine retribution in the prophetic literature.

> God's judgment is never capricious, but wholly consistent, and he acts according to moral principles which are essentially the same as those recognized among men.[24]

The difficulty with such a position is that it tends to ignore the more explosive types of divine action that occur rather frequently within the Hebrew Bible. Divine wrath, although often provoked by human misbehavior, does appear to have an uncontrollable quality to it, once it is released. Furthermore, there are certain instances in which it is amoral, or even demonic. God frequently reacts in a highly volatile manner to human sin, thus the language of divine wrath and terror. Here, Martin Buber's comment on Exod. 4.24-26 is instructive:

> The early stage of Israelite religion knows no Satan; if a power attacks a man and threatens him, it is proper to recognize YHVH in it or behind it, no matter how nocturnally dread it may be.[25]

---

the whole dichotomy between holiness and morality is anachronistic.

22. For a different reading of Exod. 4.24-26 and 12.1-13, see Lindström, *Origin of Evil*, pp. 41-73.

23. *Contra* Eichrodt who asserts that 'wrath never forms one of the permanent attributes of the God of Israel'. Eichrodt, *Theology*, p. 262.

24. Barton, 'Natural Law', p. 12.

25. M. Buber, *Moses* (London: East & West Library, 1946), p. 58.

That Deuteronomy and the deuteronomistic history continue to subscribe to early religious conceptions of holiness and bloodguilt can be proven by noting that various legislative texts in Deuteronomy (Deut. 21.1-9; 22.8; 23.10-15) and narrative texts in the deuteronomistic history (Josh. 7 and 2 Sam. 21) continue to utilize these ideas.[26] Inasmuch as other aspects of the religious worldview found in the Uzzah and Korah incidents continue to be espoused within Deuteronomy and the deuteronomistic history, it seems quite probable that the older view of divine wrath was also maintained. This is not to say that the covenantal framework of Deuteronomy and the deuteronomistic history in which the older conception of divine wrath is now embedded has had no effect upon Israel's conception of divine wrath. Clearly, divine wrath is now less magical, inasmuch as it is more closely tied to ideas of guilt and punishment. But acknowledging that divine wrath is now less magical is not the same as saying that it is completely unmagical.

Once one grants that the deuteronomistic history conceives of divine wrath as a force that can be set off accidentally, that can be stored up over time, and that has the tendency to be uncontrollable once it is set off, it becomes much easier to understand why corporate ideas are so prevalent in ancient Israelite thought. If one subscribes to the belief that divine wrath is an almost palpable entity that operates in a fashion analogous to a fire that burns out of control, it is only natural for one to advocate that punishment could be, and often is, corporate in nature (e.g., Ps. 79.5). In fact, Deut. 21.1-9, 22.8 and 23.10-15 clearly reveal this school's reaffirmation of the way in which the failure to adhere to the ancient religious notions of holiness and bloodguilt by an individual, or a part of the nation, can endanger the nation as a whole. It is precisely this ancient conception of divine wrath that helps one understand the language found in 2 Kgs 22.17 that speaks about the inability to extinguish the wrath of God once it is set in motion.

Conclusions

The deuteronomistic historian's covenantal conception of the exile, which understands the exile as a corporate punishment for the sins of Manasseh and his generation, in fact flows out of earlier religious conceptions of wrath and holiness. Although the notion of covenant expressed within the deuteronomistic history is a very sophisticated theology, it is a theology

26. Josh. 7 and 2 Sam. 21 will be discussed at length in the next two chapters.

that built upon, and continued to maintain, the basic worldview of these earlier religious conceptions. Inasmuch as ancient Israel's covenantal ideas built upon and maintained these earlier religious conceptions, ancient Israel continued to affirm that punishment was something that may have a corporate dimension. It is not at all strange that Dtr 2 attributes the exile to Manasseh and the Judeans he led astray, nor is it unexpected that the exilic generation receives punishment for their and their ancestors' sins. The deuteronomistic historian conceives of divine punishment as inherently corporate, because his whole theology is pervaded by conceptual ideas that are essentially corporate.

The next two chapters, in which we will examine the ancient religious conceptions of holiness and bloodguilt, will provide further support for this thesis.

Chapter 4

JOSHUA 7: HOLINESS VIOLATION AND CORPORATE PUNISHMENT

Joshua 7 contains a narrative that raises some very important issues concerning the concept of divine retribution in the Hebrew Bible. My translation of the text is as follows.

> But the people of Israel acted treacherously with regard to the dedicated things.[1] Achan[2] son of Carmi son of Zabdi son of Zerah, of the tribe of Judah, took some of the dedicated things, and the Lord became angry at the people of Israel. 2 Joshua sent men from Jericho to Ai which is near Beth-aven—east of Bethel—and he told them, 'Go up and spy out the land'. And the men went up and they spied out Ai. 3 Then they returned to Joshua and said to him, 'All the people should not go up, but only two or

---

1. 'Dedicated things' is a translation of the single word חרם. The word חרם clearly connotes the idea of consecration to God in many instances and surely in our story (Josh. 6.17). On the concept of חרם see the following: Mark Fretz, 'Herem in the Old Testament: A Critical Reading', in W. Swartley (ed.), *Essays on War and Peace: Bible and Early Church* (Elkhart: Institute of Mennonite Studies, 1986), pp. 7-44; N.K. Gottwald, *The Tribes of YHWH* (Maryknoll, NY: Orbis Books, 1979), pp. 543-50; M. Greenberg, 'Ḥerem', in *EncJud* VIII, cols. 344-49; Y. Kaufmann, *The Religion of Israel* (trans. M. Greenberg; New York: Schocken Books, 1972), pp. 247-54; N. Lohfink, 'חרם', in *TDOT*, V, pp. 180-99; A. Malamat, 'The Ban in Mari and in the Bible', *Proceedings of the Ninth Meeting of 'Die Ou-Testamentiese Werkgemeenskap in Suid-Afrika'* (Stellenbosch: University of Stellenbosch, 1966), pp. 40-49; S. Niditch, *War in the Hebrew Bible* (New York: Oxford University Press, 1993), pp. 28-77; G. von Rad, *Holy War in Ancient Israel* (trans. M.J. Dawn; Grand Rapids: Eerdmans, 1991), pp. 49-51; C. Sherlock, 'The Meaning of ḤRM in the Old Testament', *Colloquium* 14 (1982), pp. 13-24; P.D. Stern, *The Biblical Ḥerem* (BJS, 211; Atlanta: Scholars Press, 1991), pp. 1-226; de Vaux, *Ancient Israel*, I, pp. 258-67.

2. His name is Achar in the LXX and in 1 Chron. 2.7. This probably reflects a further growth in the narrative's attempt to explain the name of the location where this story supposedly occurred (Josh. 7.24, 26). This location is also mentioned in Hos. 2.17 and Isa. 65.10.

three squads[3] of men should go up and attack Ai; do not trouble all the people to go there, because they are few'. 4 So about three thousand men from the people went up there; but they retreated before the men of Ai. 5 And the men of Ai killed about thirty-six men and chased them from before[4] the gate as far as the Shebarim[5], slaying them at the descent. And the morale of the people melted and became like water.

6 Then Joshua and the elders of Israel tore their clothes and lay prostrate on the ground before the ark of the Lord until evening; and they scattered dust on their heads. 7 Joshua cried, 'Alas, O Lord God, Why did you even lead this people across the Jordan,[6] only to give us into the power of the Amorites and destroy us? If only we had been willing and had stayed on the other side of the Jordan! 8 O Lord, What can I say after Israel has turned its back before its enemies? 9 The Canaanites and all the inhabitants of the land will hear [of this] and will turn upon us and destroy our name from the earth. And what will you do about your great name?'

10 The Lord answered Joshua: 'Get up! Why are you lying prostrate? 11 Israel has sinned! They have transgressed my covenant that I imposed upon them; they took some of the dedicated things; they have stolen, and acted deceitfully, and placed them with their equipment. 12 Therefore, the people of Israel will not be able to withstand their enemies; they will turn their backs to their enemies, because they have become utterly dedicated. I will not be with you again unless you purge the dedicated things from your midst. 13 Go sanctify the people, and proclaim: Sanctify yourselves for tomorrow; for thus says the Lord God of Israel: Something utterly dedicated is in your midst, O Israel, and you will not be able to withstand

3.   Although the word אלף is often translated as a thousand, in certain contexts it appears to indicate a large military troop, but not necessarily one composed of a thousand men. If there were only thirty-six men killed out of three thousand this would not be a serious military defeat. On the development of the term and its various meanings in different periods, see G.E. Mendenhall, 'The Census Lists of Numbers 1 and 26', *JBL* 77 (1958), pp. 52-66.

4.   Reading מלפני instead of לפני. Here it seems likely that a *mem* has fallen out as a result of haplography with the preceding plural suffix. This reading follows J.A. Soggin, *Joshua* (OTL; Philadelphia: Westminster Press, 1972), p. 93. Soggin follows M. Noth, *Das Buch Josua* (HAT; Tübingen: Mohr, 1953), p. 38.

5.   Perhaps it should be translated as 'The Quarries' as suggested by J. Garstang, *Joshua Judges* (London: Constable, 1931), p. 152. No one is quite sure of the exact meaning or location of this site. Ziony Zevit argues that the root שבר is not associated with quarries but with ruined walls and translates the phrase as 'they pursued them in front of the gate to the ruined walls'. Z. Zevit, 'Archaeological and Literary Stratigraphy in Joshua 7–8', *BASOR* 251 (Summer 1983), p. 31.

6.   LXX reads, 'Why did your servant lead this people across the Jordan?' This would solve the difficulty of the form הֶעֱבַרְתָּ הַעֲבִיר by turning it into הֶעֱבִיר עַבְדְּךָ. One could also emend it to the infinitive absolute הַעֲבֵיר. On this form, see GKC, §113x.

your enemies until you have removed that which is utterly dedicated from your midst. 14 In the morning you will come forward according to your tribes; and the tribe that the Lord takes will come forward by clans, and the clan that the Lord takes will come forward by households, and the household that the Lord takes will come forward man by man. 15 And the one who is caught with the utterly devoted things shall be burned with fire, he and all that he has,[7] because he transgressed the covenant of the Lord and he committed an abomination in Israel.'

16 Early in the morning Joshua had Israel approach by tribes, and the tribe of Judah was taken. 17 He then had the clans[8] of Judah approach, and the clan of the Zerahites was taken. Then he had the clan of the Zerahites approach man by man,[9] and Zabdi was taken. 18 And he had his household approach man by man, and Achan son of Carmi son of Zabdi son of Zerah of the tribe of Judah was taken.

19 Then Joshua said to Achan, 'My son pay honor to the Lord God of Israel and make confession to him. Tell me what you have done; do not hide from me.' 20 Achan answered Joshua and he said, 'Truly, I have sinned against the Lord God of Israel. This is what I did: 21 I saw among the spoil[10] a beautiful Shinar mantle, two hundred silver shekels, and a

7.   Certain early interpreters such as Rashi understand the act of burning as only applying to the tent and chattels. Rashi argues that the Masoretic disjunctive accent of *zaqef* over the word בָּאֵשׁ indicates that the burning does not apply to Achan who is signified by the following word אֹתוֹ. This interpretation does not seem particularly compelling to me, but it would explain the multiple punishments of burning and stoning in v. 25.

8.   Here we follow the LXX (κατὰ δήμους) and read the plural 'clans' rather than the MT's singular מִשְׁפַּחַת.

9.   One expects 'by households' here as found in the Syriac, but the text is clearly understandable with or without the emendation.

10.   Boling sees the word שָׁלָל as evidence that there are two separate traditions that were originally unrelated. 'It appears that memories of (1) a contaminating ḥērem-violation at Jericho and (2) Achan's theft of šālāl, "booty" (the latter given a Jericho setting), have been combined by a historian in such a way as to protect Joshua from any charge of poor military judgment in the debacle of the first battle of The Ruin', R.G. Boling, *Joshua* (AB; Garden City, NY: Doubleday, 1982), p. 230. Although it is possible that the Achan story is an intrusion into the story about the conquest of Ai, I think one could interpret the word שָׁלָל in a literary way. One expects Achan to give his side of the story which might include a different perception of the facts. Achan would admit to having taken certain goods from Jericho, but in this scenario, would place this act within the law by categorizing the items he took as שָׁלָל, rather than as חרם. Furthermore, there is evidence to suggest that the Achan story is not intrusive in its present context. The book as a whole seems aware of this story of disobedience (Josh. 6.17-19 and 22.20) and it is far from uncommon for the Bible, and particularly for the deuteronomistic historian, to elucidate the consequences of

wedge of gold weighing fifty shekels, and I desired them and took them. Indeed, they are hidden in the ground in my tent, with the silver underneath.'

22 So Joshua sent messengers and they ran to the tent; and truly it was hidden in his tent with the silver underneath. 23 And they took them out of the tent and brought them to Joshua and all the Israelites; and they poured them out before the Lord. 24 Then Joshua, and all Israel with him, took Achan the son of Zerah, and the silver, the mantle, the wedge of gold, his sons, his daughters, his oxen, his asses, his sheep, his tent, and all that he had; and they brought them up to the Valley of Achor. 25 And Joshua said, 'How you have troubled us! May the Lord trouble you this day.' And all Israel stoned him with stones; they burned them with fire and stoned them with stones.[11] 26 They raised a great heap of stones over him, which remains today. Then the Lord turned from his hot anger. Therefore to this day that place is called the Valley of Achor.

past disobedience in order to preclude the possibility of such errors in the future. An excellent study of the way in which Josh. 7–8 functions as a wholistic literary unit and fits into the larger theological agenda of the deuteronomistic history can be found in C.T. Begg, 'The Function of Josh 7,1-8,29 in the Deuteronomistic History', *Bib* 67 (1986), pp. 320-33.

It should be noted that I do not object to the idea that Josh. 7 may be a composite narrative; I only object to the criteria invoked by Boling as proof for his particular reconstruction of this narrative's prehistory.

11. This verse is clearly corrupt with the double reference to stoning and the ambiguity over exactly who or what is stoned or burned. One way to solve this difficult text is to follow the LXX which reads: καὶ ἐλιθοβόλησαν αὐτὸν λίθοις πᾶς Ισραηλ. It lacks the last clause found in the MT that states, 'they burned them with fire and they stoned them with stones' and thus it eliminates the textual ambiguity. But there are reasons to give priority to the longer reading found in the MT. To begin with, the MT contains the theologically and philologically more difficult text and one could argue that on these grounds alone, it should be preferred. See Ralph Klein's succinct statement: 'The Hebrew text may have seemed difficult already to the translator. Consequently, a superior reading in LXX is not necessarily original; it may only result from the translator's glossing over a problem', R.W. Klein, *Textual Criticism of the Old Testament* (Philadelphia: Fortress Press, 1974), p. 62. Secondly, if one follows the LXX's reading, one is left with the logical difficulty of explaining why in v. 24 Achan's sons, daughters and livestock are all led up to the valley of Achor if, in fact, they are not executed; and the fact that v. 15 calls for the complete destruction of the guilty party's household. Instead, I would be more inclined to view the first mention of 'they stoned him with stones' as a later interpolation into the text. Verse 15 points in this direction because it calls for the culprit and all he owns to be burned. He or his livestock may have been stoned as well, but it would be odd if they were not burned at all. If both acts occurred, it makes more sense to have burning followed by an act of heaping stones upon the charred remains, rather than vice versa. Other evidence also suggests that the first mention of 'they

Although the aims of this project are primarily oriented toward reaching a theological understanding of Joshua 7, which is not contingent on the historicity of the passage, it seems only proper to survey briefly the historical issues that naturally arise in any discussion of this narrative. This chapter is set within the book of Joshua and thus it falls within the deuteronomistic history, the books that run from Joshua through 2 Kings. It seems likely that this narrative, along with much of the material in Joshua and Judges, is older than the framework in which it is currently set. This fact obliges us to ask about the actual historicity of the narrative and of course the historicity of the conquest narratives in general.[12] Archaeological excavations have called into doubt the likelihood that Ai was destroyed in Joshua's time.[13] This evidence forces us to abandon the view that Joshua 7 is a historically reliable account. But it should not lead us too quickly to assume that it is simply a fiction fabricated by the deuteronomistic historian. There is some evidence that this narrative has roots that are older than the seventh century BCE. The fact is that the type of warfare it describes and the idea of חרם both appear to have strong historical parallels in ancient Near Eastern culture.[14] Also the idea that some type of apostasy took place at Achor shortly after Israel's

stoned him with stones' is a later addition to the text. While סקל is used four times in Deuteronomy and seven times in the deuteronomistic history, רגם is used only once in Deuteronomy and aside from Josh. 7.25, only one other time in the deuteronomistic history. Who added the phrase with רגם and why is an interesting question. The restricting of the punishment to Achan alone could be an attempt by a very late hand to remove the theological difficulty that one encounters if Achan's children and live-stock are executed together with him. This position is advocated by B.S. Jackson, *Theft in Early Jewish Law* (Oxford: Clarendon Press, 1972), p. 62 n. 1. But it is possible that this addition is simply a gloss that crept into the text explaining that the older term סקל is equivalent to the newer term רגם. If a later editor had wanted to change the story and have only Achan killed by stoning, one wonders why he did such a poor job of editing.

12. For an excellent discussion of the data and the major theories, see J.H. Hayes and J.M. Miller (eds.), *Israelite and Judean History* (OTL; Philadelphia: Westminster Press, 1977), pp. 213-84.

13. J. Bright, *A History of Israel* (Philadelphia: Westminster Press, 3rd edn, 1981), pp. 130-33; J.A. Callaway, 'New Evidence on the Conquest of "AI"', *JBL* 87 (September 1968), pp. 312-20; R. de Vaux, *The Early History of Israel* (trans. D. Smith; Philadelphia: Westminster Press, 1978), pp. 612-20. For a full summary of all the relevant archaeological data, see Zevit, 'Archaeological and Literary Stratigraphy', pp. 23-35.

14. These features will be discussed in detail further below.

entrance into the land is strongly hinted at in Hos. 2.17, which tells us that in the prophetic future the past place of apostasy will now be called the door of hope.[15] But, unfortunately, this evidence tells us nothing about the age or the accuracy of the story reported in Joshua 7. We should be cautious about assuming that Hosea knows the story we have in Joshua 7, although he is apparently aware of a story of apostasy associated with the Valley of Achor.[16]

It should be noted that even if this text should prove to be historically erroneous or fictitious certain theological problems inherent in the narrative will remain relevant. Joshua 7 sheds light on the world-view of ancient Israel (or at least of those Israelites who produced and preserved the story as a cultural memory), even if the final verdict of the historian is that this narrative is substantially an invented memory.[17]

In this project I am trying to clarify specific aspects of the problem of divine retribution, particularly the fairness of divine retribution and the exact relationship between the individual and the community. This narrative brings up three issues of central importance to my project:

1.   Verses 24 and 25 appear to indicate that innocent family members and sentient animals are executed for Achan's crime.
2.   Verse 5 tells us that approximately 36 innocent soldiers died in the first battle against Ai. The chapter as a whole implies that these deaths would not have occurred if Achan had not taken some of the utterly devoted things into his possession. Thus these men died for Achan's crime as well.[18]

15. M. Fishbane, *Biblical Interpretation in Ancient Israel* (Oxford: Clarendon Press, 1985), p. 361. Fishbane's insight was adumbrated by H.W. Wolff, *Hosea* (trans. G. Stansell; Hermeneia; Philadelphia: Fortress Press, 1974), p. 43.

16. Additionally, we must remain cautious because Hos. 2.17 may be a late gloss inserted into the book of Hosea by someone who shares the same ideological background as the deuteronomistic historian.

17. On the power and importance of memory as opposed to actual history, see Y.H. Yerushalmi, *Zakhor: Jewish History and Jewish Memory* (New York: Schocken Books, 1989). On the difference between different types of history that various groups use and their relationship to each other, see B. Lewis, *History Remembered, Recovered, Invented* (Princeton, NJ: Princeton University Press, 1975; repr.; New York: Simon & Schuster, 1987).

18. Whether these deaths should be viewed as a punishment inflicted against Israel, or an omen to alert them to the fact that a covenantal breach has occurred, remains in doubt. But in either scenario, apparently innocent men die for the sin of Achan.

3.   Verse 12 informs us that God will not be with Israel again until
the 'utterly devoted things' are removed from their camp and
the culprit who violated the rules of holy war has been
executed. For the time that God has removed himself from the
Israelite camp, all Israel remains susceptible to attack and
destruction. Thus it appears that all Israel is suffering innocently
on account of the sin of one individual.

The exact rationale behind why the taking of חרם by Achan alone
would cause all Israel to be punished (issues 2 and 3) will be taken up
further below in the discussion of holiness and its place in ancient
Israelite religion. For now I will focus specifically on the question of why
Achan's whole family is killed for his act of taking these dedicated
goods. There are several options that scholars have proposed to explain
why Achan's family and chattels were also destroyed.

Ancient Israel was Pre-Logical

Robinson employed the concept of corporate personality as an
explanation for some of the theological difficulties raised by Joshua 7.[19]

> No one can overlook this unity of corporate personality in its more legal
> aspects. Familiar examples from the Old Testament are given when Achan
> breaks the taboo on the spoil of Jericho, and involves the whole of Israel in
> defeat and, on discovery, the whole of his family in destruction.[20]

It is interesting to note that Robinson was so sure that the concept of
corporate personality was the explanation for cases such as Joshua 7 that
he never elaborates on exactly how the notion of corporate personality
is operative in this case.[21] A close reading of Robinson's ideas reveals
that his assertion is generated by his tendency to subscribe to the now
outmoded anthropological idea that ancient Israelites had a psychic
inability to distinguish between the individual and the group. But if
ancient Israel had an inability to distinguish between the group and the
individual, then why does God order Joshua to find the specific offender
and punish him with the death penalty (Josh. 7.13-15)? Indeed, in vv. 20-
21 Achan confesses that he alone committed this crime. Furthermore, in

19. For a fuller account of Robinson's ideas and the criticisms levelled against
them, see Chapter 1.
20. Robinson, 'Corporate Personality', pp. 25-26.
21. As noted by Porter, 'Legal Aspects', p. 362.

v. 24 there is a clear distinction made between Achan, the goods he stole, his sons and daughters, and his other, wordly possessions. All of these facts suggest that ancient Israelites could and did distinguish between the real offender and other members of his family and his tribe. Thus it seems questionable at best to invoke the idea of a pre-logical mentality involving some type of psychical unity as an explanation for the execution of Achan's sons, daughters, and cattle.

People Could be Reckoned as Personal Property

There is a substantial body of evidence that suggests that the clear division that we make between persons and things (including animals) may not have existed in the ancient Near East in general.[22] Although many scholars have recognized that ancient Israel maintained a clear distinction between property (objects and animals) and people,[23] there is still much evidence that certain people were sometimes reckoned within the category of property. The fact that one could own slaves suggests that a class of people existed who were treated, at least in certain ways, as chattels (Exod. 21.4, 21). Daughters appear to belong to their fathers as a piece of valuable but disposable property (Exod. 21.7; Deut. 22.29). The Decalogue includes a man's wife among his possessions (Exod. 20.17).[24] And there is also evidence that male children may have been viewed as property that could be sacrificed by their father (Gen. 22 and Mic. 6.7), or killed as part of their father's punishment (Exod. 20.5 and 2 Sam. 21).

These points might allow us to infer that Achan's family is not

22. 'In Mesopotamia no qualitative discontinuity was perceived between the phenomenon of man and any other phenomena of the natural universe. An accidental untoward occurrence in which a person is the victim therefore did not, by virtue of that element alone, transpose the event or the procedure by which it was to be emended into some exclusive categorical sphere which would not have obtained had the victim been other than a human being.' J.J. Finkelstein, *The Ox that Gored* (Transactions of the American Philosophical Society; Philadelphia: Independence Square, 1981), p. 39.

23. M. Greenberg, 'Some Postulates of Biblical Criminal Law', in M. Haran (ed.), *Yehezkel Kaufmann Jubilee Volume* (Jerusalem: Magnes Press, 1960), pp. 5-28. Reprinted in J. Goldin (ed.), *The Jewish Expression* (New Haven: Yale University Press, 1976), pp. 18-37.

24. It should be noted that in the version of the Decalogue found in Deut. 5.17 the phrase 'you shall not covet your neighbor's house' occurs after 'you shall not covet your neighbors wife'. This word order may indicate an attempt to elevate the status of women out of the category of property. This line of interpretation is suggested by M. Weinfeld, *Deuteronomy 1–11* (AB; New York: Doubleday, 1991), pp. 317-18.

executed because they are in some way guilty, but rather, because his
crime warranted his death and the total destruction of his property as
well. According to this line of reasoning, his family was destroyed as
part and parcel of his property.[25]

This reconstruction no doubt provides at least part of the reason for
the execution of Achan's family and his cattle. As we will see, there are
other factors that help elucidate not only why Achan's family and
chattels had to be eliminated, but also help explain the death of the 36
men in the first battle of Ai and God's excommunication of all Israel
until they executed the culprit (points 2 and 3 respectively).

This Case is an Extra-Legal Case

One could argue that the severity of the punishment in Joshua 7 is
evidence that this case belongs to a group of offences that fall outside of
the normal legal system. For example, Joshua 7 may be analogous to
Lev. 21.9, in which a priest's daughter is convicted of prostitution and
sentenced to death by burning.

> As long as a person is within the covenant relationship, his offences can be
> coped with by society and dealt with by regular judicial procedure, but if
> he puts himself outside the covenant relationship, he can have no place in
> society.[26]

This solution would explain the death of Achan's whole family as a
drastic measure that was imposed in this unusual case in order to
eradicate this dangerous evil (Deut. 13.13-18).[27] The flaw in this particular
proposal resides in its suggestion that this case falls outside of the normal
purview of the legal system of ancient Israel. Inherent in such a view is
the tendency to create a false dichotomy between the categories of the

25. This view accords well with the concept of 'ruler punishment' developed by
David Daube. See p. 49 and references there. J.R. Porter applies Daube's idea of
ruler punishment to Josh. 7 and several other cases such as 2 Sam. 21. Porter states,
'If the patriarchal family is in view, then in ancient Israel a man was the lord, master
and owner of this household, human beings as well as material possessions, then what
happened to Achan's household might be no different in principle from the custom of
ancient warfare, when the wives of the defeated and slain king would become the
property of his conqueror, or from that of the sixteenth century England, whereby the
property of an executed traitor was forfeit to the crown'. Porter, 'Legal Aspects', *VT*
15 (1965), pp. 368-69.

26. Porter, 'Legal Aspects', p. 371.

27. It does not appear to be useful in solving problems 2 and 3 listed above.

ritual and the ethical. The ethical is understood to be rational and is connected to the legal system, while ritual is considered irrational, strange, marginal and exceptional.[28] This proposition is inaccurate because it imposes a modern set of assumptions about the clear separation between ethical and ritual norms onto the Hebrew Bible, which is composed of a set of documents that appear to stress the organic connection between ethical and ritual ideas.[29] Ritual laws, including the procedures found in Joshua 7, are found in biblical texts that claim to be a part of the biblical legal system (Lev. 27.28-29; Deut. 13.18). Rather than arguing for a very narrow definition of legal material in the Hebrew Bible and then being forced to exclude Joshua 7 and other troubling cases from this definition, it makes more sense to acknowledge that notions of contagion, holiness and bloodguilt are internal to Israelite law just as they are internal to much of Israelite theology. Once one acknowledges that the biblical legal system also contains ritual ideas, it becomes much easier to comprehend why the ancient Israelites executed Achan and his family. As we will see, this action was taken because ritual violations, inasmuch as they endangered the community as a whole, were considered a criminal offence punishable by the human legal system.

Two other scholars make arguments that resemble Porter's. J.J. Finkelstein views this case as particularly severe in that it threatens the 'cosmic hierarchy' and thus like 'a physical malignancy, the drastic excision of which entails the removal of some of the surrounding and apparently non-infected tissue...Achan's family and property had to be destroyed'.[30] Here Finkelstein views the punishment as a psychological maneuver to make an example of Achan, rather than a normal legal and ritual procedure, as I will argue below.

Lastly, Jacob Milgrom treats this as a case of divine retribution that happens to be executed by humans. Milgrom maintains that the deity always reserves the right to collective liability and thus one should not treat this as a case of human jurisprudence.[31] Milgrom's rationale for

28. As indicated in Chapter 1 above, often the tendency to split the ethical from the ritual is connected to the common Christian assumption that the prophets are ethically oriented spiritualists who reject ritual procedures propagated by priests and later by Pharisees.

29. The deep connection between ethical and ritual ideas that one finds in texts such as Lev. 19 and Ezek. 18 will be documented in greater detail further below.

30. Finkelstein, *The Ox that Gored*, p. 28.

31. J. Milgrom, *Cult and Conscience* (SJLA, 18; Leiden: Brill, 1976), pp. 33-35. Speaking about Israelite legislation, Milgrom informs us that 'for both cleric and

placing Joshua 7 under the rubric of divine retribution does not seem to be related to Porter's maneuver to segregate the ethical from the ritual. Milgrom, a very sensitive reader of Leviticus, would have no interest in creating such a false dichotomy. Rather, his argument appears to flow from two assumptions, both of them problematic. He presumes that all cases found within the Hebrew Bible fit neatly into one of two categories: those that fall solely under the rubric of divine retribution, and allow for communal responsibility; and others that fall solely under the heading of human retribution, and punish only the offending party. Additionally, he assumes that Israelite law is highly ethical and highly rational and thus that the Israelite judicial system would never allow a human court to impose a trans-generational punishment.[32] Although I concur with Milgrom that the deity always reserves the right for collective liability, cases such as Achan's reveal that the existing cases do not always fall neatly into one category; Milgrom's system of classification is thus dubious. To argue as Milgrom does, that this case is simply a case of divine retribution, is to force the data into a Procrustean bed. There are several instances in the Hebrew Bible that straddle this dualistic categorization, and Achan's is one such example.[33] In these

layman, master and slave, the doctrine of collective culpability is reserved to divine justice; it never functions in the jurisprudence of men'. Milgrom, *Cult and Conscience*, p. 34. Milgrom appears to be expanding on a point made by Greenberg several years earlier that the 'principle of individuality in fact governs all of biblical law'. Greenberg, 'Some Postulates', p. 30.

32. Behind this view is an apologetic bias that is based on an attempt to contrast what he sees as the high ethical standard of the biblical legal system with the less ethically developed ancient Near Eastern law codes. An insightful critique of this method of contrasting biblical to ancient Near Eastern law can be found in B.S. Jackson, *Essays in Jewish and Comparative Legal History* (SJLA, 10; Leiden: Brill, 1975), pp. 25-63. A response to Jackson can be found in M. Greenberg, 'More Reflections on Biblical Criminal Law', *Scripta Hierosolymitana* 31 (1986), pp. 1-17. A discussion of the more general problem of the exact ways in which Israel might or might not be different from her ancient Near Eastern neighbors can be found in R. Gnuse, *Heilsgeschichte as a Model for Biblical Theology: The Debate concerning the Uniqueness and Significance of Israel's Worldview* (College Theology Society Studies in Religion, 4; Lanham, MD: University Press of America, 1989). Also see J. Kaminsky, review of R. Gnuse, *Heilsgeschichte as a Model for Biblical Theology: The Debate concerning the Uniqueness and Significance of Israel's Worldview*, *JR* 71 (April 1991), pp. 255-56.

33. Here Fishbane is on the right track when he calls for caution and suggests that a simple dualistic model fails to account for all the evidence. He makes the following

medial cases humans, albeit by divine imperative, are carrying out a punishment that is collective in nature.

I acknowledge that the egregious nature of Achan's violation is a factor that can help explain the severity of the punishment inflicted on Achan's family and chattels.[34] But the fact that the Achan case involves a particularly egregious violation is not equivalent to acknowledging that it, or other cases that resemble it, fall outside of the purview of the ancient Israelite legal system (Lev. 24.10-23; Num. 15.30-31).

In order to demonstrate that Joshua 7, despite its unusual features, still falls within the normal operation of Israelite law, we must first clarify the precise role that the institution of חרם plays within our narrative. As we will see, several key difficulties can be explained by reaching a fuller understanding of the way in which חרם functions in the Hebrew Bible in general and in Joshua 7 in particular.

חרם *in the Hebrew Bible*

The term חרם is not employed in a consistent manner within the Hebrew Bible. It sometimes appears to be a voluntary practice undertaken by the Israelites (Lev. 27.28; Num. 21.2) and at other times it seems to be commanded by God (Deut. 20.17; Josh. 6.17-18).[35] On some occasions

two points: 'First it is clear that some of the early rules against vicarious punishments (like Exod. 21.31, examined earlier) are the product of deliberate exegetical revision; and, secondly, the fact that the late deuteronomic corpus must state apodictically "Fathers shall not be put to death instead of their sons, nor shall sons be put to death instead of their father; [but] everyone shall be put to death for his own sin" (Deut. 24.16) shows a considerable concern to curb this practice... In any event, the available evidence requires one to draw the qualified conclusion that while the legal corpora tend to reject vicarious punishment, this latter notion probably coexisted with other ones.' Fishbane, *Biblical Interpretation*, pp. 336-37.

34. So David Daube tells us that 'it is safe to infer that theft of anything sacred was deemed a particularly grave offense'. Daube, *Studies in Biblical Law*, p. 203.

35. In general there are many more occurrences in which God orders the חרם as opposed to instances in which it is done as part of a vow. It appears that the voluntary idea occurs almost exclusively in texts of priestly origin (Lev. 27.21, 28; Num. 18.14; Ezek. 44.29). It is fair to say that in Deuteronomy and the deuteronomistic history the institution of חרם never appears as a vow and often, although not always, is explicitly ordered by God (Deut. 7.2; 13.16; Josh. 10.40; 11.15, 20; 1 Sam. 15.2-3). For fuller bibliography on this topic, see n. 1 above. For a comprehensive chart of all occurences of the root חרם, see Fretz, 'Herem', Appendix 1, pp. 29-31. For a philological examination of this root, see Stern, *The Biblical Ḥerem*, pp. 5-17.

one is allowed to keep parts of the booty (Josh. 8.2) and at other times everything is to be destroyed (Deut. 13.16-18; 1 Sam. 15.3). It is possible that this practice changed over time,[36] or it might just be that different sources represent this institution in different ways.[37]

Joshua 7 is a narrative that speaks about a חרם that was absolute and commanded by God.[38] One would expect to find this type of חרם in the deuteronomistic history because this is the type of חרם one finds in the speeches and laws of Deuteronomy. Compare the language of the four following passages from the book of Deuteronomy with the fifth passage which is taken from the book of Joshua.

> The Lord your God has given them (these nations) before you and you shall smite them, utterly destroying them, you will not make a covenant with them nor shall you show any mercy to them (Deut. 7.2).

> You will burn the idols of their gods with fire and you will not covet the silver and gold upon them and take it for yourself, lest you become ensnared by it; for it is an abomination to the Lord your God. And you will not bring an abominable thing into your house or you will become proscribed like it; you shall completely abhor and detest it for it is a proscribed thing (Deut. 7.25-26).

> You will surely smite the inhabitants of that city with the sword, utterly destroying it and all that is in it, including its livestock. You will gather all of its booty into the center of its square and you will burn the town and all its booty as a whole burnt offering to the Lord your God. It will remain an eternal ruin and will not again be rebuilt (Deut. 13.16-17).

> You shall utterly destroy them—the Hittites and the Amorites, the Canaanites and the Perizzites, the Hivites and the Jebusites—just as the Lord your God commanded you (Deut. 20.17).

> And the city and all that is in it will be utterly dedicated to the Lord (Josh. 6.17a).

36. For example, von Rad thinks that the idea of a vow found in Num. 21.2 is more recent than the notion that חרם was a divine imperative. Von Rad, *Holy War*, p. 50.

37. For example, it is possible to argue that Josh. 6.19 is a late, perhaps priestly addition to a text which originally stressed the total destruction of the city and everything in it (Josh. 6.17).

38. By 'absolute' I only mean that everything was dedicated to God, not necessarily that everything had to be destroyed. As noted further below, Josh. 6.17 and 6.24a seem to call for utter destruction, while 6.19 and 6.24b indicate that certain objects went 'to the treasury of the (house) of the Lord'. On this problem, see the discussion further below.

It is clear that all these passages share a similar model of the institution of חרם. Nevertheless, it should be noted that there is evidence of variation within this institution. In Josh. 6.19 Joshua commands the Israelites to take the silver, gold, bronze and iron vessels that are sanctified to the Lord and bring them to his treasury, whereas in Deut. 7.25-26 the Israelites are commanded to burn such items. It is possible that Josh. 6.19 along with the second half of v. 24 are late, (perhaps priestly) additions to a text that calls for complete destruction rather than destruction of everyone and dedication of valuable objects. But it is equally possible that there are different levels of חרם that are employed at different times. There are at least two instances in Deuteronomy that allow one to plunder livestock and booty of a nation that has been put to the ban (Deut. 2.34-35; 3.6-7). Interestingly, after the misfortune resulting from Achan's sin the severity of the ban is reduced in Joshua 8 and the people are now permitted to keep the booty and the livestock (Josh. 8.2, 27).[39]

These texts make it clear that when one treats something as חרם, it means that the object is consecrated or dedicated in an almost sacrificial manner. Support for such an understanding of חרם can be found in several biblical passages. Notice the way in which Deut. 13.17 uses terminology that is strongly reminiscent of the language of sacrifice: ואת־כל־שללה כליל ליהוה אלהיך.[40] Similar sacrificial terminology can also be found in Josh. 6.17a, והיתה העיר חרם היא וכל־אשר־בה ליהוה, and in Lev. 27.28b, כל־חרם קדש־קדשים הוא ליהוה (all חרם is most holy to the Lord). The sacral character of חרם also extends to the effect it has on those who misuse it. It is clear from Deut. 7.25-26 cited above and from Josh. 6.18 cited here that when one misappropriates חרם, one runs the risk of having the tabooed status of the חרם transferred to oneself.[41]

---

39. This may be connected to a larger biblical tendency to ease the rules after God realizes that he has set an unreachable standard. Thus it might be compared to God's allowing humans to consume meat after the flood (Gen. 9.3) even though he had initially limited humankind to a strictly vegetarian diet (Gen. 1.29).

40. The term כליל is used several times in reference to sacrificial procedures (Lev. 6.15, 16; Deut. 33.10; 1 Sam. 7.9; Ps. 51.21).

41. As pointed out by Greenberg 'this is wholly analogous to the contagiousness of the state of impurity, and a provision of the law of impurity is really the best commentary on the story of Achan's crime: "This is the law: when a man dies in a tent every one that comes into that tent, and every thing that is in that tent, shall be unclean" (Num 19.14)'. Greenberg, 'Some Postulates', p. 31. It should be noted that both Stern and Sherlock object to the use of the idea of taboo and to the notion חרם of having a contagious element to it. The objection to the use of taboo is based upon

> Only be very vigilant about the utterly dedicated goods, lest you covet[42]
> and you appropriate some of the utterly dedicated goods and you make the
> camp of Israel into an utterly dedicated thing and bring trouble upon it
> (Josh. 6.18).

The sacral character of חרם and the fact that an individual who
misappropriates such an object can also become proscribed, can also be
supported by various extra-biblical parallels.

Ancient Near Eastern Analogues to the Idea of חרם

That the notion of holy war, perhaps more accurately described in
ancient Israel as YHWH war, and the idea of חרם do appear to have
analogues in other ancient Near Eastern cultures strongly suggests that
these practices did occur in certain periods and should not be viewed as
fictional concepts invented by certain biblical writers who were
romanticizing about the glorious past.[43] The single closest analogue to

the fact that the biblical concept of חרם does not correspond precisely to the idea as it
is used in Polynesian thought from whence the term derived. Sherlock, 'The Meaning',
p. 15 and Stern, *The Biblical Ḥerem*, pp. 145-49. I acknowledge this to be the case,
but still feel the term taboo can be used more loosely to mean something banned or
prohibited. The same is true of the use of the word contagion. It need not be limited to
the idea of disease, and Stern correctly criticizes those scholars who attempt to
understand the Jericho incident as primarily a form of health control. But it is
important to recognize that חרם can spread and thus can be described as something
that is contagious. For theories of חרם as a preventive health measure, see, Boling,
Joshua, pp. 207, 214-15; C. Meyers, 'The Roots of Restriction: Women in Early
Israel', *BA* 41 (1978), pp. 91-103; and Mendenhall, *The Tenth Generation*, pp. 105-
21. Stern's critique is found in Stern, *The Biblical Ḥerem*, p. 143.
    42. This part of the verse is problematic inasmuch as the Hebrew only has the
hiphil verb תחרימו with no object following it. Here I have emended the text to תחמדו
following the LXX which reads ἐνθυμηθέντες. There is other textual support for this
reading inasmuch as Josh. 7.21 and Deut. 7.25 use the verbal root חמד in passages
associated with illegally appropriating some of the חרם. A more conservative approach
to this text is suggested by Stern who translates the Masoretic text as 'lest you spread
חרם'. Stern, *The Biblical Ḥerem*, pp. 148-49. It should be noted that either reading
will support my thesis that it is Achan's misappropriation of the חרם that is the major
factor in explaining the various theological difficulties raised by this narrative. If one
adopts Stern's reading it enhances my argument because his reading, despite his
protestations to the contrary, explicitly states that חרם does have a tendency to spread
its status in a contagious fashion to those who misappropriate it.
    43. There is a large amount of literature on the problem of holy war in ancient
Israel, much of it in reaction to von Rad's very limited view of holy wars as strictly

the way in which these ideas function in our narrative can be found in the Mesha inscription which contains the following lines:

> 10 Now the Gadites had lived in the land of 'Aṭaroth forever, and the king of 11 Israel had built 'Aṭaroth for himself. But I fought against the city and took it, and I killed the entire population of 12 the city—*a satiation for Kemosh and Moab*...14 Now Kemosh said to me, 'Go seize Nebo from Israel'. So I 15 went at night and fought against it from the break of dawn until noon. I 16 seized it and killed everyone of [it]—seven thousand men, foreign men, native women, for[eign] 17 women, and concubines—for *I devoted it to* 'Ashtar Kemosh.[44]

defensive enterprises. Several scholars have argued that the notion of YHWH war is a more accurate description of the phenomenon as it occurred in ancient Israel. For more detailed discussions of the problem, see the following works: P.C. Craigie, *The Problem of War in the Old Testament* (Grand Rapids: Eerdmans, 1978), pp. 45-54; G.H. Jones, '"Holy War" or "YHWH War"?', *VT* 25 (July 1975), pp. 642-58; S.M. Kang, *Divine War in the Old Testament and in the Ancient Near East* (BZAW, 177; Berlin: de Gruyter, 1989); P.D. Miller, *The Divine Warrior in Early Israel* (HSM, 5; Cambridge, MA: Harvard University Press, 1973); R. Smend, *YHWH War and Tribal Confederation* (trans. M.G. Rogers; Nashville: Abingdon Press, 1970); M. Weippert, '"Heiliger Krieg" in Israel und Assyrien: Kritische Anmerkungen zu Gerhard von Rads Konzept des "heiligen Krieges im alten Israel"', *ZAW* 84 (1972), pp. 460-93. It is not necessary to solve the terminological difficulties inherent in this discussion in order to sustain my argument that the language found within the Hebrew Bible and other ancient Near Eastern texts frequently implies that wars were fought for and even by various deities. I recognize that later redactors schematized the notion of holy war and forced certain stories into the complex that they invented. But even though this process may have occurred, it does not nullify the fact that warfare was an inherently religious activity. I reject Jones's argument that because warfare often lacked a set ritual pattern, it should not be viewed as a holy, or sacred institution. I am more inclined to Roland de Vaux's view that 'in antiquity, then, every war was a holy war, in a broad sense'. De Vaux, *Ancient Israel*, I, p. 258. Furthermore, it should be noted that it is not only the ritual practices that surround the act of warfare that give warfare its sacrality. The descriptions of warfare in ancient Israel are pervaded by mythological patterns and images that are ultimately derived from the cultic sphere. On the mythology of holy war in ancient Israel and among her neighbors, see Miller, *Divine Warrior, passim*. On the transformation of this imagery in later biblical times, see J.J. Collins, 'The Mythology of Holy War in Daniel and the Qumran War Scroll: A Point of Transition in Jewish Apocalyptic', *VT* 25 (July 1975), pp. 596-612.

44. The emphases are mine. The translation is from K.P. Jackson, 'The Language of the Mesha Inscription', in A. Dearman (ed.), *Studies in the Mesha Inscription and Moab* (Archaeology and Biblical Studies, 2; Atlanta: Scholars Press, 1989), pp. 97-98. It should be noted that several other essays in this volume shed light on this inscription as well as on Moabite religion and culture.

This text is a clear historical witness to the existence of a kind of warfare that could be accurately characterized by the term sacred warfare and it includes a concept that is closely analogous to the biblical notion of חרם. There are two areas in this inscription that are of particular importance for my argument. The first field of focus is in lines 11-12. Mesha tells us that he killed all the people of Ataroth as a רית לכמש ולמאב. The Moabite word רית has been a point of contention among various scholars and there is still no consensus on its correct interpretation. The proposed 'satiate' would derive the word from the root רוי. Such a usage would parallel nicely with the text of Isa. 34.5-7 which twice uses a verbal form of this root in a depiction of God warring against the nations and especially against Edom.[45] It is also possible to derive the word from the root ראי and translate it as 'spectacle' like the word ראי in Nah. 3.6. As noted by Kent Jackson, 'one cannot rule out the possibility that it means something else entirely, perhaps something similar to the concept of *herem*, "dedication", "slaughter"'.[46] Regardless of its exact meaning it strongly implies that warfare is being waged for the god Kemosh, the head of the Moabite pantheon.

The other part of this inscription that deserves our attention is found in line 17 where Mesha tells us that after seizing Nebo he killed all seven thousand of its inhabitants כי לעשתר כמש החרמתה. The word החרמתה is a *hiphil* perfect first person common singular with a third person feminine singular suffix. It is from the root חרם, the same root used in the Hebrew text of Joshua 7. This text gives positive evidence to the existence of an actual historical practice of חרם, in which people and objects were dedicated to the national deity.

A similar usage of the word חרם can be found in 2 Kgs 19.11 in reference to Assyrian conquests. Here Sennacherib sends a message to Hezekiah that includes the following statement: 'Indeed you have heard what the kings of Assyria did to all the lands, utterly destroying them (להחרימם)'. Whether the Assyrian delegation actually used the verb cannot be known for sure,[47] but the fact that much of ancient warfare

---

45. It should be noted that the root חרם also occurs in Isa. 34.5.

46. Jackson, 'The Language of the Mesha Inscription', p. 112.

47. Ehud Ben Zvi argues that the Rabshakeh's speech here and in Isa. 36 are literary creations that use stock vocabulary and ideas from a later period. He compares the authors of these speeches to Thucydides who admits that he deals rather freely with the language of the historical speeches in his text. Ben Zvi does not deny that there may have been a speech by an Assyrian Rabshakeh, but does argue that the

was seen explicitly as fighting either to protect or expand various gods' territories certainly makes this a possibility.[48]

In addition there is the Akkadian term *asakku* found in certain texts from Mari.[49] A. Malamat, in discussing these texts and their relationship to the biblical idea of חרם, tells us the following about these texts:

> In several contracts, a man who goes back on terms agreed upon is likened to 'one who has eaten the *asakku*' of a particular king or god. Thus in one case the penalty exacted for failure to honour a contract on the sale of a field is likened to that of eating the *asakku* of the god Dagan, of the king Shamshi-Adad, and of the god Iatūr-Mer (ARM VIII 6.9-11). In another instance, the penalty is as meted out for eating the *asakku* of the god Shamash, of...and of the king Shamshi-Adad (Ibid. 7.9-10); and, in a third case the contract breaker is compared to one who has eaten the *asakku* of the god Itūr-Mer, of the goddess of Ḥanat, and of the king Zimri-Lim (Ibid. 85.3-5).
>
> In all these cases, the breach of contract is treated as a serious religious transgression equal to the eating of a taboo; or, in biblical terms, to the violation of a holy or banned object.[50]

Asakku is similar in connotation to the word חרם, and, according to Malamat, the person who ate the *asakku* became contaminated by it and, originally, would have been killed for this offence.[51] Furthermore, although this taboo may have originated elsewhere it also occurs in military contexts that imply that war spoils were a type of *asakku* (ARM II 13).

speeches in the Hebrew Bible are later literary creations. E. Ben Zvi, 'Who Wrote the Speech of Rabshakeh and When?', *JBL* 109 (Spring 1990), pp. 79-92. Other scholars such as Brevard Childs argue that the speeches are based closely on the words of an Assyrian Rabshakeh. B.S. Childs, *Isaiah and the Assyrian Crisis* (London: SCM Press, 1967), p. 82.

48. Ahlström, *Royal Administration*, pp. 6-9.

49. The ground-breaking study was Malamat's, 'The Ban in Mari', pp. 40-49. Discussions of *asakku* and its relationship to various biblical concepts can also be found in Fretz, 'Herem', pp. 17, 32; Stern, *The Biblical Ḥerem*, pp. 57-58, 149-152; K. van der Toorn, *Sin and Sanction in Israel and Mesopotamia* (Studia Semitica Neerlandica; Assen: Van Gorcum, 1985), pp. 41-44.

50. Malamat, 'The Ban in Mari', pp. 40-41.

51. The wording of the penalty is 'he has eaten of the *asakku* of (the gods) Shamash and Itūr-Mer, (of the king) Shamshi-Adad and (the viceroy) Iasmah-Adad, and he shall pay three and a half minas of silver (the fine for) a capital offence' (ARM VIII 1.28-31). Malamat argues that the language in this inscription implies that it must have originally been a capital offence that was later changed to a monetary fine. Malamat, 'The Ban in Mari', p. 43, parentheses his.

You have not given me my [share], as well as my lord's portion (of the
booty). The *asakku* of the god Dagan and the god Itūr-Mer, the *asakku* of
Shamshi-Adad and Iasmaḫ-Adad... He of (my) servants who steals the
booty of a soldier has eaten my *asakku* (i.e. has committed sacrilege
against me).[52]

Although it is clear that the notion of *asakku* sheds some light on the
biblical notion of חרם, it is also certain that it is not an exact analogue
because the *asakku* can belong to a king and even a soldier, as well as a
god. Also, it remains uncertain whether the violation of *asakku* ever was
a capital offence and whether it functioned as a taboo item that
transferred its proscribed status to those who violated it.[53]

The above evidence can be summarized as follows:

1. The Mesha Inscription gives extra-biblical evidence for the
   existence of an institution in which people who live in a particular city are totally exterminated as a type of offering to a
   particular god. This is closely analogous to the biblical concept
   of חרם.

2. The biblical parallel from 2 Kgs 19.11 lends further support to
   this type of practice.

3. The texts from Mari are of great importance because *asakku*
   includes inanimate objects like those stolen by Achan and
   because they specifically discuss the penalties involved when
   someone violates the rules for dealing with *asakku*.
   Unfortunately, it remains uncertain exactly how close the institution of *asakku* is to the notion of חרם as found in the Hebrew
   Bible or the Mesha Inscription.

4. All of these pieces of evidence support the contention that,
   even though the narrative in Joshua 7 may be historically
   inaccurate, it contains accurate portrayals of the way in which
   sacral warfare was practiced in the ancient Near East.

How the Sacral Character of חרם Helps Explain Joshua 7

I have argued that חרם is sacral in nature and that it has the ability
to transmit its taboo status to those who misappropriate it. That this

52. Malamat, 'The Ban in Mari', pp. 44-45, parentheses his.
53. Stern, in discussing another text also cited by Malamat (ARM V 72), argues
that it provides clear evidence for a case in which the theft of *asakku* was punished by
death. Stern, *The Biblical Ḥerem*, pp. 149-52.

factor is operational in this narrative is stated rather explicitly in Josh. 7.12.[54]

ולא יכלו בני ישראל לקום לפני איביהם ערף יפנו לפני איביהם
כי היו לחרם לא אוסיף להיות עמכם אם־לא תשמידו
החרם מקרבכם:

This verse appears to indicate that all Israel has, at least temporarily, become חרם. Verse 15, in which God orders that Achan and everything he owns be burned, suggests that the tabooed status from the misappropriated objects spread to Achan's family and possessions.[55] I maintain this to be the case in spite of the objections raised by Jacob Milgrom that this solution is untenable because it cannot explain why Achan's animals, who presumably never came into his tent, were executed; and why this contagion failed to infect Joshua's men who confiscated the stolen property (Josh. 7.22-23).[56] Milgrom's first objection can be overcome by assuming that Achan and his family probably came into regular physical contact with his flocks.[57] As for the second objection, two possible solutions can be put forward. First, one can suggest that Joshua would have sent representatives who were qualified to handle such items (perhaps certain Levites as in Num. 3.5-39). Or, alternatively, one might argue that the mere handling of proscribed objects does not contaminate an individual, rather it is the act of bringing them inside one's household, to a context in which they are expressly forbidden, that leads to the spread of their proscribed status.[58] One of the two solutions seems necessary in order to explain how ancient Israel could have carried out the ban without infecting itself with the contagion of the dedicated objects. Putting something to the ban required one to come into contact

---

54. Also note Deut. 7.26 and Josh. 6.18 (quoted above).

55. Following Greenberg, who states, 'Achan's misappropriated objects…were hidden in the ground under his tent. Therefore, he, his family, his domestic animals, and his tent, had to be destroyed, since all incurred the חרם status.' Greenberg, 'Some Postulates', p. 31.

56. This objection is raised in Milgrom, *Cult and Conscience*, p. 34 n. 127.

57. There is strong archaeological evidence supporting the idea that ancient Israelite houses 'indicate that animals shared the shelter with people… Probably the livestock was brought into the house at night.' L. Stager, 'The Archaeology of the Family in Ancient Israel', *BASOR* 260 (Fall 1985), p. 12.

58. This argument follows the lead of B.S. Jackson who tells us that 'we may assume that contact with the property in the execution of the ordained destruction did not constitute the offence'. Jackson, *Theft*, p. 61 n. 7.

with the taboo items which were either killed (humans and animals), or
burned (all other property) (Deut. 7.25-26; 13.16-18). The language used
in Deut. 13.18 does not say that one cannot touch the חרם, but rather
that 'none of the חרם will cling to your hand' (ולא ידבק בידך מאומה מן־
החרם). Josh. 6.18 also implies that it is not touching it that is problematic,
but misappropriating it (ולקחתם מן־החרם, lest you take from the חרם). And
while it is true that Deut. 7.25-26 says not to bring any such object into
one's house (ולא־תביא תועבה אל־ביתך), it clearly implies that someone is, at
least for a short time, handling it. Contrary to Milgrom, it does seem that
these dedicated objects transmitted their tabooed status to Achan's
whole household and his chattels and thus they had to be removed
'from the ordinary world of men in the same way that the city of
Jericho itself had been'.[59]

Although I attribute the necessity for eliminating Achan's family and
his chattels primarily to the idea that the tabooed status of the items that
he illicitly procured was transmitted to him and his whole household, I
would not discount the idea that other factors could be at work. It is
certain that the writers who produced these narratives were not
systematic theologians who were precise about the exact mechanism
behind a given set of circumstances.[60] Thus it is possible to postulate that
a synergism of various factors contributed to the punishment of Achan's
family and destruction of his chattels. These could include the idea that
people might sometimes be treated as property, and the fact that
Achan's sin was particularly egregious.

It is now time to turn our attention to the question of how Achan's
misappropriation of the חרם is connected to the death of the 36 men
(Josh. 7.5) and to Israel's temporary excommunication from God (Josh.
7.12). It seems that these two issues are intertwined inasmuch as it
is God's abandoning Israel that leads to the death of the 36 men. But

59. Porter, 'Legal Aspects', p. 370.
60. Nor are we moderns always completely systematic or precise in expressing
our rationale behind various punishments. Very few people can explain why our
society punishes criminals in the ways we do. Furthermore, the rationale behind the
concept of any form of punishment can be conceived very differently by different
elements in a single society. A liberal might speak of the rehabilitative function of
punishment and a conservative will likely speak of the punitive aspect, while others
might speak of the necessity to detain prisoners as simply a protective device. Yet, it is
possible to argue that all these factors are involved in a given punishment in varying
degrees. For a basic introduction to this problem, see C.L. Ten, *Crime, Guilt, and
Punishment* (Oxford: Clarendon Press, 1987).

theologically speaking, one must attempt to clarify what religious ideas underpin ancient Israel's conception of a system of divine retribution in which the sin of one man could lead to such disastrous consequences for the 36 men as well as for the nation as a whole.

One could propose that the answer is to be found in Josh. 7.12, which tells us that Israel has become חרם. The difficulty with this suggestion is that it is clear from the course of the narrative that, although they may be categorized as חרם, they are infected at a lower level that can be corrected by purification and removal of the חרם from their midst (Josh. 7.13).

The proper way to solve this enigma is to place the concept of חרם within the larger theological idea of holiness. Although different sources within the Hebrew Bible have different understandings of the idea of holiness, they do share certain basic assumptions about this notion.[61] The particular religious state that Israel is told time and again to maintain is described by the word 'holiness'.[62] The concept of holiness in the Hebrew Bible cuts across the Western dichotomy of the spiritual versus the physical; one's physical state is part of one's spiritual state. The idea of a spirituality that is distinct from the body and the material world, an idea that seems so obvious for most moderns to grasp, is not found within the Hebrew Bible.

Israel is commanded to be holy because God is holy, and because this holy God lives in proximity to the people of Israel (Lev. 11.44; 19.2; 20.26; Deut. 7.6; 14.2; 23.10-15; 26.19; 28.9; Isa. 12.6; Jer. 2.3; Ezek. 20.41). Israel's failure to maintain the proper level of holiness will eventually cause God to abandon his dwelling place and thus leave Israel vulnerable to attack from external forces (Ezek. 8–11).[63] If Israel maintains a proper state of holiness, it continues to be protected by the divine presence that abides in her midst (Pss. 46 and 48).

Although the above statement on holiness seems easy enough to understand, unfortunately it does not reveal all of the subtleties of this unusual concept. Holiness and the consequences that flow from it often operate in what could be termed an amoral universe. There are numerous instances in the Hebrew Bible that reveal this amoral dimension to

61. An excellent comparison of the differences between P and D can be found in Weinfeld, 'Pentateuch'.

62. See n. 20 in Chapter 3 above for fuller bibliography on the concept of holiness.

63. J. Milgrom, *Studies in Cultic Theology and Terminology* (SJLA, 36; Leiden: Brill, 1983), pp. 75-84.

God's behavior (Exod. 4.24-26; Lev. 10.1-7; Num. 16.19-22; 25.11; 2 Sam. 6.6-8).[64] It would be fair to describe holiness as analogous to an electrical charge that can be quite useful when channeled properly and quite dangerous when handled improperly. Neither electricity nor holiness will act any differently simply on the basis of one's interior state or intentions. Just as a person might unawares come into contact with a live electrical charge and accidentally receive a severe or even fatal shock, so too, one could offend God's holiness in an accidental or unconscious manner (Lev. 4).

As indicated above, in order for Israel to function as a mediator for God's holiness, Israel must create an environment that is sanctified so that the deity will manifest itself. This requires that Israel construct a shrine and its utensils according to a precise model revealed by God to Moses (Exod. 25.9, 40; Num. 8.4).[65] It also requires that various ritual procedures be executed properly. But God's environment was not only affected by the actions or inactions of various cultic officials, but was also affected by any Israelite who even accidentally committed a breach of the laws of holiness.[66] It is on this basis that ancient Israel recognized and accepted a type of communal responsibility that held individuals responsible, at least at some level, for the misdeeds of other Israelites. Israel was held communally accountable for maintaining a fit environment in which God could manifest himself, and through this manifestation could radiate blessing to the rest of the terrestrial world. Maintaining the proper environment entailed three basic responsibilities:

1. The community as a whole was obligated to make every attempt possible to avoid polluting themselves or their land. This vigilance included being watchful of even accidental cases of pollution.

---

64. Otto clearly recognized this amoral or non-rational aspect inherent in the idea of holiness and captures it well with his notion of *mysterium tremendum*. In his discussion of the *mysterium tremendum* he broaches the subject of the ὀργή, or wrath of YHWH and tells us that 'this wrath has no concern whatever with moral qualities'. Otto, *The Idea of the Holy*, p. 18.

65. A similar claim seems to be made about David's plans for the Temple in 1 Chron. 28.11-19.

66. According to P, it appears that even a non-Israelite could affect God's environment in a negative way if he ate impure things within the land of Israel (Lev. 17.15). Again note Weinfeld's argument, 'Pentateuch', p. 249.

2. If a breach of the purity rules occurred, the community as a whole must first determine what offence was committed and then identify the sinner who committed it, if at all possible.
3. They must make sure that every breach is atoned for properly. This may require a sacrificial act, a fine, a confession, or some combination of these. In more severe cases it requires the removal of the individual offender from the group by either excommunication or execution.[67]

The rationale behind this elaborate system is summed up quite nicely by the following quotation:

> One becoming impure as the result of an offense against the deity introduced a kind of demonic contagion into the community. The more horrendous the offense, the greater the threat to the purity of the sanctuary and the surrounding community by the presence of the offender, who was a carrier of impurity. This person required purification if the community was to be restored to its ritual state, which, in turn, was a precondition set down by the resident deity for his continued presence among the people. The deity had made a vital concession to the Israelites by consenting to dwell amidst the impurities endemic to the human situation (Lev. 16.16). If his continued residence was to be realized, YHWH required an extreme degree of purity (Exod. 25.8).[68]

---

67. I have relied quite heavily on Jacob Milgrom's ideas about the nature of sin and its relationship to the cult in ancient Israel. I believe Milgrom's comment about the Day of Atonement can be applied to the cult in general and can illuminate many of the texts that are often spoken of whenever the concept of corporate personality is invoked. He says, 'Thus it is discovered that the complex of sanctuary rituals that comprise the Day of Atonement (better rendered: "Purgation Day") predicate the priestly conviction that divine retribution operates on the basis of collective liability: every person is responsible for Israel's destiny because every sinful or impure act pollutes the sanctuary; the demons of the pagan world are replaced by man who, by his covenanted violations, can force God to abandon His sanctuary'. Milgrom, *Studies in Cultic Theology*, p. xii. Milgrom's central idea is that failure to guard against sin and to neutralize sins by ritual action causes God to abandon his sanctuary, thus wreaking havoc on Israel. Interestingly enough, Milgrom claims that the חטאת sacrifices are not really for the atonement of the sinner, but for the cleansing of the sanctuary where the sin has come to roost. The sinner is already forgiven through his remorse. It is the pollution of the sanctuary, which happens whenever any Israelite sins, that requires the sacrifice. See especially *Studies in Cultic Theology*, pp. 77-84, in which Milgrom also explains the difference between intentional and unintentional sins.

68. Levine, *Presence*, p. 75. It should be noted that Levine has a running dispute

When the purity of God's environment was violated it could lead to a swift and severe reaction by God against the individual offender (Lev. 10.1-7) or sometimes against the nation as a whole (Josh. 7). This was not an arbitrary punishment:

> There is a reason for YHWH's wrath. It was not mere displeasure at being disobeyed. His wrath was a reaction based on a vital concern, as it were, for his own protection.[69]

The above quotations elucidate the rationale behind the loss of the 36 men in the first battle of Ai and the temporary excommunication of the entire community until they located and disposed of the actual offender. Israel as a whole was responsible for Achan's crime and thus could be legitimately punished, at least until Achan (who was the primary offender) was executed for his sin.

Having shown how a fuller understanding of the ideas of חרם and holiness help elucidate certain theological problems posed by the

with Milgrom about the exact nature of sin and purification. Levine, in contrast to Milgrom, argues that the individual is cleansed during the חטאת ritual and that both the sanctuary and the sinner are inhabited by demons that are dismissed through a magical ceremony. I do not feel qualified to settle the dispute about how magical the Priestly legislation is per se, or if other ancient Near Eastern rituals are more magical. Milgrom presents some evidence of the ways in which originally magical rituals were toned down and tamed by the biblical writers. Milgrom's approach has an apologetic tendency that stresses the superiority of Judaism to its pagan neighbors and thus often overlooks how magical many of the biblical rituals, in fact, are. Note Milgrom's quote in reference to the ritual of the red heifer in Num. 19: 'More than a half millennium earlier the priestly legislators of this ritual severed its pagan roots and remodelled it to accord with their norms and praxis'. J. Milgrom, 'The Paradox of the Red Cow', *VT* 31 (January 1981), p. 72. Much of this debate appears to turn on how one interprets the magical language and rituals that are part of the text. Are these only a part of the pre-history of a text that is now no longer magical, or are they old magical ideas that are utilized in a new and different magical system? The latter appears to be the view of Levine. Either position is compatible with my argument inasmuch as both authors agree that sin is a communal problem because it could cause God to abandon his sanctuary, thus leaving Israel vulnerable to external attack. The debate is over the nature of the threat to God and the way that expiation functions. Is it, as Milgrom maintains, solely God who decides when to abandon his sanctuary and what types of procedures are effective in cleaning his environment; or is it, as Levine maintains, that 'the sacrificial blood is offered to the demonic forces who accept it in lieu of God's "life", so to speak, and depart'? Levine, *Presence*, p. 78.

69. Levine, *Presence*, p. 78.

narrative found in Joshua 7, it is now time to ask what, if any, connection exists between the idea of חרם and covenant. It should be , noted that Joshua 7 twice uses the language of transgressing God's covenant (Josh. 7.11, 15) and thus implies that there is a relationship between the notion of covenant and the ideas of holiness and חרם. The exact relationship between these various concepts is nicely stated by Philip Stern:

> The חרם stems ultimately from a foreign milieu where the Hebrew concept of covenant was not operative. There is no hint of it in the Mesha Inscription; nor had it a place of importance in the Mesopotamian world of thought which led to *asakku akālu*. The notion of חרם flows from more fundamental religious conceptions than the covenant. As the root implies the חרם is a form of holiness and flows from the immediate nature of the divine, while covenant is an external result of YHWH's action in history.[70]

Although the ideas of חרם and holiness do not presuppose the existence of the idea of covenant, the notion of covenant does presuppose and grow organically out of these earlier ideas. Implicit within the idea of covenant in the Hebrew Bible is the idea of election and the responsibilities that this notion entails. The earliest conception of these responsibilities is tied up with the notion of holiness. But it is only after the idea of holiness is incorporated into the larger schema of covenant that Israel reaches a fuller understanding of itself. It is within a covenantal framework that Israel comes to realize that its relationship to God is necessary for Israel to mediate divine blessing to all the other nations of the world (Gen. 12.3; 22.18; Exod. 19.6). The temple, which is God's residence, is portrayed as the *axis mundi* and the place from which fertility and blessing issue to the rest of the terrestrial world (Ezek. 47).[71]

In addition to providing a much broader theological scope to Israel's relationship to God, the notion of covenant binds all the legal and religious norms that we find in the Pentateuch to the notion of holiness. In doing so the laws are no longer purely human; they are now divine imperatives. When one breaks a covenantal law, one commits a religious sin, not just a legal offence. When one acts in accord with a covenantal law, one participates actively in God's world-sustaining activity. This

70. Stern, *The Biblical Ḥerem*, pp. 155-56.
71. On the connection between fertility and blessing, and the Temple, see J.D. Levenson, *Theology of the Program of Restoration of Ezekiel 40–48* (HSM, 10; Atlanta: Scholars Press, 1976), pp. 7-24.

covenantal system and the consequences that follow from it are succinctly described by Anthony Phillips:

> As has been recognized, the covenant was deemed to have been entered into both with each individual Israelite and with Israel as a people. Thus on its breach, both individual and communal liability arose, a man being liable not only for his own acts, but also, by reason of his membership in the covenant community, for the acts of others. Further, the same criminal act could result in two different sources of punishment, human or divine. Thus YHWH could directly punish the individual or the community for breach of the covenant stipulations, and the community itself was under a duty to execute the criminal in order to propitiate YHWH and so avert or bring to an end divine punishment.[72]

The concept of covenant which appears to have developed out from these earlier religious conceptions has ultimately come to frame these ideas. Thus the notions of חרם and holiness are now elements within the larger deuteronomistic covenantal theology. But they do not simply reside within this theological framework as totally eviscerated ideas; rather, they continue to remain alive and well. In fact, the notion of covenant is in many ways a natural development of the fundamental religious insight found within these earlier religious conceptions: ritual and legal norms are not separable. Israel's intuition into the unity of law and religion, expressed so clearly within covenantal theology, implies that Israel's judicial system of retribution is pervaded by religious ideas such as holiness and the contagious nature of sin. Inasmuch as these earlier religious ideas continue to maintain their power, it should come as no surprise that Israel's theology continues to understand retribution as something that often has corporate implications.

Conclusions

1. Various factors may help explain the execution of Achan's family and chattels. These include the fact that in ancient Israel a man's extended family was sometimes treated as part of his property, that Achan

---

72. A. Phillips, *Ancient Israel's Criminal Law: A New Approach to the Decalogue* (Oxford: Basil Blackwell, 1970), p. 32. Phillips does not draw a close connection between covenant and holiness as I do. He thinks that the Priestly legislation with its focus on ritual purity is a rejection of pre-exilic notions of communal liability. He connects such a movement toward individual responsibility to the recitation of the Temple entrance liturgies (pp. 186-87). Furthermore, Phillips does not view the Achan case as a criminal case, but as a violation of the military ban (p. 40).

committed a particularly serious offence, and that חרם has the ability to transmit its taboo status to other objects around it.

2. The idea that חרם has the ability to transmit its taboo status to other objects around it is particularly important in gaining a deeper understanding of this narrative. Not only does this factor provide the most likely explanation for the execution of Achan's family and possessions, but it can also elucidate the death of the 36 men at the first battle of Ai and the conditional excommunication of Israel by God.

3. It is not the concept of חרם alone, but the way in which this idea is related to the larger concept of holiness, that helps one understand why Achan's violation of the חרם led to God's abandonment of Israel and thus to the loss of the 36 men in the first battle of Ai. When the חרם was brought illicitly into the camp, it violated the rules of camp purity and thus led to God's abandoning of the Israelites. This is not an arbitrary act on God's part, but is done because God's environment in the camp is no longer in a proper ritual state, which in turn forces the deity to leave. Without divine protection, Israel remains vulnerable to attack.

4. The concepts of חרם and of holiness eventually contributed to the rise of a covenantal theology. The current narrative of Joshua 7 is in fact set within the deuteronomistic history which is pervaded by the notion of covenant. While the notion of covenant eventually came to frame these early religious ideas, these early religious ideas have strongly influenced the way in which this covenantal theology understands Israel's relationship with God.

5. This relationship is based upon the community's responsibility to maintain a proper environment in which God can be made manifest. This responsibility, which grows out of earlier religious conceptions, means that the whole community can be held liable for the sins of its individual members. Furthermore, it also entails the idea that individuals may harm those in the vicinity, if they breach the rules of proper ritual procedure.

The purpose of this chapter was to clarify the corporate notions of retribution found in Joshua 7. I did this by explicating the ways in which the ideas of חרם, holiness and covenant function in ancient Israelite thought, and specifically how these notions pervade the narrative in Joshua 7. By elucidating the deeper religious ideas that undergird Israelite conceptions of divine retribution one comes to see that the Achan case, which upon initial inspection appears to be enigmatic, has an internal coherence to it. Furthermore, although many modern thinkers would criticize the system of punishment advocated by Joshua 7 as inherently unfair because it does not treat each person as an autonomous individual, one wonders whether this narrative might not offer an implicit critique of the modern predisposition to view individuals as autonomous entities who only relate to their society when they freely choose to do so.

Chapter 5

2 SAMUEL 21.1-14: BLOODGUILT AND CORPORATE PUNISHMENT

In the last two chapters I focused upon the notions of divine wrath and holiness in order to substantiate my claim that corporate ideas occur frequently in the Hebrew Bible because the larger theological systems have preserved various ancient religious ideas that are inherently corporate. Before closing this section of the book there is one other ancient religious idea that merits our attention: bloodguilt. To facilitate our discussion of this concept, once again I will focus the discussion upon a specific text from the deuteronomistic history. The text is 2 Sam. 21.1-14.

> There was a famine in the land in the days of David three years, year after year; and David inquired of the Lord. The Lord said, 'There is bloodguilt upon[1] Saul and upon his[2] house, because he put the Gibeonites to death'. 2 So the king summoned the Gibeonites and said to them. (Now the Gibeonites were not of the people of Israel, rather they were of the remnant of the Amorites, but the Israelites had sworn to them, and Saul had sought to destroy them in his zeal for the people of Israel and Judah.) 3 David said to the Gibeonites, 'What can I do for you? How can I make atonement that you may bless the heritage of the Lord?' 4 The Gibeonites said to him, 'It is not a matter of silver or gold between us[3] and Saul and his household; and it is not for us to put to death anyone in Israel'.[4] He said,

1. Reading עַל rather than the MT's אֶל.
2. Following the LXX. McCarter following Driver suggests that the ה from the following word, הַדָּמִים, belongs with the word בֵּית as the third person masculine singular form according to the older orthography. McCarter, *II Samuel*, p. 437; S.R. Driver, *Notes on the Hebrew Text of the Books of Samuel* (Oxford: Clarendon Press, 1890), p. 268; H.P. Smith, *The Books of Samuel* (ICC; New York: Charles Scribner's Sons, 1904), p. 375. Also see GKC, §91e.
3. Reading with the *qere*.
4. This reading follows the logic that the Gibeonites did not have full rights within the Israelite community. As H. Cazelles says, 'It is an affair of blood. But owing to the supremacy of Israel, the Gibeonites could not exact the blood revenge which the justice of YHWH required, which was the only valid expiation which would

'What are you saying I should do for you?' 5 They replied to the king,
'The man who destroyed us and planned to eradicate us[5] from having any
place within the territory of Israel—6 let seven of his sons be given over to
us[6] that we may impale[7] them before the Lord at Gibeon on the mountain[8]
of the Lord'. The king said, 'I will agree'.

7 But the king had mercy on Mephibosheth, the son of Jonathan, the
son of Saul, because of the oath of the Lord that was between them,
between David and Jonathan the son of Saul. 8 The king took the two sons
of Rizpah the daughter of Aiah that she bore to Saul, Armoni and

---

accord with David's desire to appease the divinity.' H. Cazelles, 'David's Monarchy
and the Gibeonite Claim', *PEQ* 87 (1955), p. 170. It is possible to read the phrase as
'we have no need to kill anyone (else) in Israel (beside Saul's descendants)'. For a
fuller exploration of the relationship between the Israelites and the Gibeonites, see
J. Blenkinsopp, *Gibeon and Israel* (Cambridge: Cambridge University Press, 1972).

5.   Emending ואשר דמה־לנו נשמדנו to ואשר דמה להשמידנו following McCarter,
Driver and Wellhausen. Smith, *Samuel*, p. 375, Driver, *Samuel*, p. 269, and McCarter,
Samuel, p. 438.

6.   Here one may either follow the *qere* and read this as a *hophal* or one can
repoint the *kethib* and read it as a *niphal*. Either way it is a passive form and would be
translated in the same manner.

7.   The root of this word is יקע and its exact meaning is unclear. It is used in
Gen. 32.26 of Jacob's dislocated thigh and in Num. 25.4 it occurs in a text as a
means of execution. McCarter suggests crucifixion but notes that there are many
alternative possibilities (ritual dismemberment, hurling down, to expose *et al.*).
McCarter, *II Samuel*, p. 442. It is not clear that crucifixion existed before the Persian
period, but it is possible. For a fuller discussion see M. Hengel, *Crucifixion*
(Philadelphia: Fortress Press, 1977), pp. 21-32. The act of impaling people existed at
least since Assyrian times and thus I have chosen this term. Hanging already dead
people on display can be found in 1 Sam. 31.10. It has been suggested that Gibeon is
a center for the cult of the sun god ŠMŠ. If this is so it might help explain the
unusual form of execution as exposure to the sun in order to satisfy ŠMŠ, who may
have been a god invoked in the original treaty with the Israelites. There may be further
proof for this in the fact that in Num. 25.4 the Lord asks Moses to take all the heads
of the people and והוקע אותם ליהוה נגד השמש (impale them to the Lord in the face of
the sun). For more on this idea see J. Dus, 'Gibeon—eine Kultstätte des Šmš und die
Stadt des benjaminitischen Schicksals', *VT* 10 (1960), pp. 353-74; J. Heller, 'Die
schweigende Sonne', *Communio Viatorum* 9 (1966), pp. 73-79 and Blenkinsopp,
Gibeon and Israel, pp. 41-52.

8.   The MT reads, 'before the Lord at Gibeah of Saul the chosen of the Lord'. I
follow McCarter's suggestion that בהר was wrongly read as בחר and that once this
occurred Saul was added as a gloss and thus בנבעון became בגבעת. This suggestion
gains some support from the LXX which reads Γαβαων Σαουλ, which suggests that
the word Saul is a later gloss that arose from the misreading of בהר. McCarter,
II Samuel, p. 438.

Mephibosheth; and the five sons of Merab[9] daughter of Saul, whom she bore to Adriel son of Barzillai the Meholathite. 9 He-handed them over to the Gibeonites, and they impaled them on the mountain before the Lord. The seven of them[10] died together. They were executed in the first days of the harvest[11] at the beginning of the barley harvest.[12] 10 Rizpah the daughter of Aiah took sackloth and spread it out for herself on a rock at the beginning of the harvest until the waters poured on them from the heavens; she did not let the birds of heaven set upon them during the day nor the wild beasts by night. 11 When David was told what Rizpah the daughter of Aiah, the concubine of Saul had done, 12 David went and took the bones of Saul and the bones of Jonathan his son from the men of Jabesh-gilead, who stole them from the plaza of Beth-shan, where the Philistines had hung them on the day that the Philistines had killed Saul on Gilboa. 13 He brought up from there the bones of Saul and the bones of Jonathan his son, and they gathered the bones of those who were impaled. 14 They buried the bones of Saul and Jonathan his son in the land of Benjamin, in Zela, in the tomb of Kish, his father. They did everything that the king commanded, and afterwards God was appeased concerning the land.

Before discussing the theological implications of this text, it is necessary to clarify certain basic issues surrounding this episode and its placement within the deuteronomistic history. It is likely that this chapter was originally connected to 2 Samuel 9.[13] There are several pieces of

9. The MT reads Michal but 2 Sam. 6.23 informs us that Michal was childless so this is obviously problematic. 1 Sam. 18.19 tells us that Merab was given to Adriel the Meholathite as a wife and it seems most likely that this is the correct reading. It is possible to argue that the reading Michal could be maintained and that the passage in 2 Sam. 6.23 only tells us that Michal had no more children, not that she was totally barren. Although I do not find this view convincing, it is argued in a sophisticated manner by J.J. Glück, 'Merab or Michal', *ZAW* 77 (1965), pp. 72-81.

10. Reading with the *qere*.

11. The Lucianic recension of the LXX reads ἐν ἡμέραις ζειῶν ἐν ἀρχῇ θερισμοῦ κριθῶν. It is possible that this text hides an original transliteration of the old Canaanite month named Ziv and that the text originally read, 'in the days of Ziv, at the beginning of the barley harvest'. This suggestion was made by S.P. Brock, 'An Unrecognized Occurence of the Month Name Ziw (2 Sam. XXI 9)', *VT* 23 (January 1973), pp. 100-103.

12. McCarter suggests that originally the word מחלחת was introduced into this verse by accident in anticipation of its occurence in v. 10. The מ was then associated with the previous word and the ב was reintroduced but on the previous word rather than where it belonged. From this McCarter deduces that originally the MT read הקציר הראשון that is 'the former harvest'. McCarter, *II Samuel*, p. 439.

13. My argument in the following paragraph is heavily indebted to Kapelrud, 'King and Fertility', pp. 113-22.

evidence to support this contention. To begin with 2 Sam. 8.16-18 is
very similar to 2 Sam. 20.23-26 in that both describe the most important
officials in David's kingdom. Although the lists are not identical, it is
probable that they are variants of a single list and that they function as
an *inclusio*, thus telling us that this material was shifted from its initial
position.[14] Additionally, 2 Sam. 21.14 ends with the words אחרי־כן which
are a bit awkward in their current position, but would work quite nicely
if shifted to the beginning of 2 Samuel 9 (cf. 2 Sam. 2.1; 8.1; 10.1; 13.1).
From a narrative viewpoint, there are good reasons to support the idea
that 2 Sam. 21.1-14 belonged before 2 Sam. 9.1. David's question in 2
Sam. 9.1 makes much more sense after he has eliminated Saul's other
descendants. And Shimei's statement in 2 Sam. 16.7-8 which includes
the phrase השיב עליך יהוה כל דמי בית־שאול (the Lord has recompensed you
[literally: has caused to return upon you] for all the blood of the house
of Saul), is more understandable in the light of David's elimination of
Saul's other progeny. After all, David was not responsible even
indirectly for Saul or Jonathan's death on Mount Gilboa (1 Sam. 31),
nor was David directly involved in the death of Ish-bosheth (2 Sam. 4).
All of these facts provide strong support for the idea that this passage
was moved from its original location. What they do not tell us is why it
was moved and how it ended up in its current position.

It has been suggested that this story was temporarily suppressed
because it portrayed David in a bad light,[15] or because it tells of child
sacrifice,[16] an institution that was condemned by the first redactor(s) of
the deuteronomistic history. It has further been suggested that the
material between 2 Sam. 20.23 and 2 Sam. 24.25 'is neither part of the
Deuteronomistic history nor related to the earlier literature it
embraced'.[17] If this story proved to be alien to the deuteronomistic
history, then one could object to any attempt to use it to as an example
of corporate thinking by the deuteronomistic historian. It could be
posited that this narrative was dropped out of the original edition
precisely because it contained ideas of divine retribution that were seen
as untenable to the deuteronomistic historian.

There are several reasons why one should not exclude this passage
from the deuteonomistic history. To begin with, it is most unlikely that

14. See McCarter, *II Samuel*, p. 257.
15. Smith, *Samuel*, p. 374.
16. Kapelrud, *King and Fertility*, p. 113.
17. McCarter, *II Samuel*, p. 16.

2 Sam. 21.1-14 was intentionally omitted due to its controversial nature and then later re-incorporated. Anyone who makes such an argument has the onus of explaining precisely who omitted it and why, and who re-incorporated it and why. Although this passage is somewhat controversial in its portrayal of David's treatment of Saul's extended family, it surely is not as damaging to David's image as the David and Bathsheba incident reported in 2 Samuel 11–12. Furthermore, one could argue that the story reflects positively on David who preserves the life of Mephibosheth (2 Sam. 21.7) and sees to the proper burial of Saul and Jonathan (2 Sam. 21.11-14). Kapelrud's suggestion, that this story was omitted because it contains ideas of child sacrifice, is not highly compelling. Even if one granted that this narrative is in fact a case of child sacrifice, a contention that remains very dubious, there is little evidence that the editor of the deuteronomistic history would suppress a passage just because it contains this motif (cf. Judg. 11.34-40). The strongest argument in favor of treating this narrative as alien to the deuteronomistic history is employed by those who claim that the material in 2 Sam. 20.23–24.25 looks like a series of appendices that were added at the end of the book. '2 Sam. 21-24 is full of additions, which gradually accumulated *after* Dtr.'s history had been divided into separate books.'[18] But as McCarter notes, in the 'Lucianic' manuscripts of the LXX, 1 Kings begins with 1 Kgs 2.12, and Josephus begins book 8 of his *Antiquities* at this point as well.

> By this arrangement II Samuel ends with David's death, just as I Kings ends with Ahab's, I Samuel with Saul's, Joshua with Joshua's, Deuteronomy with Moses', and Genesis with Jacob's and Joseph's.[19]

Thus it is reasonable to presume that the oldest division between the books is the one preserved in the Lucianic manuscripts of the LXX and that therefore one cannot see these passages as simply an accumulation of appendices at the end of a book. Equally dubious is McCarter's attempt to compare the status of these materials to the accumulation of certain poetic materials immediately before the death of Jacob in Genesis and Moses in Deuteronomy. McCarter notes that if this is the case it is odd that the material did not come immediately before 1 Kgs 2.1-11.[20] Furthermore, McCarter's contention that the material between

18. Noth, *Deuteronomistic History*, p. 124 n. 3. Emphasis is his.
19. McCarter, *II Samuel*, p. 17.
20. McCarter, *II Samuel*, p. 17.

2 Sam. 20.23 and 2 Sam. 24.25 'is neither part of the Deuteronomistic history nor related to the earlier literature it embraced'[21] is called into question by his own statement two pages later in which he informs the reader that 2 Sam. 21.1-14 'was probably moved to the end of the story of Abishalom's revolt from an original position before 9.1-13 by a Deuteronomistic editor'.[22] If 2 Sam. 21.1-14 is unrelated to the earlier literature that the deuteronomistic historian inherited, how could it have originally been attached to 2 Sam. 9.1-13; and if it was never part of the deuteronomistic history, why was it moved by a deuteronomistic editor?

That 2 Sam. 20.23–24.25 contains miscellaneous materials, does not mean that these texts are alien to the deuteronomistic history, or ended up in their current place by accident or because a later redactor re-inserted them. Although I do not pretend to be able to solve all the difficulties surrounding these narratives and their current placement, I can suggest a few alternative possibilities. It is possible to argue that the story about David's census (2 Sam. 24) ended up in its current position because it is concerned with the site of Solomon's temple, and thus it occurs closer to the building of the actual temple which it foreshadows.[23] If this proved to be true, one could argue that this story attracted the narrative in 2 Sam. 21.1-14 by association, either because they are both narratives that deal with David overcoming God's wrath, or it could be an attempt to explain why the sanctuary at Gibeon was eventually overshadowed by the newer sanctuary at Jerusalem.[24] Another likely scenario is that 2 Sam. 20.23–21.14 was moved to its present position in order to highlight David's loyalty to Saul's house by drawing a stronger connection between 1 Sam. 20.11-17 and 2 Samuel 9.[25] But just

21. McCarter, *II Samuel*, p. 16.

22. McCarter, *II Samuel*, p. 18.

23. As suggested by H.W. Hertzberg, *I & II Samuel* (OTL; London: SCM Press, 1964), pp. 415-16.

24. This idea is offered as a possibility by Blenkinsopp who tells us that 'we might be able to suppose, without being able to offer proof, that the second narrative had the purpose of legitimizing the new sanctuary to be established on the Jebusite threshing floor over against the renowned Gibeonite cult centre'. Blenkinsopp, *Gibeon and Israel*, p. 94. Further proof for this hypothesis might be found in 1 Chron. 21.29-30 which informs us that David was prevented from going to Gibeon to seek God because he was terrified by the sword of the angel of the Lord. This can be viewed as an attempt to explain how it was that Jerusalem came to overshadow Gibeon by divine choice.

25. An idea that is suggested by McCarter, *II Samuel*, pp. 18 and 262-65.

because 2 Sam. 21.1-14 was moved away from its original position does not mean that it was discarded by the deuteronomistic historian and then re-inserted by a later editor. It may simply point to the fact that the editor inherited a document consisting of 2 Sam. 21.1-14 and 2 Samuel 9, which for literary or political[26] reasons he chose to divide into two separate stories. As we will see in the theological analysis immediately below, the corporate ideas of retribution espoused by this particular narrative are not at all alien to the book of Deuteronomy or to the deuteronomistic history.[27]

The Execution of Saul's Descendants and Corporate Punishment

This narrative poses two interrelated difficulties that are of direct relevance to the aims of this project. These two difficulties are easily posed in the form of two questions:

1. What factors explain why Saul's descendants are punished for Saul's mistreatment of the Gibeonites?
2. Why does all Israel suffer a famine because of Saul's mistreatment of the Gibeonites?

There have been several ideas generated by various scholars to elucidate why Saul's descendants are killed for his mistreatment of the Gibeonites. The most straightforward suggestion is that this is simply a case of political expediency on David's part; he eliminated all the rivals to his throne except for Mephibosheth, who is lame and therefore not capable of playing the role of king. The difficulty with such a solution is that although David obviously benefitted from the death of Saul's progeny, 'there is nothing in the text to suggest that he engineered the situation to be rid of potential rivals' and there 'is no proof of machiavellian plotting on his part'.[28]

---

26. One could argue that the original tenor of the whole document was condemnatory toward David in that he dealt unjustly with Saul's descendants (1 Sam. 24.22-23, 21-22 in English) and thus that the editor broke the document in pieces to change the general tone of the narrative and highlight David's loyalty to Jonathan (1 Sam. 20.11-17).

27. It is interesting to note that this was already recognized by H.P. Smith who, while insisting that this narrative was a later editorial insertion, tells us that 'few sections of the Old Testament show more clearly the religious ideas of the time'. Smith, *Samuel*, p. 374.

28. R.P. Gordon, *I & II Samuel* (Library of Biblical Interpretation; Grand Rapids:

Kapelrud looks to the connection between royalty and fertility to explain the nuances of this narrative.[29] Obviously, David would have very good reasons to eliminate Saul's descendants, as they were rivals to his throne and as long as they lived they were a continuing threat to the stability of his dynasty. But if David purged them because they were a threat to the stability of his throne, it would reflect badly on him. As Kapelrud notes, the king in the ancient Near East was responsible for the general fertility of his country (Ps. 72). When fertility failed, it called into question the legitimacy of the ruler and often forced the ruler to take extraordinary measures. These measures might include human sacrifice or, if things were particularly bad, royal human sacrifice (2 Kgs 16.3). By killing Saul's progeny, David could accomplish two ends with a single action: he would restore the kingdom's fertility by offering a royal sacrifice and would eliminate several other legitimate claimants to the throne at the same time.

The greatest weakness in this explanation is that it ignores the logic of the narrative which informs us that the famine is due to the improper treatment of the Gibeonites by Saul. Clearly there are elements of Canaanite mythology in the background of this passage,[30] but Kapelrud gives them too great an emphasis. Kapelrud's conjecture calls for one to read motives into the text that are not explicitly there, and at the same time to disregard the rationale that the text supplies to explain these executions.

The most viable explanation for the death of Saul's progeny is in fact the rationale provided within the text itself. The first verse of this

---

Zondervan, 1988), pp. 300-301. Although there is no direct evidence that David engineered this situation specifically to rid himself of potential rivals, it is nearly impossible to maintain that he was innocent in every instance in which rivals are killed. Just because David manages to eliminate various rivals and still appear innocent does not mean that he is utterly blameless in all these cases. For a persuasive argument about David's complicity in the deaths of Abner and Eshbaal, see J.C. VanderKam, 'Davidic Complicity in the Deaths of Abner and Eshbaal', *JBL* 99 (December 1980), pp. 521-39.

29. Kapelrud, 'King and Fertility', pp. 118-21.

30. Note especially Cazelles, 'David's Monarchy', and Blenkinsopp, *Gibeon and Israel*, pp. 92-94. They both point to factors such as the time of the year in which the execution occurred, the connection between the mourning rights of Rizpah and the rites surrounding Baal's death, the exposure of the corpses until the rains arrive, and that the particular form of execution may be a type of dismemberment related to the way Anat deals with Mot.

passage tells us explicitly that the motivation behind the famine and the consequent punishment of Saul's descendants is:

ויאמר יהוה אל־שאול ואל־ביתה דמים על־אשר־המית את־הגבענים:[31]

> The Lord said, 'There is bloodguilt upon Saul and upon his house, because he put the Gibeonites to death.'

The notion that blood has a life of its own after it is spilled appears to be quite prominent in the Hebrew Bible (Gen. 4.10; Lev. 17.4; 1 Kgs 2.5). When innocent blood is spilled, it pollutes the land until one makes proper expiation (Num. 35.33 and Ps. 106.38). Expiation is made by spilling the blood of the offender (Gen. 9.6), or if the offender cannot be discovered, expiation is made by other ritual means (Deut. 21.1-9). An additional idea that is also commonly associated with the notion of spilling innocent blood is that the guilt from the spilled blood can adhere to the guilty party (Deut. 19.10 and 1 Kgs 2.32), and can potentially spread to the descendants of the guilty party (2 Sam. 3.29; 1 Kgs 2.31).[32] The verses just cited use the term בית אב to describe this larger corporate group that is susceptible to the spread of bloodguilt. Since Saul is the patriarch of his family, it is not surprising to find the term ביתה rather than בית אב in 2 Sam. 21.1. This tells us that the bloodguilt had spread to his extended family and thus we should not be surprised that some of his progeny are executed for his crime.[33] Additionally, it should be noted that unatoned for blood is explicitly connected to the idea of famine and

31. See nn. 1 and 2 above for the textual emendations.

32. The literal expression implies that the blood actually attaches itself to the guilty party. On the idea that blood can adhere to someone and exert powerful consequences on them or their descendants, see Koch, 'Doctrine of Retribution', pp. 57-87; *idem*, 'Der Spruch "Sein Blut bleibe auf seinem Haupt" und die israelitische Auffassung vom vergossenen Blut', *VT* 12 (1962), pp. 396-416; Reventlow, 'Sein Blut komme über sein Haupt', pp. 311-27. For a discussion of this idea in relation to the New Testament, see H. Kosmala, 'His Blood on us and on our Children', *ASTI* 7 (1970), pp. 94-126. It should be noted that the tendency for guilt to spread to the larger household is a general property of sinful behavior, but seems to occur with particular frequency in instances of murder.

33. It seems likely that the number of Saul's descendants that are executed is not equivalent to the number of Gibeonites that Saul killed. Rather, it is symbolically representative of the number of killed Gibeonites. One cannot help but connect this passage to Gen. 4.15 in which we are told that sevenfold vengeance will be taken if anyone kills Cain. It is also interesting that in the plague in 2 Sam. 24 seventy thousand Israelites are killed (2 Sam. 24.15). Clearly the number seven is a sacred number and one that symbolizes wholeness. Cazelles, 'David's Monarchy', p. 172.

infertility in the land (Gen. 4.11-12; Num. 35.34; Deut. 21.1-9),[34] thus strongly suggesting that this factor is of major importance in 2 Sam. 21.1-14 in which there is a famine in the land.[35] The precise connection between bloodguilt and infertility is rather complicated. In its oldest form one suspects that it is a miasmic phenomenon in which the innocent blood taints the land, thus rendering it infertile. But over time the miasmic qualities of blood have become inextricably linked up with two notions discussed in the last chapter, holiness and covenant. God has covenantally agreed to dwell within the land of Israel and his presence is connected to the fertility of the land. But because God is holy, he — requires that the Israelites maintain the purity of his environment. This notion is expressed most clearly in Num. 35.33-34, which tells us that unatoned blood pollutes the land, and that this is not acceptable because God dwells in this land. The almost identical concept can be found in deuteronomic and deuteronomistic texts as well (Deut. 19.10; 21.8-9; 22.8; Jer. 19.4; 26.15).[36] Of course, failure to keep the land free of impurity is cause for God to abandon the land, which in turn leads to infertility. This is both a punishment and an omen inasmuch as it is an attempt to notify the inhabitants of a given land that they should rectify their behavior (Amos 4.6-11).

Another aspect of the idea of bloodguilt is the way it functions for the family that experienced the loss. Here the notion of the גאל הדם, or redeemer of the blood, is of central importance. The גאל הדם is the representative appointed by the family who is responsible for seeking the life of the guilty party.[37] Here one should note the argument made by David Daube that the גאל הדם may not function as an institution that is oriented toward vengeance, but rather, may be directed toward compensation.

---

34. This idea continues on into the rabbinic period. The rabbis draw an explicit connection between drought and the sin of שפיכות דמים as noted by R. Patai, 'The Control of Rain in Ancient Palestine', *HUCA* 14 (1939), pp. 267-68.

35. As will be noted below, famine and infertility are also closely allied with the notion of covenant.

36. I say almost identical because it appears that in the priestly texts it is the land itself that becomes polluted and in the deuteronomic and deuteronomistic texts it is the people of Israel who inhabit the land who become infected with the bloodguilt. This disinction is noted by J. Milgrom, *Numbers* (The JPS Torah Commentary; Philadelphia: The Jewish Publication Society, 1990), p. 509.

37. For more extensive discussion of the organization of Israelite social life and the function of the בית אב and the גאל הדם, see de Vaux, *Ancient Israel*, I, pp. 1-12.

The murderer has obtained control over the murdered man's soul. So the
גאל הדם has to redeem the dead man from the power of the murderer. By
killing the murderer, he takes back the victim's soul.[38]

In this particular case, since Saul is no longer alive, the killing of Saul's
progeny may be the only way for the Gibeonites to regain possession of
the souls of their dead kin. This in fact would link up nicely with another
factor that is clearly at work in this passage, the idea that someone's
progeny may be viewed as a personal extension of his self.[39] Interestingly
enough, it is J.R. Porter, a critic of the notion of corporate personality,
who advocates the idea that Saul's descendants were in fact vicarious
representatives of Saul himself.[40] He suggests that we could leave the
consonantal text of 2 Sam. 21.5 intact and repoint it so that it reads:
נִשְׁמְדֶנּוּ מֵהִתְיַצֵּב בְּכָל-גְּבֻל יִשְׂרָאֵל: (let us destroy him [i.e. Saul] from remaining
within the whole territory of Israel). If this were the correct reading, it
would show 'the strength of the idea that it was the actual individual

38. Daube, *Studies in Biblical Law*, p. 124.

39. It is at this point that David Daube's idea of 'ruler punishment' again comes
into focus. Although I do think that the notion of ruler punishment is a factor in this
narrative, I find Daube's and Porter's definition of ruler punishment to be overly
narrow. As noted in Chapter 4 n. 25 above, they both see ruler punishment as an
attempt to punish a person by diminishing his or her personal property. However, in
2 Sam. 21 Saul's descendants are personal extensions of himself and who continue
to carry on his name and thus they are candidates for Saul's punishment. That Saul's
descendants are not simply property can be seen from the fact that the Gibeonites tell
David that their claim against Saul is not a monetary matter (2 Sam. 21.4).
Furthermore it appears that Saul's personal property remained in a consolidated form
after his death and there is nothing in 2 Sam. 21.1-14 that suggests that this changed
due to the claim of the Gibeonites (2 Sam. 9.9; 16.4; 19.30-31, 29-30 in English).
Daube, *Studies in Biblical Law*, pp. 154-89.

40. Porter, 'Legal Aspects', pp. 377-78. Although Porter would not view this
suggestion as support for corporate personality, it does in fact support aspects of
Robinson's argument inasmuch as it advocates that there are corporate dimensions to
the Israelite legal system. In his analysis of 2 Sam. 21.1-14 Porter says, 'Again,
ancient concepts of blood and sin are to the fore here rather than any notion of
"corporate personality"'. I agree with him whole-heartedly that this case is pervaded
by ideas of the contagiousness of blood and sin. My disagreement with Porter centers
on the question of whether the particular way in which the ideas of sin and blood
function in the Hebrew Bible involves an aspect of corporateness. I acknowledge that
ideas of psychical unity are problematic; nevertheless, I think it is fair to say that this
narrative contains elements that could be accurately labelled as 'corporate' in nature.
For further discussion, see Chapters 1 and 4 above.

who was being punished, even though through his family'.[41]

From the above discussion it has become clear that there are numerous factors which operate at various levels that help explain why Saul's descendants are executed. These factors should not be viewed as atempts to explain away corporate ideas in ancient Israel; rather they are part and parcel of the rationale that resides behind ancient Israel's notion of corporate punishment. Some of these factors are more central and some are operating further in the background. For example, factors such as David's political ambitions and the connection between fertility and royalty may play some role in the narrative and in its earlier forms, but the current form of the text suggests that we should be cautious about putting too much stress on these more marginal factors. The factors that play the most important part in elucidating why Saul's progeny are executed for his sin are:

1. Bloodguilt in ancient Israel functions in a miasmic manner and thus spreads from the guilty party to his whole household.
2. Saul's descendants function as vicarious representatives of Saul in that they embody and perpetuate his life force and his name.

Now we can turn to the second problem: why did all Israel suffer a famine because Saul mistreated the Gibeonites? The first step in attempting to understand the punishment is to clarify the crime that Saul committed against the Gibeonites. It should be noted that while the text presumes that the reader knows precisely what Saul did to the Gibeonites, it is by no means self-evident to the modern reader of the text. We do know that the Gibeonites were protected by a treaty that they made with the Israelites (Josh. 9). It may in fact be the case that they do not have full rights (Josh. 9.23-27; 2 Sam. 21.4), but it is clear that the Israelites were obligated to come to their defense if they were threatened militarily (Josh. 10.6).[42] It is probable that Saul's mistreatment of the Gibeonites is somehow connected to the massacre of the priests at Nob

---

41. Porter, 'Legal Aspects', p. 378.

42. Here I reject the argument made by Whitelam that the inability of the Gibeonites to kill Saul's sons on their own implies that no covenantal relationship existed between Gibeon and Israel. It is possible to make a covenant that gives little power to one party, but still requires the superior party to protect the life of the vassal (Deut. 20.10-11; Josh. 9.26-27). Furthermore, even a group that had full rights might not have been capable of executing the sons of a former monarch. K.W. Whitelam, *The Just King* (JSOTSup, 12; Sheffield: JSOT Press, 1979), pp. 112-21.

which may have been a Gibeonite enclave (1 Sam. 22.6-23).[43] The fact that the men who assassinated Saul's son Ish-bosheth were from Beeroth (2 Sam. 4), a Gibeonite city (Josh. 9.17), appears to point to an ongoing feud between Saul's house and the Gibeonites. Additional evidence for this feud may be found in 2 Sam. 4.2-3, which tells us that Beeroth is reckoned as part of Benjamin and that the people of Beeroth fled to Gittaim. Perhaps they fled there as a result of a 'hostile action of Saul against this alien group'[44] that Saul took in order to strengthen his strategic position against the Philistines.[45]

Although we remain unsure of the exact nature of Saul's activities in relation to the Gibeonites, it is clear from 2 Sam. 21.1-14 that he violated the terms of the covenantal agreement recorded in Joshua 9. This becomes evident when we notice that famine is often associated with covenantal violations both inside the Hebrew Bible (Deut. 28.23-24, 42, 47-57) and in the ancient Near East in general.[46] Thus the treaty between Esarhaddon and his vassals includes the following paragraph:

> May Adad, the canal inspector of heaven and earth put an end [to vegetation] in your land...let there be no sound of the grinding stone or the oven in your houses, let barley rations to be ground disappear for you, so that they grind your bones, (the bones of) your sons and daughters instead of barley rations.[47]

This same text informs the reader that those who break the treaty are cursed to receive a punishment of non-burial.

> May Ninurta, leader of the gods, fell you with his fierce arrow, and fill the plain with your corpses, give your flesh to eagles and vultures to feed upon.[48]

That Saul's progeny also remain unburied together with the notice about the famine strongly indicates that Saul broke the covenant that

---

43. Hertzberg, *I & II Samuel*, pp. 382-83, and Blenkinsopp, *Gibeon and Israel*, p. 67.

44. Blenkinsopp, *Gibeon and Israel*, p. 9.

45. A. Malamat, 'Doctrines of Causality in Hittite and Biblical Historiography: A Parallel', *VT* 5 (1955), pp. 1-12.

46. For more extensive analysis of this idea, see F.C. Fensham, 'The Treaty between Israel and the Gibeonites', *BA* 27 (September 1964), pp. 96-100; and Malamat, 'Doctrines'.

47. Translated by D.J. Wiseman in *ANET*, p. 538.

48. *ANET*, p. 538.

ancient Israel made with the Gibeonites (Josh. 9). This alone would explain why the nation as a whole suffers a famine for three years. A treaty such as this one would have been ratified by an oath that invoked curses upon each nation involved in the agreement as a corporate entity. These curses would have been backed up by the gods of both nations, who are called upon to punish either offending nation. And, of course, one of the usual punishments for a covenantal violation is a famine, especially because a famine can function as an omen that would force the guilty party to see his error and repent. The notion that a famine can function as a type of alarm to notify a population of a covenantal breach is an idea that occurs several times in the Hebrew Bible (Lev. 26.18-20; Deut. 11.17; Amos 4.6-9).

Furthermore, it is not simply a matter of one Israelite who broke the treaty and mistreated the Gibeonites. It is Saul, who as king is representative of the nation as a whole. That the king's actions can bring about either positive or negative consequences on the nation as a whole is a given within the ancient Near East. That this holds true of Israel as well is easily demonstrated by the fact that it is the new king, David, who is responsible for putting an end to the famine that is currently afflicting the nation as a whole due to the past misdeeds of the last king, Saul.[49] This case in fact has a close resemblance to the case discussed in Mursilis's plague prayer.[50] A plague is raging in Hatti land and Mursilis discovers that one of its prime causes is that his father Suppiluliumas broke a treaty with the Egyptians, and thus angered the Hattian storm god who witnessed the signing of that treaty. As the new king he has both inherited the guilt of his father's misdeeds and he, as the peoples' mediator between them and the gods, is the party who is responsible for appeasing the deity and putting an end to the plague. Malamat concisely summarizes the affinities between Mursilis's plague prayer and 2 Sam. 21.1-14:

> It does not seem to have mattered how much time elapsed between the conclusion of a treaty and its violation; nor that the effect of the sin may have occurred a considerable time later, even after the death of the king who violated the treaty. In any case the transgression was not absolved with

---

49. For a more extended discussion of the representational role of the king, see the discussion of the figure of Manasseh in Chapter 2.

50. *ANET*, pp. 394-96. For a comparison between these two texts, see Malamat, 'Doctrines'.

the death of the guilty king. In both sources, the Hittite and the Biblical, the guilt was laid to a king, who, as representative of the entire people, seems to have been held responsible for a disaster of national proportion.[51]

It should be noted that within the plague prayer Mursilis mentions that he 'has already made restitution twentyfold... But, if ye demand from me additional restitution, tell me of it in a dream and I will give it to you.'[52] It seems highly probable that David, like Mursilis, is primarily interested in discovering the cause of the famine and the way in which he can appease God and thus bring this crisis to a resolution.[53] Thus he journeyed to Gibeon, a known cult center and a location apparently famous for incubating dreams and receiving oracles (1 Kgs 3.5).[54] It appears that it was precisely such an oracle that let David know that there was a famine in the land because Saul had violated a treaty that existed between the Israelites and the Gibeonites.

One other point that highlights the importance of the notion of covenant in explaining the connection between Saul's treatment of the Gibeonites and the famine in the land is that the punishment of Saul's sons may also be partially attributed to a covenantal violation. Again I cite the Esarhaddon treaty which informs us that those who violate this covenantal oath should suffer the destruction of their future progeny: 'May Zarpanitu, who grants offspring and descendants, eradicate your offspring and descendants from the land'.[55] Such ideas appear within the Hebrew Bible as well (Deut. 28.55; 1 Kgs 14.10; 16.11). The exposure of the corpses in order that they might be eaten by wildlife further corroborates the fact that we are dealing with a covenantal violation. It is found within the Bible several times in reference to kings who acted against God's wishes (1 Kgs 14.10-11; 16.1-4; Jer. 19.7), and in the Esahaddon treaty as well: 'May Palil, lord of the first rank, let eagles and vultures eat your flesh'.[56]

What is perhaps most interesting about 2 Sam. 21.1-14 is that this particular narrative reveals that one cannot always make a clear-cut distinction between where the earlier religious ideas leave off and the

51. Malamat, 'Doctrines', p. 12.

52. *ANET*, p. 396.

53. This line of reasoning is suggested by Kapelrud, 'King and Fertility', p. 118.

54. For a fuller discussion of Gibeon as a cult site, see Blenkinsopp, *Gibeon and Israel*, pp. 84-97.

55. *ANET*, p. 538.

56. *ANET*, p. 539.

later covenantal ideas begin. The notions of bloodguilt, holiness, and the idea that later descendants embody the life force of earlier ancestors all play a vital role in explaining various corporate ideas exhibited by this narrative. But when one looks at issues such as the famine, one remains unsure whether this element is more closely allied with ancient ideas of bloodguilt, or with later ideas of covenant. In the end, it is not necessary to choose between these two options; rather it is more productive to see that this narrative testifies to the fact that corporate ideas had their roots in various ancient religious conceptions that have now been taken up and framed within a larger theological system that is strongly covenantal.

Conclusions

Several different types of corporate punishment are operative in this particular case. These include: the idea that King Saul committed a sin which led to the death of his progeny; that this sin committed by Saul led to a famine against the whole nation of Israel; that Saul's successor, David, inherited the consequences of this sin and thus was responsible for its atonement. All of the above features prove that corporate ideas are operational and even common within the Hebrew Bible.

There are three key factors that play a role in this narrative:

1. The notion of bloodguilt and its ability to adhere to one's person and one's household helps explain why Saul's progeny suffer for his sin and perhaps why specifically a famine occurs.
2. The idea that Saul's children embody and perpetuate his life force and his name clearly plays a role in explaining why it is legitimate to execute Saul's progeny for his error.
3. The notion of covenantal violation is of central importance in explaining the connection between the famine and Saul's sin against the Gibeonites. It also helps explain why David is responsible for rectifying Saul's past mistreatment of the Gibeonites and perhaps sheds light on the gruesome method of execution as well.

This narrative is important inasmuch as older religious ideas of bloodguilt and the notion that one's progeny embodies one's life force are set within a more theologically developed framework created by the deuteronomistic historian. The core of this framework is the notion of covenant and all that it implies about the relationship between God and Israel. Thus, these older religious ideas have been recalibrated and, some might argue, somewhat toned down by their placement within the deuteronomistic history. It is no longer a matter of blood acting in a strictly mechanical way, as argued by Klaus Koch;[57] rather the miasmic quality of blood is understood as something that is related to the issue of holiness. It is also probable that the notion of holiness itself has changed over time from a miasmic conception that operated in an automatic fashion to a system that is more closely controlled by divine choice.[58] This change in the concept of holiness has occurred because holiness itself is now linked to a larger system of covenantal ideas.

Acknowledging that various ancient religious conceptions have been affected by their placement into Israel's covenantal theology is not equivalent to saying that they are now rendered powerless. Israel's covenantal ideas grew out of the soil of these ideas and they continued to exert themselves quite strongly. The idea of corporate punishment has now been given a more sophisticated covenantal explanation, but it is still evident that this notion originated in the matrix of older religious notions of sin, bloodguilt, holiness and divine wrath. While recognizing that covenantal theology tempers and in some ways transmutes these older religious conceptions, one should remember that the preservation of corporate aspects within the religion of ancient Israel is itself a testimony to their great power. In fact, one of the most striking features of Israel's covenantal theology is its strongly corporate orientation.

Over the course of the last several chapters, I have argued that corporate ideas should not be viewed as exceptional within ancient Israelite thought. In fact, they are quite common and very important. Corporate ideas pervade Israel's covenantal theology and are employed in Israel's attempt to understand some of its greatest national tragedies. And it is no surprise that the larger theological systems that ancient Israel produced made use of corporate notions of punishment. Rather, one would expect to find these corporate ideas inasmuch as many of the most ancient religious conceptions that gave birth to and eventually became embedded within these larger theological systems were strongly corporate in orientation.

After showing the persistence, centrality and ubiquity of these corporate ideas, we now must shift our attention to another set of theological ideas that also merit further inquiry. Certain streams of tradition within ancient

---

57. For Koch's arguments and the various criticisms levelled against his position, see Chapters 1 and 3.

58. For a fuller discussion of this problem, see n. 68 in Chapter 4.

Israel paid much greater heed to the individual and perhaps even rejected some of the corporate ideas that I have been discussing. Obviously, the existence of such passages will affect one's final evaluation of the status of corporate ideas within ancient Israel. The investigation of passages that focus upon the individual will be conducted with the following questions in mind: What precisely do these texts imply about individuals and their relationship to the community? Are such passages truly individualistic, or just more attentive to the individual than many other passages within the Hebrew Bible? Do some (or all) of these passages explicitly, or implicitly, reject the corporate ideas that I have been focusing upon? And finally, can one make sense of a theology that appears to encompass corporate, as well as individualistic, emphases?

Part II

Chapter 6

INDIVIDUALISM WITHIN DEUTERONOMY
AND THE DEUTERONOMISTIC HISTORY

Over the course of the last five chapters, I have argued the following points: (1) that corporate types of punishment occur often in ancient Israel; (2) that one should not be surprised to find such thinking because ancient Israel's covenantal ideas are fundamentally corporate in nature; (3) that ancient Israel's covenantal ideas are fundamentally corporate because they developed from and continued to utilize earlier theological notions such as wrath, holiness and bloodguilt, ideas that all operate in a corporate manner.

It is now time to ask in what ways were these ancient corporate ideas qualified by their placement into the larger theological frameworks in which they now reside? Did the conception of the individual and his or her relationship to the community remain the same from the time of David until the time of Daniel? The biblical period covers quite a few centuries, and it would be surprising if no developments had occurred in the field of societal relationships. Furthermore, the Hebrew Bible consists of a small library of diverse texts that represent the views of different factions within ancient Israel.[1] Therefore, one would expect to find more than one conception of the relationship between the individual and the community within a corpus like the Hebrew Bible.

As will be demonstrated shortly, there are several pieces of evidence within the Hebrew Bible that suggest that an alternative theology to the one that stresses corporate punishment and reward can, in fact, be found within the biblical corpus. This evidence consists mainly of passages that stress the individual and his or her direct relationship to God. Biblical scholars appear to agree that these passages are of great theological importance, inasmuch as they focus the theological lens upon the

---

1. See M. Smith, *Palestinian Parties and Politics that Shaped the Old Testament* (London: SCM Press, 2nd edn, 1987).

individual. But there is considerable debate over how innovative and radical these passages are.

Certain scholars see them as a natural unfolding of ideas that were latent within the older corporate conceptions. Thus Scharbert, in his discussion of the formula found in Exod. 34.6 and later restated in numerous passages in more refined and individualized terms, makes the following insightful comment:

> The history of the formula does not show us a development from collectivism to individualism, but rather, a general theological clarifying and unfolding of a thought that was there from the beginning.[2]

Furthermore, scholars who follow this line of reasoning tend to interpret these passages as working in relation to, rather than in rejection of, the older corporate ideas.

> In interplay with this solidarity thinking we find a living individuality which, as distinct from individualism, is to be understood as the capacity for personal responsibility and for shaping one's life. This does not stand in mutually exclusive opposition to, but in fruitful tension with, the duty of solidarity, and as such affects the individual and motivates his conduct.[3]

On the other hand, many scholars, including some contemporaries, maintain that the Hebrew Bible contains two opposite views of divine retribution: a superior one that portrays divine retribution as individualized, and an inferior one that operates on a principle of corporate responsibility. Furthermore, the apparent tensions between those biblical texts that stress the communal aspects of punishment and those that stress the individual aspects of punishment are resolved by placing the various biblical statements surrounding divine retribution into a chronological framework. This viewpoint understands the growth of individualism within the biblical corpus as an evolutionary movement in which the individual slowly emerges from the murky depths of communal obscurity and gradually gains autonomy. Antonin Causse comments that, 'with the prophets of the eighth and seventh centuries there is a transition from primitive collectivism to moral individualism'.[4] Often

---

2. Josef Scharbert, 'Formgeschichte und Exegese von Ex 34,6f. und seiner Parallelen', *Bib* 38 (1957), p. 149.

3. W. Eichrodt, *Theology of the Old Testament* (trans. J.A. Baker; Philadelphia: Westminster Press, 1967), II, p. 232.

4. In S.T. Kimbrough, Jr, *Israelite Religion in Sociological Perspective* (Studies in Oriental Religions, 4; Wiesbaden: Otto Harrassowitz, 1978), p. 62.

Jeremiah and Ezekiel are given credit for discovering or clearly proclaiming this supposed great religious transformation.[5] Thus von Rad
declares the following in his analysis of new elements within prophecy of
the Babylonian and Persian periods:

> Ezekiel countered the complaint that JHWH lumped the generations
> together in wholesale acts of judgment by roundly asserting the contrary—
> each individual stands in direct relationship to God, and JHWH has the
> keenest interest in the individual and the decisions which he takes, because
> he wants to preserve his life (Ezek. 18). In advancing this view, Ezekiel
> abandoned the old collective way of thinking. How modern and revolu-
> tionary the prophet appears here, this very prophet whose thinking is at the
> same time so conditioned by sacral orders! Jeremiah too has heard it said
> that the children had to bear their fathers' guilt, and he too used what was a
> radically individualistic view to counter the saying (Jer. 31. 29-30).[6]

That von Rad considers this new individualized thinking superior to
the 'now rotten collectivism'[7] can be gathered from the fact that he
praises this movement as modern and progressive, unlike the outmoded
'sacral orders' found in Ezekiel's thought. A similar viewpoint is
expressed by Daube in his characterization of Genesis 18 as a midway
point between the regressive ideas of corporate punishment and the
progressive ideas of individualized punishment:

> Probably, communal thinking was so deep-rooted that Abraham could
> think in no other way; the method of judging a city as one unit was so
> unreservedly accepted that he never questioned it as such. He noticed what
> deplorable results this system might produce: but he did not discover its
> real flaw, the ultimate source of those deplorable results...While he
> expressed horror at the idea that 'the righteous should be as the wicked',
> his own proposal implied neither more nor less than that the wicked should
> be as the righteous. Fettered by the communal principle, he was unable
> to take the direct steps from communal responsibility to individual
> responsibility.[8]

---

5.   G.A. Cooke, *The Book of Ezekiel* (ICC; Edinburgh: T. & T. Clark, 1936),
pp. 194-96. H. Ringgren, *Israelite Religion* (trans. D.E. Green; Philadelphia: Fortress
Press, 1966), p. 286.

6.   G. von Rad, *Old Testament Theology* (trans. D.M.G. Stalker; New York:
Harper & Row, 1965), II, p. 266.

7.   These words are found in von Rad's treatment of Ezek. 18 in his first volume.
G. von Rad, *Old Testament Theology* (trans. D.M.G. Stalker; New York: Harper &
Row, 1962), I, p. 394.

8.   Daube, *Studies in Biblical Law*, p. 157.

This theory of a radical shift toward individuality has also been used by scholars in order to date materials in the Hebrew Bible that are difficult to date by other criteria (e.g., certain psalms). Such an argument assumes that texts that stress the individual must be late because they are concerned with the individual and such concern could only have developed in the later biblical period. Thus Claus Westermann in his discussion of Psalm 23 makes the following observation:

> Its transfer to the individual's relationship with God indicates a change towards a greater prominence for the individual, such as we see elsewhere in later Old Testament writings, particularly Ezekiel. Therefore we can certainly conclude that Psalm 23 is a late composition.[9]

My thesis in this chapter is that, with a few qualifications, scholars such as Scharbert and Eichrodt are, in fact, closer to the truth of the matter than those such as von Rad and Daube. Although there is evidence of some movement toward an innovative new theology that individualizes retribution, to read this movement as a radical shift toward individualism that completely rejected older corporate notions is problematic. It both oversimplifies the relationship between corporate and individualistic ideas by portraying these two sets of ideas as poles in an evolutionary schema, and it often leads scholars to read every passage that highlights the individual as automatically rejecting corporate ideas.

The weakness of this particular scholarly view can be easily demonstrated by testing the accuracy of the portrait of Israelite religion that such a theology inevitably produces. The evidence used to support the contention that there was a radical shift toward individualism in the late biblical period comes primarily from passages such as Deut. 24.16, Jer. 31.29-30 and Ezekiel 18. These passages do in fact come from the later period and do, at first glance, appear to advocate a new individualism. The difficulty with using passages such as these to argue

---

9. C. Westermann, *The Living Psalms* (trans. J.R. Porter; Grand Rapids: Eerdmans, 1989), p. 129. Anthony Phillips sees the temple entrance liturgies (e.g. Pss. 15 and 24) which appear to speak of some type of individual confession, as post-exilic and thus as proof of the post-exilic rejection of communal liability. Phillips, *Ancient Israel's Criminal Law*, pp. 186-87. Also note the rationale provided by Soggin for his dating of certain parts of the book of Job. 'A post-exilic dating seems advisable for the body of the book. The problems are seen in an individualistic key, and we know that this approach is sometimes to be found during the exile.' J.A. Soggin, *Introduction to the Old Testament* (trans. J. Bowden; Louisville: Westminster/John Knox, 3rd edn, 1989), p. 453.

that individualism blossomed in the later biblical period, is that these passages are drawn from biblical books that contain equally strong statements of communal solidarity with respect to punishment and to hope for future restoration. It seems rather strange that in this period of supposed growing emphasis upon the individual, the author(s) of P, who is either influenced by, or has influenced the material in Ezekiel is completing his work in which the concept of communal solidarity is very important (Lev. 4).[10] Thus the priestly writings affirm 'the old doctrine of collective responsibility: when the evildoers are punished they bring down the righteous with them'.[11]

The book of Deuteronomy, believed by most scholars to have been first composed in the mid to late seventh century BCE and finally edited in the exilic period,[12] constantly stresses the solidarity of the nation as a whole (Deut. 7.6-11; 28.1–32.43). In Deuteronomy individuals gain their ultimate purpose in life only in relation to the community because God covenantally binds himself to the nation as a whole and not to its membership singly (Deut. 26.16-19).[13] This same focus on the nation and its fate is also found within the deuteronomistic history (Josh. 22.20 and 1 Kgs 8). A quick review of Chapter 2 will remind the reader of just

10. Here I strongly disagree with Halpern's reading of P as a theology that 'seems to put limits upon, if not eliminate, vertical and horizontal corporate identity'. B. Halpern, 'Jerusalem and the Lineages in the Seventh Century BCE: Kinship and the Rise of Individual Moral Liability', in B. Halpern and D. Hobson (eds.), *Law and Ideology in Monarchic Israel* (JSOTSup, 124; Sheffield: JSOT Press, 1991), p. 14. Halpern bases his claim that P discredits inter-generational retribution on the text in Num. 26.11 that tells us the sons of Korah did not die with him. Inasmuch as this text is most probably an attempt to explain the fact that the sons of Korah eventually became singers in the temple, it is questionable to extrapolate P's theology of divine retribution from this verse alone. Other texts such as Lev. 20.5 and 26.39 suggests that priestly circles continued to maintain at least some form of inter-generational retribution.

11. J. Milgrom, *Leviticus 1–16* (AB; New York: Doubleday, 1991), pp. 49-50.

12. A good summary of the various arguments surrounding the book of Deuteronomy and its dating can be found in E.W. Nicholson, *Deuteronomy and Tradition* (Oxford: Basil Blackwell, 1967). He notes that although some scholars dissent, a majority agree to the seventh century date (p. 1).

13. Here I disagree with Mendenhall who disproportionately highlights the role of the individual in the covenantal community. While speaking about the individual Israelite, Mendenhall makes the following dubious assertion: 'The covenant placed him directly in relationship to YHWH, to whom alone he swore allegiance, and from whom he received protection'. Mendenhall, 'The Relation of the Individual', p. 100.

how frequently the deuteronomistic history focuses on the fate of the nation as a whole rather than upon the individuals who compose that nation. It should be mentioned that the final redactors of the deuteronomistic history appear to have influenced the shape of the book of Jeremiah and thus Jeremiah is likely to contain communal ideas as well (Jer. 32.18).[14]

The difficulties inherent in the evolutionary approach become even clearer when one examines the religious texts of the Persian and Hellenistic periods. If, in fact, the individual began to emerge during the late sixth century BCE, then why did this individualism leave so slight an impression upon the vast literature that was produced during the second temple period? If there was a progressive growth toward individualism, one would expect to find the development of a belief in resurrection of the person as a whole, or in an afterlife for the individual soul.[15]

14. Friedman's view, that Jeremiah probably authored both editions of the deuteronomistic history, is highly dubious. Friedman, *Who Wrote the Bible?*, pp. 145-48. It seems that Jeremiah is at odds with those who produced the book of Deuteronomy (Jer. 2.8 and 8.8-9). Bright's comment on Jer. 8.8 is correct: 'The law referred to is a written law, no doubt primarily Deuteronomy, but perhaps other bodies of law as well'. J. Bright, *Jeremiah* (AB; Garden City, NY: Doubleday, 1965), p. 63. Also note Blenkinsopp's comments on the tension between Jeremiah and the advocates of deuteronomic law in J. Blenkinsopp, *Prophecy and Canon* (Notre Dame: University of Notre Dame Press, 1977), pp. 35-39. That there is disagreement between Jeremiah and the deuteronomic law can be gathered from the fact that he never advocates cultic centralization.

Certain scholars such as H. Weippert and W. Holladay think that the distinctive language found in the prose sermons of Jeremiah show that he authored these sermons and that he influenced the language of the deuteronomistic school. Although these two scholars have demonstrated that the language in the prose sermons of Jeremiah is distinct from other forms of deuteronomistic language, this fact does not prove that Jeremiah authored these sermons, but does indicate a more complicated redactional process involving either a branch of the deuteronomistic school that worked solely on Jeremiah, or a post-deuteronomistic source. For a fuller discussion, see R.P. Carroll, *The Book of Jeremiah* (OTL; Philadelphia: Westminster Press, 1986), pp. 38-50; and E.W. Nicholson, *Preaching to the Exiles* (Oxford: Basil Blackwell, 1970), pp. 1-138.

15. The question of how early ancient Israel knew of a concept of resurrection is still debated. I see it as a late development beginning no earlier than the time of Ezekiel and only becoming widespread in the late second temple period. For a different position, see L.J. Greenspoon, 'The Origin of the Idea of Resurrection', in Halpern and Levenson (eds.), *Traditions in Transformation*, pp. 247-321. I agree with Greenspoon that the concept of resurrection itself appears to have developed over

Certainly, exact retribution in an afterlife or a resurrected existence in which accounts are set right is an excellent way in which to balance out the injustices apparent in this life, and thus to justify God. But instead of developing a concept of individualized resurrection or of an individualistic afterlife in which the injustices of this world could be set aright, much of the literature of this period, including eschatological texts that are particularly concerned with the problem of evil, are focused upon God's intervention for the community as a whole or for a purified remnant. The few texts that speak of a resurrection of the dead (e.g. Ezek. 37) portray it as a communal concept.[16] It is not until 400 years later that the idea of resurrection is applied in a more individualistic fashion (Dan. 12) and even here it still occurs in a text that is concerned with the fate of the people Israel.[17] Even rabbinic Judaism, which fully accepted the resurrection of the dead and also the immortality of the soul, continued to stress that communal aspects still operated within these notions that might at first glance appear to be radically individualistic.[18] Furthermore, it is evident that the rabbis subscribe to the notion that a single individual can bring guilt upon the collective as a whole (*Lev. R.* 4.6; *b. Sanh.* 43b–44a; *T. d. Eliyy.* 12).[19] All these factors point to the

time. Originally the reward of the righteous is resurrection (Isa. 26.13-19). Later (Dan. 12.2), both the righteous and the wicked are resurrected, and the righteous are rewarded while the wicked are punished.

16. One could read Ezek. 37 in terms of a metaphor that is used to describe the rebirth of the nation rather than as a reference to resurrection of the dead, although clearly the belief in resurrection must be latent in order for the metaphor to be understood.

17. J.J. Collins, 'Apocalyptic Eschatology as the Transcendence of Death', *CBQ* 36 (January 1974), pp. 21-43. O.S. Rankin, *Israel's Wisdom Literature* (New York: Schocken Books, 1969), pp. 130-36.

18. Note the saying from *m. Sanh.* 11.1 that 'All Israel have a share in the world to come', which is now found as an introduction to each chapter of the tractate *Avot* in the prayerbook. This text strongly implies that membership in the community is what entitles the individual to life in the next world. A similar argument could be made for at least some parts of the New Testament, which utilize language that connects salvation to membership in the believing community (1 Cor. 12).

19. This is not to say that there are not individualistic elements in rabbinic theology as well (*b. Mak.* 24a). It is clear that the rabbis have both collective and individualist ideas and do not really work out the discrepancies in a systematic manner. For further discussion, see the following works: L. Jacobs, *Religion and the Individual* (Cambridge: Cambridge University Press, 1992), pp. 1-9 and 113-20; M. Kadushin, *The Theology of Seder Eliahu* (New York: Bloch, 1932), pp. 163-211; Marmorstein,

inadequacy of an evolutionary theory that posits a radical shift toward individualism in the late biblical period.

But even if one rejects the thesis that there is a radical movement toward individualism, that does not mean that there is no movement toward individualism, or that there were no challenges to the older corporate view of retribution found in the texts that we examined in the last four chapters. The question is: what is the exact nature of these individualizing movements and how does one read them when they are set within a corpus of material that still preserves the more traditional corporate views of divine retribution?

In order to wrestle with this issue properly, it will be necessary to analyze each passage more carefully. Because I have dealt primarily with passages from Deuteronomy and the deuteronomistic history it seems best to begin by analyzing the exact nature of those passages that highlight individualism within this corpus and then subsequently the passages in Jeremiah and Ezekiel.

Deuteronomy 24.16 and 2 Kings 14.6

Deut. 24.16 reads as follows:

> The fathers shall not be put to death for the children, nor shall the children be put to death for the fathers; every person shall be put to death[20] for his own sin.

This text is often invoked in discussions about the new individualism that arose in the late biblical period. Thus the passage has been read as an indication 'that in the book of Dt the transition is already being made from a collective to an individual retribution'.[21] But if this is so, then why is the book of Deuteronomy permeated by the notion of communal responsibility (e.g. Deut. 5.1; 17.2-7)? It is clear that all Israel is responsible for keeping the commandments and that failure by part of the community does indeed endanger the whole community (Deut. 13.7-12).

The Doctrine of Merits, pp. 3-188; A. Melinek, 'The Doctrine of Reward and Punishment in Biblical and Early Rabbinic Writings', in H.J. Zimmels, J. Rabbinowitz and I. Feinstein (eds.), *Essays Presented to Chief Rabbi Israel Brodie on the Occasion of his Seventieth Birthday* (London: Soncino, 1967), pp. 275-90; Schechter, *Aspects of Rabbinic Theology*, pp. 170-98; E.E. Urbach, *The Sages* (trans. I. Abrahams; Cambridge, MA: Harvard University Press, 1987), pp. 420-44.

20. Emending יומת to יומת in agreement with the *qere* found in 2 Kgs 14.6.

21. Gammie, 'Theology of Retribution', p. 12.

The same problem can be raised in relation to the deuteronomistic history. It contains a passage in 2 Kgs 14.6 that is almost identical to Deut. 24.16. 2 Kgs 14.5-6 reads as follows:

> And when he had secured his kingship, he smote his servants who had killed his father the king. But he did not execute the sons of the killers, just as it is written in the book of the law of Moses, in which the Lord commanded, 'Fathers will not be executed for the children, nor will children be executed for the fathers; but each man will be executed for his own sin'.

Yet the deuteronomistic history as a whole is pervaded by narratives that record the transference of punishment from the father to the son(s) (Josh. 7; 1 Sam. 2.30-36; 2 Sam. 12.14; 21.1-14; 1 Kgs 21.29; 2 Kgs 5.27 etc.). One only need refer to the extensive discussion in Chapter 2 above to see that the exilic redactor of the deuteronomistic history used corporate ideas to explain the downfall of Judah as the result of Manasseh's sins (2 Kgs 21.10-15; 23.26-27; 24.2-4). If there was a decisive movement toward individualism in the exilic period, why does this tendency fail to manifest itself in the theology of Dtr 2 who worked in this period?

In order to clarify this problem it will be necessary to analyze both Deut. 24.16 and 2 Kgs 14.6 at length and determine their relationship to each other. Two recent treatments of Deut. 24.16 have attempted to illuminate the meaning of this text based on hypothetical reconstructions of what the author was thinking when he either penned or redacted this verse into the larger context in which it is currently set. Carmichael argues that all of ch. 24 is concerned with legislation brought to mind by the sojourn in Egypt.[22] Thus he would see this verse as possibly objecting to the slaying of the first-born (a theme not mentioned in Deuteronomy), or connected with the potential admittance of Egyptians to the congregation of the Lord (Deut. 23.8-9).

Carmichael's arguments are intriguing but not compelling. He merely proves that one can find connections between the various laws, but he fails to demonstrate that these connections are intentional rather than accidental. I strongly suspect that his loose associative method could be

---

22. C.M. Carmichael, *The Laws of Deuteronomy* (Ithaca, NY: Cornell University Press, 1974), pp. 202-26. More recently Carmichael has attempted to relate this same legislation to the narrative in Gen. 34. He does not clarify whether he has, in fact, retracted his other opinion or not. C.M. Carmichael, *Law and Narrative in the Bible* (Ithaca, NY: Cornell University Press, 1985), pp. 270-77.

used just as effectively if one randomly reordered the laws between Deuteronomy 12–26.[23]

Michael Fishbane makes a similar, although not identical argument:

> Presuming the intelligence of the legal draftsman, one might hazard the speculation that the principle of rejecting vicarious punishment was incorporated into this legal unit in order to counter tendencies to exact vicarious retributions in cases of economic collapse. In such cases, it is implied, fathers may neither be dunned nor killed (in compensation) for the debts of their sons, nor vice versa: each person is rather to be regarded as a self-contained economic unit.[24]

Fishbane bases his aggadic interpretation upon the fact that the laws surrounding Deut. 24.16 deal with economic oppression (vv. 10-15 and 17-22). He argues in a rather ingenious fashion that the author of Deuteronomy 24, who was engaged in rewriting the legislation found in Exod. 22.20-23, was repulsed by the legislation in v. 23 that speaks of turning the oppressors' wives into widows and their children into orphans.

> Thus Deut. 24.14-16 eliminates this horrific divine punishment—reducing the oppressor's punishment to a 'sin' before God—and extends the topos of oppression into one of transgenerational economic exploitation, something that presumably lay within the power of a lender but which is categorically proscribed.[25]

Fishbane's proposed interpretation of how v. 16 fits into its context seems to ignore the fact that Deut. 24.16, which uses the third person and speaks rather abstractly, disturbs the unity and flow of a series of apodictic laws that use the second person and deal with proper treatment of poor and/or marginal people within society (Deut. 24.10-15; 24.17-22).[26] Rather than positing ingenious, but highly forced interpretations to explain why this law is in its current position, it is easier to assume that it is a late editorial insertion. Fishbane acknowledges this as a possibility when he tells us that Deut. 24.16 'is contextually disruptive'.[27] If this is in fact the case, it seems best to begin our investigation of this

---

23. For a powerful critique of Carmichael's method of interpretation, see B.M. Levinson, 'Calum M. Carmichael's Approach to the Laws of Deuteronomy', *HTR* 83 (July 1990), pp. 227-57.

24. Fishbane, *Biblical Interpretation*, pp. 339-40.

25. Fishbane, *Biblical Interpretation*, p. 341.

26. H.G. May, 'Individual Responsibility and Retribution', *HUCA* 32 (1961), pp. 116-17.

27. Fishbane, *Biblical Interpretation*, p. 341.

verse by first clarifing exactly what situation this legislation was originally intended to remedy.

It is at this point that Moshe Greenberg's analysis of this verse comes into view.[28] Greenberg argues that Deut. 24.16 should not be interpreted as a general theological injunction that condemns the principal of communal responsibility and the concept of corporate guilt that it entails. Rather, this passage is concerned only with the human criminal justice system and in no way deals with the concept of divine retribution. As evidence Greenberg notes that Deut. 24.16 uses the *hophal* form of מות, which is reserved for judicial execution.[29] But if Deut. 24.16 simply prohibited human courts from punishing whole families, tribes or clans for the crime of an individual or a small group of individuals, then one wonders what would have generated such a law. According to Greenberg, 'the principle of individual culpability in precisely the form taken in Deut. 24.16 is operative in the earliest law collection of the Bible'.[30] Greenberg posits that Deut. 24.16 is in fact a firm rejection of a principle that had always been assumed in ancient Israel: in judicial cases only the guilty party is punished. But why would someone living in the seventh or possibly sixth century BCE take the time to write a law that had been accepted in principle for centuries?

The very existence of Deut. 24.16 suggests the probability that there were certain judicial cases in which punishment was carried out transgenerationally and which this legislation hoped to halt.[31] The question is, which cases are involved?

---

28. Greenberg, 'Some Postulates', pp. 29-34.

29. Greenberg, 'Some Postulates', pp. 29-30. This is also the view of Ibn Ezra and Rashbam. It should be noted that Greenberg's point is further supported by the fact that Deut. 24.16 is set within the extensive block of civil, religious, social and criminal legislation that runs from Deut. 12–26, rather than in the more theological sections of Deuteronomy (i.e. Deut. 1–11 or 27–31).

30. Greenberg, 'Some Postulates', p. 30. A similar assertion is made by von Rad: 'The principle of personal responsibility was by no means unknown in the earlier times. The whole Book of the Covenant knows nothing of such corporate liability within the family.' G. von Rad, *Deuteronomy* (trans. D. Barton; OTL; Philadelphia: Westminster Press, 1966), p. 152.

31. One might argue that Deut. 24.16 is analogous to many other laws in Deuteronomy that record an ancient principle and are not generated by a specific innovation. Although this is possible, the close relationship between Deut. 24.16 and 2 Kgs 14.6 strongly suggests that Deut. 24.16 was penned in response to a specific legislative problem. See the discussion immediately below.

To solve this puzzle, one must begin by noting that inquiry into this problem has been hampered by Greenberg's attempt to force all the data into two utterly distinct categories: judicial cases in which punishment is always individualized, and cases involving divine justice which entail corporate punishment.[32] In general, Greenberg is correct, but he overstates his case when he implies that this distinction always holds in ancient Israel. For example, Daube argues rather convincingly that Exod. 21.31 is a later addition to a text that originally implied that if someone owned an ox that was known to gore, and that ox gored someone else's child, the court would kill the child of the ox's owner. If this observation is correct then one might have some evidence of corporate responsibility in a judicial case.[33] Furthermore, as I argued in Chapter 4, there is not always a clear-cut distinction between cases executed by humans and by God (e.g., Josh. 7).

It is probable that Deut. 24.16 was in fact generated in order to redefine a case that fell into the grey area between human and divine justice. The specific behavior that this legislation wished to eradicate was the tendency of new kings to purge their rivals' and enemies' families. That Deut. 24.16 was originally intended to restrain kings from killing the families of rivals is strongly indicated by 2 Kgs 14.5-6. This passage is the one text in the whole deuteronomistic history that cites Deut. 24.16, and it cites it in reference to the fact that Amaziah spared the children of the conspirators who killed his father. This indicates that Deut. 24.16 was an attempt to limit the ability of the monarch who had previously had the right to execute trans-generational punishments because he had arrogated to himself the right to act like a deity.[34] That the king in Israel originally possessed such power is clear from numerous texts within the Hebrew Bible that indicate that Israelite kings routinely purged all their competitors and their families with them (Judg. 9.5; 2 Sam. 21.1-14; 1 Kgs 16.11; 2 Kgs 10.11; 11.1). Furthermore, one should remember that the king was no ordinary citizen (Pss. 2.7; 72; 89.20-38; 110).[35] He

32. Jacob Milgrom makes a similar claim that I discuss and refute on pp. 77-78.

33. Daube, *Studies in Biblical Law*, pp. 154-89. Also found in Fishbane, *Biblical Interpretation*, pp. 211-12, 336.

34. Thus Milgrom in reference to the concept of collective retribution correctly observes that 'the Israelite king, no differently than his Hittite prototype, does arrogate to himself this divine prerogative'. Milgrom, *Cult and Conscience*, p. 34 n. 126.

35. On the important status of the king, see Chapter 2. Bibliography can be found in Chapter 2, n. 52.

was, in fact, beyond the power of the judicial courts (2 Sam. 11–12; 1 Kgs 21), and could even institute new legislation (1 Sam. 30.21-25; 2 Kgs 23.21; 2 Chron. 19.5-11).[36] Amaziah, so it seems, was the first Israelite king who reversed this practice (2 Kgs 14.6). Thus Deut. 24.16 would have originally been an attempt to limit the judicial powers of the king.[37]

This argument would be further bolstered if one could prove that the law in Deut. 24.16 was generated by the *story* about Amaziah's restraint reported in 2 Kgs 14.5-6 and not vice versa. This argument is not an attempt to claim that 2 Kgs 14.6 was written before Deut. 24.16 which it cites, but rather that *the story* reported in 2 Kgs 14.6 was the major motivating factor behind the legislation found in Deut. 24.16. The fact that this law was not commonly followed by other earlier kings, in combination with the fact that it is invoked only in connection with Amaziah, a king who is neither early, nor well known, tends to point in this direction. That Deut. 24.16 grew out of the tradition surrounding Amaziah is a view expressed already three decades ago by H.G. May and B. Lindars:

> It was the later Deuteronomist, responsible for the insertion of Deut. 24.16, who gave the legislation an historical precedent...by adding the notation in 2 Kings 14.6 that Amaziah did not kill the children of the servants who slew his father, because of the legislation in the book of the law of Moses, quoting from Deut. 24.16. The later Deuteronomist felt the need of giving such historical precedent. The fact that he quotes Deut. 24.16 is no evidence that Amaziah himself was acquainted with the Law, but only that the writer knew it.[38]

> Although the deuteronomic historian praises Amaziah for his observance of this law, it is far more probable that Amaziah's notable restraint was one of the factors that paved the way for it.[39]

Although there is evidence to suggest that Deut. 24.16 was originally intended to limit the judicial power of ancient Israel's kings, in its current canonical context this verse must be read as a more general piece of

36. Whitelam, *The Just King*, pp. 207-20.
37. The Jewish biblical commentator Seforno also maintains that this law is especially concerned with kings and their tendency to kill the children of those who rebel against them. He recognizes that the early kings did this and Amaziah was the first to act differently.
38. May, 'Individual Responsibility and Retribution', p. 117.
39. B. Lindars, 'Ezekiel and Individual Responsibility', *VT* 15 (October 1965), p. 455 n. 2.

legislation that prevents *judicial* punishment from being transferred across generations. Deut. 24.16 is not at all concerned with God's actions and must not be read as an attempt to overturn the traditional corporate conception of divine retribution. Furthermore, the idea that it was unjust for human courts to transfer punishment across generations was not a new idea in ancient Israel, and thus Deut. 24.16 does not substantiate the argument made by those scholars who claim that there was a radical new growth in individualism in the late biblical period.

My analysis of Deut. 24.16 may be summarized as follows:

1. Deut. 24.16 is not at all concerned with the concept of divine retribution.

2. This piece of legislation was probably generated by the story of Amaziah's sparing the children of those conspirators who killed his father and, thus, was originally concerned with limiting the monarch's power by preventing the king from inflicting corporate punishments on his enemies and rivals.

3. Although the current setting of Deut. 24.16 turns it into a broader piece of legislation that prohibits the transference of judicial punishment across generations, this is not a new idea in ancient Israel.

4. Although Deut. 24.16 does prohibit the transference of judicial punishments across generations and thus may reveal some movement toward a more individualistic model of retribution, it has been misinterpreted by those scholars who claim that this passage is part of a larger cultural movement toward a type of individualism that not only rejected trans-generational *judicial* retribution, but also rejected corporate notions of *divine* retribution.

Other Passages that Might Indicate a Growing Individualism

There is other evidence within the book of Deuteronomy that must be discussed in relation to the question of whether there was a steady evolutionary growth toward a greater individualism in ancient Israel. The first text that I will discuss in this section is the formula found in Exod. 20.5-6 and Deut. 5.9-10:[40]

---

40. For more extensive discussions of these passages, their relationship to Exod. 34.6-7 and to other passages that use similar language, see the following: R.C. Dentan,

פקד עון אבות על־בנים ועל־שלשים ועל־רבעים לשנאי:
ועשה חסד לאלפים לאהבי ולשמרי מצותי:

Visiting the iniquity of the fathers upon the children, to the third and fourth
generation of those who hate me, but showing steadfast love to the
thousandth generation of those who love me and keep my commandments.

It has been noted that this formula occurs in several places throughout
the Bible and that it is likely that its most original formulation is to be
found in Exod. 34.7:

פקד עון אבות על־בנים ועל־בני בנים על־שלשים ועל־רבעים:

As one can see this verse lacks the additional word לשנאי found in
Exod. 20.5, Deut. 5.9 and 7.10. This extra word is paralleled by the
word לאהבי, which occurs in Exod. 20.6, Deut. 5.10 and 7.9, but is not
found in Exod. 34.7. The existence of these two extra words has led to
speculation that a later (deuteronomic) editor added these words in order
to bring the retributional theology implied in these verses into line with
his theological agenda. Certain scholars who see these words as extra
additions argue that the editor who changed the phraseology of the text
is allowing for the possibility that an evil person may have a righteous
child and vice-versa.[41]

> The addition would, in other words, have the purpose of making clear that
> if there is solidarity in guilt between the generations, it is because the
> children choose to follow their parents' example, and not because the guilt
> of one generation is transmitted to the next by virtue of the way God
> administers justice.[42]

'The Literary Affinities of Exodus 34,6f.', *VT* 13 (January 1963), pp. 34-51;
T.B. Dozeman, 'Inner-Biblical Interpretation of YHWH's Gracious and Compassionate
Character', *JBL* 108 (Summer 1989), pp. 207-23; B.M. Levinson, 'The Human Voice
in Divine Revelation: The Problem of Authority in Biblical Law', in M.A. Williams,
C. Cox and M.S. Jaffee (eds.), *Innovation in Religious Traditions* (Berlin: de
Gruyter, 1992), pp. 35-71. Y. Muffs, 'Reflections on Prophetic Prayer in the Bible',
Eretz-Israel 14 (1978), pp. 48-54 [Heb.]; K.D. Sakenfeld, *The Meaning of Ḥesed in
the Hebrew Bible* (HSM, 17; Missoula, MT: Scholars Press, 1978), pp. 112-39;
Scharbert, 'Formgeschichte', pp. 130-50; Weinfeld, *Deuteronomy 1–11*, pp. 293-300.

41. See Fishbane, *Biblical Interpretation*, pp. 335, 343-344; A.D.H. Mayes,
Deuteronomy (NCB; Grand Rapids: Eerdmans, 1981), p. 167; K. Koch, *The Growth
of the Biblical Tradition* (trans. S.M. Cupitt; New York: Charles Scribner's Sons,
1969), p. 47; Weinfeld, *Deuteronomy and the Deuteronomic School*, pp. 316-19.

42. J. Blenkinsopp, 'Abraham and the Righteous of Sodom', *JJS* 33 (Spring
1982), p. 124.

If this supposition proved to be true, it could be used as evidence of a movement toward individualism in the later period of ancient Israelite history.

There are also several other pieces of evidence found within the book of Deuteronomy that may indicate a growing attentiveness toward the individual Israelite. Richard Adamiak[43] notes that the portrayal of the wilderness tradition in Deuteronomy exhibits a marked ambiguity.[44] Deut. 6.20-25, 7.17-26, 8.1-20, 11.2-7 and 29.2-5 all speak about the wilderness generation as the same generation that Moses is now addressing, whereas 1.34-40 and 2.14-16 describe the wilderness generation as marked for complete destruction. Adamiak fruitfully explores this textual tension and proceeds to argue that Deuteronomy contains two strata, each with a different view of divine retribution. The early stratum speaks about the wilderness generation as the same generation that entered the land ('While those of you who held fast to the Lord are all alive today', Deut. 4.4). Furthermore, the description of this period is ambiguous rather than solely negative. The wilderness is the place where God tests and humbles the Israelites and where he exhibits his great power to sustain them (Deut. 8.1-16). Although this tradition often speaks of Israel's rebelliousness (Deut. 9.6-24), these failures to listen to God are not the reason for the long sojourn in the desert. The wilderness period is not conceived as a punishment in this stratum.

Adamiak contrasts the wilderness tradition just described with what he believes is a later deuteronomistic stratum that speaks of the complete annihilation of the wilderness generation (Deut. 1.34-40; 2.14-16). This latter tradition sees the wilderness period as a punishment imposed on Israel for its disobedience to the divine imperative to go up and take the land. This negative wilderness tradition is further elaborated in the P sections of the spy story (Num. 13–14).

Adamiak argues that each stratum is ultimately influenced by the historical period in which it was written, and thus the various portrayals of the wilderness period are motivated by each stratum's understanding of the way in which divine retribution operates. The earlier stratum, according to Adamiak, was produced during the seventh century BCE in a time when Israel (or more properly Judah) still possessed (part of) the

---

43. R. Adamiak, *Justice and History in the Old Testament* (Cleveland: John T. Zubal, 1982).

44. On the wilderness tradition more generally and its place in the Pentateuch, see G.W. Coats, *Rebellion in the Wilderness* (Nashville: Abingdon Press, 1968).

land, but was besieged by political turmoil. The possibility of losing the land was real, and in the eyes of the author(s) of the first edition of Deuteronomy this potantial exile was linked to the worship of foreign gods and disobedience to the law of Moses. According to Adamiak, it was precisely this theological interpretation of the contemporary geopolitical situation that led the author(s) of this stratum to portray the wilderness generation as rebellious but still worthy of inheriting the land. Adamiak nicely sums up the parallelism between this portrayal of the wilderness generation and the situation of this stratum's audience:

> Just as the wilderness generation was able to overcome its earlier wickedness and take possession of the land, so will its seventh century descendants be able to retain the land if they observe the law.[45]

The theological paradigm that motivates this description of the wilderness period is one that stresses God's forbearance. Although the people often fail to obey God's ways (Deut. 9.12) and continue to put him to the test (Deut. 6.16), he remains patient and gives them yet another chance to prove themselves deserving of his favor.[46] In a similar fashion, the author is offering his audience another chance to stay in the land, if only they will keep the terms of God's covenant as stipulated in the book of Deuteronomy.

Adamiak then goes on to claim that there is a direct connection between the portrayal of the wilderness generation as guilty but still worthy and the tendency in Deuteronomy to modify the older ideas of collective retribution and replace them with a system of individual retribution. It is precisely here that Adamiak's theory becomes relevant to my project. Adamiak sees Deuteronomy as a book that 'asserts the principle of individual retribution: Each is punished for his own sins without regard for the sins of his ancestors'.[47] The reason that this earlier edition of Deuteronomy stresses the individual so much 'is that if the nation is being punished for the sins of its ancestors, then no degree

---

45. Adamiak, *Justice*, p. 65.

46. Adamiak adduces several mitigating factors that help explain how the author of this edition of Deuteronomy could allow a sinful Israel to possess the land. These include the promise to the patriarchs (Deut. 7.8), the sinfulness of the Canaanites (Deut. 9.5), Moses' punishment as a vicarious punishment of the people (Deut. 1.37 and 3.26), and the fact that the deuteronomic covenant may supersede the Sinaitic covenant and thus put the wilderness generation in a temporarily sinless position. Adamiak, *Justice*, pp. 57-61.

47. Adamiak, *Justice*, p. 66.

of faithfulness can avert its destruction and all Deuteronomic exhortations are rendered nugatory'.[48]

According to Adamiak, once the exile had occurred and the book of Deuteronomy became incorporated into the deuteronomistic history, the author(s) of this history revised Deuteronomy's portrayal of the wilderness period.[49] Now this period bore a wholly negative stamp and no one who belonged to it was allowed to come into the land. Rather, a new generation arose that had not yet sinned, and they took possession of the land. These exilic editors reworked the wilderness tradition in the face of the massive destruction of the exile and used the wilderness generation as a metaphor for the generation that went into exile. More importantly, they created the idea that the possessors of the land were in fact sinless, and thus indicated to their exilic audience that the only hope for repossessing the land was complete communal obedience to the laws laid down in Deuteronomy. Thus the exilic edition 'reasserts the principle of collective responsibility'.[50]

Although Adamiak's main focus is on the shifting sands of the description of the wilderness era, his argument reveals that there are theological tensions between the individualism stressed in some passages within Deuteronomy and the collective idea of punishment asserted time and again both within Deuteronomy and the deuteronomistic history. Adamiak not only explores this theological shift, but provides us with a historical rationale for why it occurred.

One other passage that must be addressed in reference to the possibility that the book of Deuteronomy is focused on the individual Israelite and is a strong advocate of individualized retribution is Deut. 29.15-20 (English 16-21).

> For you know that we lived in the land of Egypt and that we crossed through the midst of the nations through which you passed. 16 You saw their detestable objects, their idols of wood and stone, of silver and gold, that were with them. 17 Perchance there is among you a man or a woman,[51]

---

48. Adamiak, *Justice*, p. 66.

49. That Deuteronomy and the deuteronomistic history were in tension with each other and were in fact only incorporated together in the exilic period is argued very cogently by Levenson, 'Who Inserted the Book of the Torah?', p. 203-33. For a thorough discussion and critique of Levenson's argument, see Friedman, *Exile*, pp. 1-43.

50. Adamiak, *Justice*, p. 88.

51. Anthony Phillips notes the fact that the author of the deuteronomic code 'made women equal members of the covenant community with men, and so liable for

or a family or a tribe, whose heart is even now turning away from the Lord our God to go and serve the gods of those nations—perchance there is among you a root bearing venom and wormwood. 18 When he hears the words of this oath he will bless himself, thinking in his heart 'I will be safe even though I walk in the stubborn ways of my heart'[52] (sweeping away the moist and the dry together). 19 The Lord will be unwilling to forgive him; rather the Lord's anger and passion will smoke against that individual. Every curse written in this book will descend upon him and the Lord will blot out his name from under heaven. 20 The Lord will single him out from all the tribes of Israel for calamity, in accordance with all the curses of the covenant written in this book of the law.

This passage clearly belongs to a different stratum from the immediately following passage. It seems very likely that vv. 21-27 should be dated to the exilic period. Such a dating is based on three reasons scintillatingly stated by Jon Levenson:

> The author has ceased speaking of an individual, as in the immediately preceding lines (*bā'îš hahû*, v. 19), abruptly changing into discourse about the nation. Further, it is assumed that the nation has been overthrown, like Sodom and Gomorrah (v. 22), in divine punishment for its sins. As was not the case in 28.45ff., here exile is not a terrible possibility, but an inevitability, which has already occurred (v. 27)... After a pious gloss in 29.28, which must be a later interpolation, comes 30.1-10... It is assumed that Israel must return to YHWH (vv. 2, 8, 10), experience an inner conversion, which will encourage YHWH to 'turn' Israel's fortunes for the better (v. 3). Again, retributive exile is presupposed.[53]

---

breach of the criminal law, the covenant stipulations of the Decalogue being understood to have been addressed to adult members of both sexes'. Phillips, *Ancient Israel's Criminal Law*, p. 16. Although Phillips does not note it, this could in itself be taken as evidence of a growing individualism in ancient Israel.

52. Weinfeld offers an alternative translation: 'Since I intend to keep my evil thoughts to myself no one will know and none will punish me'. He prefers this because it preserves the proper sense of the particle כִּי and he feels that the phrase שרירות לב refers primarily to 'thought or reflection'. Although I tend to agree that 'even though' is a problematic translation of the particle כִּי, I find Weinfeld's translation difficult as well. To translate the verb אלך as 'I intend to keep' seems rather unlikely. I am more inclined to translate it as involving some type of action and v. 17 connects the same verbal root to the action of 'serving the gods of those nations'. The verse is difficult and remains a bit enigmatic regardless of which translational path one takes. Weinfeld, *Deuteronomy and the Deuteronomic School*, pp. 105-106.

53. Levenson, 'Who Inserted the Book of the Torah?', p. 208. Levenson is following N. Lohfink, 'Der Bundesschluss im Land Moab', *BZ* 6 (1962), pp. 44-45.

All of the above factors strongly suggest that Deut. 29.15-20 is a pre-exilic passage.[54] This passage is concerned with dispelling the notion that the communal nature of the covenant would allow the sinner to be protected by the righteousness of the general community. It is somewhat reminiscent of the temple sermon in Jeremiah 7, a passage that certainly contains deuteronomistic diction, in which Jeremiah warns the worshippers in the temple that the existence of the temple is not, in and of itself, a guarantee of safety. The stress on the individual fits well with Adamiak's theory that an author writing in the late pre-exilic period would have had a vested interest in stressing individual responsibility, thus giving people in that and later generations the will to repent and be obedient. This particular passage may even be going farther than Adamiak envisioned. It may, along with Deut. 7.10, be in fact one of the few passages in the Hebrew Bible which proclaims that God singles out the wicked person and punishes him or her quickly and harshly.

It is clear that the texts discussed in this chapter do place a greater emphasis upon the individual. But it is less clear that this attention to the individual demonstrates the existence of a new movement that completely rejected the older corporate ideas of retribution. It seems probable that these passages are attempts to clarify and qualify the older corporate notions of retribution, rather than eliminate them. For example, Deut. 5.9 is an attempt to qualify the notion of trans-generational punishment by suggesting that this phenomenon is only operative in cases in which children follow in the evil ways of their ancestors. In fact, it is possible to argue that this is more of a clarification of an idea that was always implicit in the earlier passages concerned with trans-generational retribution, rather than an innovation that completely changed the concept.[55]

The argument made by Adamiak about the theological rewriting of the wilderness motif, by no means an irrefutable argument, does indicate that at least one stream of tradition attempted to modify the classical corporate focus of divine retribution. But it should be noted that when

54. Here I disagree with von Rad, who argues that this passage must belong to the latest stratum in the book because it portrays Deuteronomy as a book (v. 19). Von Rad, *Deuteronomy*, p. 180.

55. This is how *Targum Onqelos* interprets Ex 34.7. מסער חובי אבהן על בנין ועל בני בנין מרדין על דר תליתי ועל דר רביעי: (visiting the guilt of the fathers upon the *rebellious* sons and granchildren to the third and fourth generation). Also see Scharbert, 'Formgeschichte'.

Adamiak says that this stream of tradition was innovative, inasmuch as it focused upon the individual, his point is not that this stream of tradition advocates a notion of totally individualized divine retribution, but that it rejects the idea of trans-generational corporate retribution. His argument is that certain motifs in Deuteronomy signal an attempt by seventh-century writers to muster the people to obedience by freeing them from the sins that their ancestors had committed. Thus, although he uses the language of individualized divine retribution, he means generationally individualized. As noted above, the idea that God will not visit the sins of the ancestors on a completely innocent generation may be more of a qualification than a rejection of trans-generational retribution. It does not deny the principle, but does say that it is inoperative in instances where the children are innocent. Furthermore, even when Adamiak argues for the existence of a rather innovative theology that modifies certain corporate ideas, he recognizes that this theological movement was not potent enough to displace the older corporate notions of punishment permanently. He acknowledges that the older corporate ideas came back into vogue during the exilic period. If Adamiak's argument proved to be correct, it would at most provide evidence for a stream of tradition that intended to modify the older corporate ideas, but it would not support the idea that at a certain point in Israelite history corporate thinking died out completely and was replaced by individualistic thinking.

Other than Deut. 24.16, the most powerful evidence within Deuteronomy and the deuteronomistic history for a new concern to limit punishment solely to the guilty party is found in Deut. 7.9-10 and 29.15-20. These passages are strongly reminiscent of Job 21.19-24, and all three texts may reflect a growing dissatisfaction with the idea of transference of punishment.[56] But it is more likely that these texts do not reject the idea that a sinner's children may receive punishment, but the idea that the sinner may totally escape punishment by having it transferred to others. If this is the case, these texts are not rejecting the notion

---

56. If these texts reject trans-generational retribution, this rejection may stem from a misunderstanding of this concept. There is evidence that the transference of punishment may have been a sign of God's mercy upon the sinner, rather than of God's unfair behavior toward the children of the sinner. Muffs, 'Reflections on Prophetic Prayer', pp. 50-54. The basic thesis of Muffs's article has been expanded and translated into English in Y. Muffs, 'Who Will Stand in the Breach?: A Study of Prophetic Intercession', in *Love and Joy* (New York: Jewish Theological Seminary of America, 1992), pp. 9-48.

of trans-generational retribution; rather they are an attempt to qualify this notion. This qualification was made because certain people apparently thought they could escape punishment by transferring it to future generations, or by hiding behind the righteousness of the larger community.

Thus the passages that I have been examining in this chapter do contain evidence of a deeper appreciation of the individual, but they do not signal a rejection of the older corporate ideas. Nonetheless, this new focus upon the individual helped create a more nuanced theology in which greater attention was now paid to the individual, while not losing sight of the fact that the individual was not an autonomous entity, but a member of the larger community of God. It is precisely this theological insight into the tripartite relationship between God, the community as a whole, and the individuals who compose that community, that created much of the depth found in the theologies of P and D. In these theological systems the reward for individual adherence to the commandments is a national prosperity in which the individual shares as a citizen of the nation. Individuals are important to God, but their individuality is derived from membership in the community at large. God is not concerned with the individual qua individual, but with the individual as a member of a particular nation, Israel. To see that this is the case one need only look through the Pentateuch, the deuteronomistic history, or the prophetic corpus to see that the fate of various individuals who are discussed in the text is always related to the history of the nation as a whole. This overwhelming interest in the fate of the nation suggests that we should be extremely cautious before we begin proclaiming that the focus on the community has suddenly been eclipsed by God's new concern with the individual.

Conclusions

1. There are passages within the book of Deuteronomy that indicate challenges to the standard communal view of divine retribution.

2. Some of these texts may in fact be emphasizing ideas that were quite ancient (Deut. 5.9). Other texts are likely innovative in their stress upon individuals and their place in the divine economy (Deut. 29.15-20).

3. This new stress upon the individual does not signal a complete rejection of older corporate ideas. This tendency to pay greater attention to the individual should be understood as an attempt to qualify the older corporate ideas.

4. Although there is evidence of a growing awareness of the importance of the individual, there is also evidence that texts from the later biblical period continue to highlight the importance of the community. The fact that there are passages within the latest strata of the Hebrew Bible that support the idea of communal responsibility (Dan. 6.25; Est. 9.7-10), and the fact that this view is still alive well into New Testament times (Mt. 23.29-36; Jn 9.2; 1 Thess. 2.14-16) and beyond (*Lev. R.* 4.6; *b. Sanh.* 43b-44a; *T. d. Eliyy.* 12), suggests that those passages that stress the individual never intended to dismiss the importance of the community.

5. One must take into account both those passages that emphasize the importance of the individual and those that stress communal dimensions of experience. Such a reading produces a profound theological insight into the tripartite relationship between God, the community as a whole, and the individuals who compose that community.

Chapter 7

JEREMIAH 31.29-30 AND EZEKIEL 18

Having pursued our investigation of corporate notions up to this point, it only seems fitting and proper that we turn to two other texts: Jer. 31.29-30 and Ezekiel 18. Although neither passage is found in the deuteronomistic history, there is evidence to suggest that both passages are textually related to Deut. 24.16. Furthermore, these two texts are almost always invoked in any theological discussion concerning the place of the individual in ancient Israel. The major question that remains is, how innovative is the theology advocated within these passages? Quite often these passages are seen as indicating a major turning point in Israel's theological understanding of the individual and his or her relationship to God. Thus the following series of quotes illustrates the way in which some scholars conceive of these two texts as quite radical and innovative.

> Other documents of the seventh–sixth century restrict human punishment to individual perpetrators, but allow that divine retribution may exceed this limit. Yet both Jeremiah and Ezekiel, at the start of the sixth century, accept a doctrine limiting even divine retribution to the individual.[1]

> Whereas in the earlier period the community was the main object of the preaching and working of the prophets, the individual now came to the fore in religious teaching. This individualistic trend is particularly evident in Ezekiel and can best be studied in his sayings about individual repentance.[2]

> The Deuteronomistic theology of history had still reckoned with the effect of an evil that criss-crossed the generations, and made it a basic factor in its whole way of looking at history. Ezekiel is very different: in his passage dealing with righteousness, he starts by opposing to the contention that evil works on throughout the generations the counter-thesis…that each individual life belongs to JHWH (Ezek. xviii. 4).[3]

---

1. Halpern, 'Jerusalem and the Lineages…', pp. 14-15.
2. J. Lindblom, *Prophecy in Ancient Israel* (Philadelphia: Fortress Press, 1962), p. 387.
3. Von Rad, *Old Testament Theology*, I, pp. 392-93.

Other scholars, while acknowledging that these two texts do indeed offer certain new and important ways to understand the place of the individual in ancient Israel, are much more cautious in their evaluation of exactly how innovative these two passages are. Such scholars try to understand these texts as correctives to, rather than rejections of, older forms of corporate thinking.

> To these prophets the responsibility was not to be put on an impersonal community, and still less on the community of a former generation. Every individual had his share of responsibility for the life of the community. He was not merely a fragment of the corporate whole; he was a responsible individual. Yet let it not be forgotten that this emphasis of the teaching of Jeremiah and Ezekiel was a corrective to the false opposite emphasis of their day. Jeremiah did not render obsolete all thought of man as a member of society, and we should never father on to him a mere individualism, as though he regarded men as a tray of sand, with no cohesion, and simply a collection of units.[4]

> Except valuable criticism and an unacceptable theory of JHWH's relation to the individual, Ezekiel brought nothing substantially new to the idea of reward or to that of corporate and individual responsibility.[5]

> Even though Ezekiel's real concern is the fate of the nation as a whole, the way in which he uses legal language as if he were speaking about the fate of individuals is itself a striking feature of his teaching. He does not give us a new doctrine of individual responsibility.[6]

In order to clarify the precise import of these two biblical passages, we must analyze each one in depth. It is my contention that such in-depth analysis will provide strong support for the following theses. (1) Although each passage does challenge the standard view of divine retribution, it is very dubious that either passage means to reject all aspects of corporate thinking. (2) Although the language of these passages is at times individualistic, the fact that both oracles are spoken to the larger community suggests that one should be cautious before assuming that the theology advocated in these passages is radically individualistic. (3) Even if one reads these passages as in fact rejecting all earlier corporate notions in favor of a radical individualism, it is very unclear that such a theology is superior to the theology implied by the older corporate conceptions.

---

4.   H.H. Rowley, *The Faith of Israel* (London: SCM Press, 1956), p. 105.
5.   Rankin, *Israel's Wisdom Literature*, p. 73.
6.   Lindars, 'Ezekiel and Individual Responsibility', p. 461.

Jeremiah 31.29-30

Jeremiah 31.29-30 reads as follows:

> In those days they shall no longer say: 'The fathers have eaten sour grapes, and the children's teeth are set on edge'. But [they will say][7] every one will die for his own sin; each person who eats sour grapes, his teeth shall be set on edge.[8]

This passage, unlike Deut. 24.16, is speaking about divine retribution rather than judicial punishment. This is clear from the general tenor of the passage as well as from the fact that the text uses the *qal* ימות, instead of the *hophal* used in cases of judicial execution.[9] Jer. 31.29-30 categorically rejects the idea of trans-generational divine retribution. Furthermore, it may even advocate a system of individualistic retribution (each man will die for his own sin).[10] Should it prove true that Jer. 31.29-30 is opposed to the concept of trans-generational retribution, then the theology of these verses would seem to be in conflict with the general spirit of the book of Jeremiah as a whole. The book of Jeremiah again and again affirms that divine punishment is not a strictly uni-generational affair (Jer. 2.30; 3.25; 6.11-12; 13.14; 16.10-13; 18.21-23; 32.18-19 etc.). If Jer. 31.29-30 is interpreted as advocating not only uni-generational retribution, but the more radical idea of exact and individualistic retribution within a

---

7.　There is strong evidence that the phrase כי אם should be read as part of an elliptical formula (cf. Jer. 16.14-15 and 23.7-8). This translation will be discussed in greater detail further below.

8.　The Hebrew word תקהינה translated here as 'set on edge' has been interpreted in many different ways including blunted, dulled, numbed, ached and made crooked. It seems most likely that it refers to the gritty feeling that is caused by the thin coating that covers one's teeth after one eats something that is very sour. W. Eichrodt, *Ezekiel* (OTL; Philadelphia: Westminster Press, 1970), p. 234. For a full discussion see M. Greenberg, *Ezekiel, 1–20* (AB; Garden City, NY: Doubleday, 1983), pp. 327-28.

9.　Greenberg, 'Some Postulates', pp. 29-30.

10.　Jer. 31.29-30 has often been read as a total rejection of any form of corporate liability. For example: 'The priestly legislation therefore realized the prophecies of Jer. 31.29f. and Ezek. 18.1ff. that an individual would only be liable for his own acts, and not for the acts of others by virtue of his membership of the community'. Phillips, *Ancient Israel's Criminal Law*, p. 185. Or 'Jeremiah too has heard it said that the children had to bear their fathers' guilt, and he too used what was a radically individualistic view to counter the saying (Jer. 31.29f.)', Von Rad, *Old Testament Theology*, II, p. 266.

single generation, then the tension is magnified (5.1; 7.20).

Before attempting to elaborate upon the theory of retribution that Jer. 31.29-30 is advocating, it will be helpful to clarify the historical and literary issues that surround this passage and its current place in the book of Jeremiah. The scholarly consensus is that the book of Jeremiah can be divided into three types of materials, each one potentially coming from a different source.[11] These are usually designated by the sigla A, B and C. A designates the authentic poetic material that Jeremiah preached to the people of Jerusalem.[12] B signifies the biographical narratives and is often attributed to Baruch who was Jeremiah's amanuensis. The remaining prose material, which has a strong resemblance to the language found in Deuteronomy and the deuteronomistic history (Joshua–2 Kings), is referred to by the letter C.[13] Jeremiah 30–33 appears to be a distinct corpus concerned with consolation and restoration. Chapters 30–31 consist of a series of loosely connected salvation oracles that have been strung together by various topics (e.g. consolation and restoration), or catchwords (e.g. 'Behold, the days are coming', 31.27, 31, 38). Although individual oracles within this corpus may have actually been spoken by Jeremiah (31.2-6, 15-21), much of the material in these chapters has a strong resemblance to the restoration oracles in Second Isaiah and may be influenced by those who edited the book of Deuteronomy (Deut. 4.25-31; 30.1-10). Thus it seems almost certain that

11.   For a brief history of scholarship and full bibliography, see B.S. Childs, *Introduction to the Old Testament as Scripture* (Philadelphia: Fortress Press, 1979), pp. 339-54. For a more extended discussion see the following commentaries: Bright, *Jeremiah*; R.E. Clements, *Jeremiah* (Atlanta: John Knox, 1988); Carroll, *Jeremiah*; W.L. Holladay, *Jeremiah 2* (Hermeneia; Minneapolis: Fortress Press, 1989); L.G. Perdue and B.W. Kovacs, *A Prophet to the Nations* (Winona Lake, IN: Eisenbrauns, 1984).

12.   Carroll points out that although scholarship has always often assumed that the A materials are the *ipsissima verba* of Jeremiah, this effect could be solely the creation of the editors who have attributed these disparate pieces of writing to a single author.

13.   Holladay and others like H. Weippert contend that the language of C differs from deuteronomistic language and that it stands close enough to the A material to be considered Jeremianic. Carroll acknowledges that C contains language that moves beyond the deuteronomistic style but sees the editing process as much more complicated and thus believes it is dubious to attribute the C materials to Jeremiah, Baruch or anyone in the pre-exilic period. See W.L. Holladay, 'A Fresh Look at "Source B" and "Source C" in Jeremiah', in Perdue and Kovacs (eds.), *A Prophet to the Nations*, pp. 213-28; Carroll, *The Book of Jeremiah*, pp. 38-50.

the current form of chs. 30–31 is in fact exilic, and it seems best to attribute this editing process to either the B or C source. It is difficult to be more precise inasmuch as many of the processes by which the book of Jeremiah reached its current form are either unknown, or hotly contested.

But the question of editing is not identical to the question of composition. It is at this point that several difficulties come into focus. Although a later group of editors created the structure of chs. 30–31, it is possible that elements within these chapters are original sayings of the prophet Jeremiah. If so, one must inquire whether Jeremiah could have authored vv. 29-30. If Jeremiah did not author this saying, then one must ask who did, and why was it attached to the book of Jeremiah?

Any attempt to deal with the authorship of Jer. 31.29-30 must begin with the relationship between this passage and Ezekiel 18. Both passages are attempts to refute a common proverb that was currently circulating among the people of Israel. The difficulty is that there is little evidence to argue with any surety whether Jer. 31.29-30 was composed earlier, or later, than Ezekiel 18. On literary grounds one should not assume that the short form of Jer. 31.29-30 automatically indicates that it is older than the more expansive text of Ezekiel 18. It could just as easily be an extract from the longer passage in Ezekiel 18. Furthermore, it is conceivable that both texts could have developed independently during the same period. It is not difficult to suppose that two different groups each produced a response to a quip that was then circulating around the community.

Several scholars have argued that Jer. 31.29-30 must be exilic and thus not written by Jeremiah. Although the conclusion might be correct, the logic of these arguments is not particularly strong. Nevertheless, it is worth examining some of these arguments in-depth because they reveal both the tendency to look for coherence in prophetic theology and the presumption that passages that focus attention on the individual must be seen as stemming from a different stratum than those passages that are corporate in nature. For example, R.P. Carroll attributes all of the oracles in chs. 30–31 'to the anonymous circles during and after the exile which cherished expectations of restoration'.[14] But his rationale is based upon the following assumption:

14.   Carroll, *The Book of Jeremiah*, p. 569.

Since he had proclaimed the complete destruction of the city, land and people without residue it is difficult to see how Jeremiah could perform such a volte-face, as is entailed in attributing 30–31 to him.[15]

Such an argument presumes a psychological consistency in the figure of Jeremiah, who incidentally, according to Carroll, is beyond historical reach.[16] One can certainly question whether it is advisable to base one's interpretive strategy on the notion that a figure like Jeremiah must be psychologically and theologically consistent. Jeremiah appears to be a highly tortured person who seems to exhibit various shifts in mood (Jer. 15.15-21; 20.7-13). Furthermore, there is room in the tradition of Jeremiah for oracles of hope and restoration (Jer. 1.10).[17] Some of these oracles of hope are directed to the North and thus could have been penned by Jeremiah (Jer. 31.2-6, 15-21).[18] Finally, it should be remembered that after the partial exile of Judah in 597, Jeremiah held out hope that the king and the people might submit to Babylon, and in doing so, earn the right to remain in the land (Jer. 27.12-15; 38.17-23).[19]

Holladay, who generally disagrees with Carroll, concurs with Carroll's assessment that Jer. 31.29-30 is an exilic text, but bases his argument on a very different rationale. Holladay argues that many sayings in chs. 30–31 come from Jeremiah himself (30.1-7, 10-21, 31.1aβγb, 2-9, 15-22, 27-28, 31-34).[20] Once Holladay has decided to include Jer. 31.31-34 in his collection of original oracles, he is forced to explain the supposed disparity between the corporate focus of this oracle and the individualistic focus of the oracle that immediately precedes it.

15. Carroll, *The Book of Jeremiah*, p. 569.

16. 'The fictional Jeremiah created by the tradition is temperamentally incapable of uttering such images of love and merrymaking—the last representations of him in the tradition are of his haranguing the communities in Egypt (44) and cursing the Babylonians (51.59-64). Those are characteristic poses of the man Jeremiah and it is against a backdrop of such images that the sudden shift to love poetry and songs supportive of the people is so unlikely'. Carroll, *The Book of Jeremiah*, pp. 588-89.

17. On the importance of the idea of hope in Jeremiah, see W. Brueggemann, *Jeremiah 26–52* (International Theological Commentary; Grand Rapids: Eerdmans, 1991), pp. 39-47.

18. L. Boadt, *Jeremiah 26–52, Habakkuk, Zephaniah, Nahum* (Old Testament Message, 10; Wilmington, DE: Michael Glazier, 1982), p. 36.

19. For evidence of the existence of the original post-597 theology of Jeremiah's book and discussion of how it was brought into line by later exilic redactors who were involved with the Ezekiel traditions, see Seitz, *Theology in Conflict*, pp. 204-96.

20. Holladay, *Jeremiah 2*, p. 22.

The notion of individual responsibility appears to some degree to contradict
the corporate restoration set forth in vv. 31-34; indeed the passage seems
to be intended as a corrective to the message of corporate restitution.[21]

On this basis, Holladay argues that the text of vv. 29-30 'is secondary to
Ezekiel 18 and is the attempt (by priestly circles?) to correct the implications of the "new covenant" passage'.[22] His argument rests on the
following logic. The oracle in vv. 31-34 was spoken by Jeremiah.[23]
Verses 31-34 are primarily focused on corporate matters. The oracle in
31.29-30, which is focused upon the individual, is in tension with the
oracle in vv. 31-34. Jeremiah must have a consistent theology of
retribution. By definition the oracle in vv. 29-30 cannot belong to
Jeremiah if vv. 31-34 belong to him.

Holladay's approach to this passage is generated by his fundamental
assertion that there is in fact a tension between the individualism of
vv. 29-30 and the corporate focus of 31-34. That the notion of individual
retribution is inherently in conflict with hopes of corporate restoration
can be called into question.[24] The use in v. 29 of the plural verb יאמרו,
which refers back to the House of Israel and the House of Judah in
v. 27, demonstrates that this oracle, as well as much of the surrounding
material, is addressed to the nation as a whole and proclaims the imminent rebirth of national prosperity (Jer. 30.4; 31.1, 31-34; 32.38). Thus

21. Holladay, *Jeremiah 2*, p. 163.
22. Holladay, *Jeremiah 2*, p. 163.
23. It should be mentioned that one cannot help but think that Holladay's move
to attribute the oracle in Jer. 31.31-34 to the prophet himself is primarily based upon
this oracle's importance to early Christianity (2 Cor. 3.6 and Heb. 8). Implicit in such
an assumption is the notion that the *ipsissima verba* of a prophet are truer, and of
higher revelatory status, than the additions to prophetic books. Such logic can also be
glimpsed in Bright's commentary upon this same passage: 'As regards its authenticity, one can say that it ought never to have been questioned'. But when one looks
for the reason why one should not question this oracle's authenticity, one finds both
an acknowledgment of the improbability that it preserves the *ipsissima verba* of the
prophet, followed by a plea to attribute it to the prophet because 'it is one of the
profoundest and most moving passages in the entire Bible'. Bright, *Jeremiah*, p. 287.
24. Carroll also seems to argue for a radical discontinuity between vv. 29-30 and
31-34. In reference to vv. 29-30 he comments that 'as a note of realism among the
golden dreams of a utopian future it is quite out of place'. Carroll, *Jeremiah*, p. 609.
A similar interpretation is put forward by Ludwig. Relying upon Volz and Rudolph,
he tells the reader that 'the purely negative tone of verse 30 hardly fits the tenor of the
rest of the book of consolation'. T.M. Ludwig, 'The Shape of Hope: Jeremiah's
Book of Consolation', *CTM* 39 (September 1968), p. 538.

the tension between vv. 29-30 and 31-34 is far less radical than often argued, and consequently Holladay's evidence for asserting that Jer. 31.29-30 is an exilic composition is not very secure.

Interestingly enough, neither Carroll nor Holladay highlight the strongest piece of evidence that this oracle was produced by the later deuteronomistic redactors who handled the book of Jeremiah, rather than by Jeremiah himself. This is the fact that Jer. 31.30 uses the phrase איש אם בעונו ימות which is quite similar to the phrase found in Deut. 24.16 איש בחטאו יומתו. This language is so close that it points to the likelihood that both were produced within exilic deuteronomistic circles. But one should bear in mind that even though Jer. 31.29-30 utilizes almost identical language to that found in Deut. 24.16, this does not prove conclusively that Jeremiah could not have written it. And certainly there is no evidence to support the notion that there is a radical tension between Jer. 31.29-30 and 31.31-34 and thus claim that the two texts must be from different strata.

Whether this oracle was authored by Jeremiah after the traumatic events of 597, or by later deuteronomistic editors after the tragic events of 587, it is clear that Jer. 31.29-30 is addressed to an audience that has experienced a great tragedy. Furthermore, the community interpreted this event as an undeserved punishment which they received because of the sinful actions of their ancestors.[25] They expressed their assesssment of their situation through a simple proverb. In their use of the proverb, the people identified themselves with the children in it. Just like the innocent children, they too were innocent of any wrongdoing and were suffering for the misdeeds of their ancestors. Inasmuch as they believed their punishment was totally undeserved, they were hopelessly unmotivated to do anything about their current state.

The author of this oracle responds to this general sense of despair with an eschatological proclamation about the coming days, which is intended to instill a new sense of hope in the people. That this oracle is an eschatological oracle of hope which looks to a new time can be seen by the introductory statement found in v. 29 which states, 'In those days', which refers to the eschatological future proclaimed in the phrase, 'Behold, the days are coming, says the Lord, when...' (Jer. 31.27, 31, 38; 33.14). This is a time in which once again the people will be living in

---

25. Although it is possible that the lament is a specific reference to the misdeeds of Manasseh's generation, I tend to think it should be understood in the more generic sense of those generations that lived before the present one.

the land of Israel (Jer. 32.42-44), with a restored temple cult (Jer. 33.17-22), and a renewed Davidic monarchy (Jer. 33.14-16, 23-26). Verses 29-30 are part of this proleptic proclamation that announces a new era in which things will not only be renewed, but different. The difficulty with this passage is clarifying both who will be changing and exactly what will be different in the future.

Much of this difficulty hinges on how one understands the words כי אם at the beginning of v. 30. Quite often it is translated as 'but' (NJPSV, NRSV, JB), which implies that this Jeremianic passage proclaims an idealized future in which divine retribution will be distributed in a more just manner, thus precluding any future complaint on the part of the people. This exegesis of the passage acknowledges that the current situation is one in which divine punishment has a corporate, and in particular a trans-generational, dimension. Only in the future will God change the way he relates to Israel, and only then will he judge each person on his or her own merits.[26] This interpretive option has the following points in its favor. It fits in nicely with many of the surrounding texts that each focus on God's new action in relation to the people of Israel (Jer. 31.7-14, 27-28, 31-34). It makes sense of the declaration 'each man will die for his sin' by attributing this to God. And finally, one could argue that it resolves the internal contradiction between this passage and those passages that stress corporate punishment (Jer. 2.30; 3.25; 6.11-12; 13.14; 16.10-13; 18.21-23; 32.18-19 etc.), by acknowledging that God had previously acted inequitably, but in the near future things would be different.

The difficulties with this position are twofold: (1) the form of the text leads one to expect the people to say something in the future, but on this reading, they will simply no longer complain because God will now act equitably; (2) such a reading acknowledges that God did, in fact, act inequitably in the past.

The second line of interpretation understands the phrase כי אם as part of an elliptical formula that begins with the words לא יאמרו עוד and is completed with כי אם. In this reading the כי אם implies כי אם יאמרו.[27] Thus the passage describes a change in what the people will say, rather than a

26. Several commentators follow this line of interpretation including Bright, *Jeremiah*, p. 283; Holladay, *Jeremiah 2*, p. 154; May, 'Individual Responsibility and Retribution', pp. 114-15.

27. This view is expressed by J. Schoneveld, 'Jeremiah 31:29,30', *VT* 13 (July 1963), pp. 339-41, and by A. Graffy, *A Prophet Confronts his People* (AnBib, 104; Rome: Pontifical Biblical Institute, 1984), 35-38.

change in how God will act, in this future time. Evidence for this type of elliptical formula can be found in other passages in Jeremiah (Jer. 3.16-17; 7.32; 16.14-15; 19.6; 23.7-8), as well as in other places in the Hebrew Bible (Gen. 32.29; 35.10; Isa. 62.4). This interpretation of v. 30 leads to the following conclusion:

> The refutation looks forward to the time when they will speak differently. The change which is announced in this text is a change in knowledge of YHWH's ways. In the future time of salvation they will no longer put all the blame for the events of 587 on their ancestors, but will recognize that they too had a share in the guilt.[28]

Thus, the only change is one of perception, not of the way in which divine retribution operates. The drawbacks of this reading are the inverse of those of other reading. (1) The phrase 'each man will die for his sins' seems rather awkward as part of the people's new proverb. (2) One must explain the tension between this text and other texts in Jeremiah that indicate that God punishes corporately.

In spite of these drawbacks, I think that the merits of the second line of interpretation outweigh its drawbacks and thus indicate that it is the correct line of interpretation. The second line of reasoning has the following points in its favor:

1. It does not imply that God had, in fact, acted in an apparently unjust manner in the past and will change to a fair system of retribution only in the future. Thus, God neither changes, nor acts arbitrarily.

2. It makes clear why the text not only rejects the proverb but offers an alternate proverb in its place.

3. It reduces the apparent friction between vv. 29-30 and 31-34, inasmuch as both passages can be seen as projections about a forthcoming change in the people's perception and awareness of God and how he acts.

4. This line of interpretation brings the theology of Jer. 31.29-30 into line with the theology espoused in Ezekiel 18. Rather than being forced to view Jer. 31.29-30 as advocating a theology of retribution that will only be true in the future, while Ezekiel 18 advocates this theology of retribution in the present, both texts are seen as advocating the current validity of an equitable system of divine retribution.

---

28.   Graffy, *A Prophet Confronts his People*, p. 37.

In terms of the drawbacks, the following can be said. It is by no means impossible to see the phrase, 'each man will die for his iniquity' as part of the new proverb, inasmuch as this formulaic usage of כי אם is generally followed by the new saying or name (Gen. 32.29; 35.10; Isa. 62.4; Jer. 3.16-17; 7.32; 16.14-15; 19.6; 23.7-8).[29] Or, alternatively, one could suggest that it is an interpolation or expansion that eventually found its way into the text because it clarified what the people had really been complaining about.

The second objection, about the relationship between this passage and other texts in Jeremiah that take a more corporate view of divine punishment (Jer. 2.30; 3.25; 6.11-12; 13.14; 16.10-13; 18.21-23; 32.18-19 etc.), will require a much longer answer. One way to solve this difficulty is simply to acknowledge that Jer. 31.29-30 comes from a deuteronomistic exilic editor who disagreed with the retributional system generally advocated by the book of Jeremiah and thus offered his alternative system as a corrective.[30] Evidence for such an approach would come from scholars who argue that later editors had a tendency to simply add on corrective glosses to texts without eliminating or changing the original. Thus one ends up with two contrary notions that are both asserted, often side by side. Such an argument is made about the passage found in Jer. 32.17-19.

> Ah Lord God! It is you who made the heavens and the earth by your great power and by your outstretched arm! Nothing is too hard for you, 18 who shows steadfast love to thousands but requites the sin of fathers into the bosom of their children after them. O great and mighty God whose name is the Lord of Hosts, 19 great in counsel and mighty in deed, whose eyes watch all the ways of people, repaying each person according to his deeds and with the fruit of his deeds.

In reviewing the various types of aggadic exegesis within the Hebrew Bible, Michael Fishbane makes the following observation about this passage:

> The sequence of 32.18-20 was interrupted with the exegetical revision which states that YHWH's greatness (cf. v. 18b) actually lies in the fact that 'He deals with each person according to his actions' (v.19b).[31]

29. Graffy, *A Prophet Confronts his People*, p. 38.
30. Note May's comment on Jer. 31.29-30: 'It is true that it is strange in Jeremiah's mouth, but... [it] is quite consonant with... the wider context of Jeremiah's "biographer"'. May, 'Individual Responsibility and Retribution', p. 115.
31. Fishbane, *Biblical Interpretation*, p. 342.

While Fishbane's interpretive strategy is productive in many instances, one must question whether such a strategy, at times, imposes a modern notion of consistency upon a text. One wonders whether Weinfeld is not closer to the truth when, in commenting upon this perceived tension between Jer. 32.18 and 19, he notes that 'a contradiction is revealed of which the compiler was unaware'.[32] Does the expression 'paying back according to one's deeds' exclude any form of trans-generational retribution? Hosea uses very similar language in 4.9 and 12.3 to announce the coming exile of the whole population. Yet it is dubious to assert that such language implies that Hosea thought that the innocent children would be spared (Hos. 2.6; 9.16).[33]

Because it remains possible that the composers of texts that seem contradictory to us understood them in a harmonious fashion, we must proceed with caution before pronouncing that Jer. 31.29-30 is a complete rejection of the older theology of divine retribution that often encompassed corporate ideas. I would argue that many of the interpretive problems surrounding Jer. 31.29-30 and its relationship to other aspects of biblical thought have arisen because of the following hermeneutical assumption: this oracle's primary intention is to announce a theology in which divine retribution will be individualized.

> Although in the future nobody will suffer for any misdeeds other than their own, there will be those who misbehave to the point of being executed! Everybody will bear the responsibility of their own actions.[34]

> But he [Jeremiah] rejects the common wisdom of the ages and announces a new order of responsibility. All will not suffer for the sins of the few. Each will bear the responsibility for his or her own conduct.[35]

Both of these quotes indicate a strong preference for reading the oracle as an announcement of a doctrinal shift from corporate toward individualized retribution. By focusing almost exclusively on the individualistic language found within this oracle, one fails to see that the primary thrust of the passage is not to assert a new theory about individualized divine

32.   Weinfeld, *Deuteronomy 1–11*, p. 371.

33.   A similar problem can be raised in relation to Lam. 5.7 which blames the ancestors for the exile and Lam. 5.16 in which the exiles confess their guilt. Are these mutually exclusive categories? Texts such as Exod. 32.34, Lev. 26.39, Jer. 16.10-13 and Ezek. 20.23 indicate that one might suffer for both one's sins and one's ancestor's sins. See n. 35 Chapter 2 below.

34.   Carroll, *Jeremiah*, p. 609.

35.   Boadt, *Jeremiah 26–52*, pp. 54-55.

retribution, but rather, to attempt to counter the hopelessness of those who experienced a great tragedy. To achieve this goal the prophet had to help the people reach a new understanding of their situation. This new understanding could only be reached when each individual Israelite acknowledged his or her personal responsibility for the current state of the nation. By blaming their ancestors for their condition, they were asserting that it was useless to do anything to alleviate their condition. As long as this generation felt that it was suffering unjustly, it would feel that nothing could be done because God's ways were unfair and arbitrary. The despair and helplessnesss of the exilic situation can be seen rather clearly in Lamentations 5. To overcome this sense of helplessness and empower the people, it was necessary that they first acknowledge their guilt and then turn toward God.

> So we can see that the citation of the principle 'every one shall die for his own sin…' (v. 30) was not intended as a reformulation of a legal principle but a demonstration of the total transformation made possible for Israel through the gift of repentance. Israel's suffering in exile and Judah's devastation were not part of an inexorable fate from which there could be no escape, but they had been necessary punishments from God. Because renewal and restoration were possible, so repentance and renewal of commitment to God were wholly possible and meaningful actions.[36]

Thus it is not God who changes the way that he acts, but the people who come to understand that God had acted justly when he punished them for their misdeeds. Strangely enough, the act of accepting their culpability for the exile will empower the nation, both as individuals and as a unit, to work toward the restoration. Although acknowledging one's guilt may initially be more depressing, it ultimately gives one a sense of control over one's personal condition. The oracle in Jer. 31.29-30 is primarily aimed at instilling new hope for the future into the nation. It does this by indicating that the nation and the individuals who compose it can only regain control over their destiny by acknowledging that they are responsible for their current predicament. To argue that the *primary purpose* of the oracle was not to propound a new doctrine of divine retribution, does not mean that this oracle does not modify

---

36. Clements, *Jeremiah*, p. 189. Although I concur with this statement made by Clements, it should be noted that he does not understand the passage as an attempt to help the nation acknowledge its guilt. He argues that the people are in their current state of despair because they feel that they were justly punished and thus beyond any hope of restoration.

secondarily older conceptions of divine retribution. Before exploring the tension between this oracle and the older corporate conceptions, we must first clarify this oracle's theory of divine retribution. This is not an easy task inasmuch as there are two levels at which one can address this problem: There is the intent of the passage and there is the literal language employed by the passage. I do not believe that Jer. 31.29-30 had any intention of advocating an utterly individualized conception of divine retribution. The whole context of chs. 30–31 is one pervaded by themes of *corporate* restoration (Jer. 30.4; 31.1, 31-34; 32.38). Furthermore, the proverb used by the people in v. 29 indicates that their complaint is about God punishing their generation for the sins of their ancestors. Verse 30 functions as a rejection of the people's assertion that God is visiting the sins of earlier generations upon them.

The use of the individualistic language can be explained in the following way. In order to motivate the population and refute the proverb, the prophet utilized the text in Deut. 24.16 which speaks about the problem of the transference of sins across generations. The language of Deut. 24.16 is individualistic and also judicial. The prophet changed the judicial language into language that is more appropriate in reference to God by switching the stem of the root מות from the *hophal* to the *qal*. But he maintained the individualistic language for two reasons: (1) it functions as a rhetorical device employed to motivate the individual addressee to stop brooding and take responsibility for his or her current state; (2) it creates an interpretive link with Deut. 24.16.[37] This interpretive link allows the author of Jer. 31.29-30 to reflect upon the issue of God's justice by refracting it through the lens of Deut. 24.16, a text that contains a divine imperative that prohibits humans from punishing criminal offenders trans-generationally. This maneuver creates a type of pietistic, inner-biblical exegesis in which the author of Jer. 31.29-30 demonstrates that God must act equitably toward humankind, because God's legislation makes it clear that only the guilty party must be punished and not the innocent progeny. Thus God who authored

---

37. I acknowledge that this interpretive link only exists once one has decided that Deut. 24.16 is earlier than Jer. 31.29-30 and that this may not be the case. Although there is no conclusive evidence that Deut. 24.16 is earlier than Jer. 31.29-30, Jer. 31.29-30 makes much more sense if one assumes that it is expanding upon the text of Deut. 24.16. The text of Ezek. 18, discussed below, seems to provide stronger evidence that it is explicitly building upon Deut. 24.16.

Deut. 24.16 and created the standard of human justice must surely abide by his own legislation.[38]

Thus the primary purpose of the oracle, which was to help the nation realize and acknowledge its responsibility, was accomplished by refuting the validity of the concept that punishment can be transferred across generations. But the language employed by the text signals not only a rejection of trans-generational retribution, but also a rejection of the idea that guilt can be transferred from one individual to another within a single generation. It is important to recognize that this passage challenges the validity of both trans- and intra-generational retribution. But it is equally important to realize that passages such as Jer. 31.29-30 and Ezekiel 18 (which will be discussed below), may have arisen as *ad hoc* creations that grew out of pastoral necessity. This is not to deny their importance, but to caution us about their intent. There is little evidence to support the idea that they were written as systematic statements of theology that were produced in an effort to reject the older corporate ideas. It is much more likely that the same person maintained both sets of theological ideas, expressing one set in certain pastoral circumstances and the other in a different set of pastoral circumstances. Even if one rejects this latter idea, that these alternate theological systems could coexist in the same prophet, one should remember that, canonically speaking, they do coexist. That there is a movement toward greater recognition of the place of the individual in relation to divine retribution cannot be denied. But neither should one deny that this individual's very self-understanding was derived from his or her relationship to the community. It was the community that produced the various theologies of divine retribution. One should not forget that even those trends that stressed the growing importance of the individual viewed the individual as a member of the community, not as an autonomous entity before God. Furthermore, one should bear in mind that just as there are movements in certain late texts, such as Jer. 31.29-30, to place a greater

---

38.   This particular theological maneuver is somewhat analogous to a Chasidic story told about Rosh Hashanah. It is said that when Rosh Hashanah falls on the Sabbath it is very good. Why? Because Rosh Hashanah is the day on which God writes the destinies of all people. Yet God is not allowed to write on the Sabbath (it is considered work) except to save a life. Therefore God must write all people in the book of life when Rosh Hashanah falls on the Sabbath. This story can be found in L.I. Newman, *The Hasidic Anthology* (New York: Charles Scribner's Sons, 1934), p. 399. In both this story and the passage from Jeremiah, there is an attempt to force God to act according to the standards he has set for the human community.

emphasis upon the individual, at this same period other texts are being composed which place a tremendous emphasis on the nation as a whole. Rather than seeing these trends as belonging to different chronological periods or assuming that they must stem from different sources, it might be more useful to see them as related phenomena. Israel is developing both a deeper theological understanding of the corporate unity of the group and of the way in which the individuals who compose that group participate in that unity. This point is made quite nicely by Paul Joyce.

> We do not deny that certain developments in the understanding of responsibility may be discerned in the biblical material. However, it is important to acknowledge that there seem to be developments both in the direction of increased emphasis on individual responsibility and also in the opposite direction, towards a more collective emphasis.[39]

This analysis of Jer. 31.29-30 reveals the following:

1. Jer. 31.29-30 is not an attempt to describe a coming change in God's behavior, but rather a coming shift in man's awareness of God's behavior.
2. Jer. 31.29-30 is primarily an attempt to give hope to the exilic generation by forcing them to acknowledge their guilt and take control of their future.
3. Nevertheless, the passage is innovative in certain respects. It intentionally rejects the notion of trans-generational retribution, and the individualistic language it uses implies that it rejects all forms of punishment displacement.
4. It is dubious that the author of Jer. 31.29-30 intended to refute the general tendency of Israelite religion to hold the community liable for the sins of its individual members. It is more likely that the passage was an *ad hoc* piece that was produced out of homiletic necessity.
5. It is important to realize that the same thinker may have affirmed two different sets of ideas about the way in which God punishes people. This is especially true of a prophetic thinker who may have developed his thought in relation to specific pastoral situations, rather than as a systematic theological treatise.

---

39. Joyce, *Divine Initiative*, p. 85.

Ezekiel 18

Ezekiel 18 reads as follows.[40]

> The word of the Lord came to me: 2 Why are you using this proverb concerning[41] the land of Israel, 'The fathers have eaten sour grapes, and the children's teeth are set on edge?'[42] 3 As I live, says the Lord, this proverb will no longer be spoken by you in Israel. 4 Behold, all persons[43] are mine; the person of the father as well as the person of the son is mine: the person that sins shall die.
>
> 5 If a man is righteous and he acts justly and rightly— 6 if he does not eat upon the mountains or lift up his eyes to the idols of the House of Israel, does not defile his neighbor's wife or approach a woman in her time of impurity, 7 does not oppress anyone, but restores his debt-pledge,[44]

40. There is an extensive amount of bibliographical material on the book of Ezekiel. One can consult the major commentators for this information. I will list only those books and articles most relevant for my discussion. Eichrodt, *Ezekiel*, pp. 213-49; Gammie, *Holiness in Israel*, pp. 45-70; Greenberg, *Ezekiel, 1–20*, pp. 325-47; Joyce, *Divine Initiative*, pp. 33-87; R.W. Klein, *Ezekiel: The Prophet and his Message* (Studies on Personalities of the Old Testament; Columbia: University of South Carolina Press, 1988), pp. 97-112; Matties, *Ezekiel 18*; W. Zimmerli, *Ezekiel 1* (Hermeneia; Philadelphia: Fortress Press, 1979); M. Fishbane, 'Sin and Judgment in the Prophecies of Ezekiel', *Int* 38 (1984), pp. 131-50; J.B. Geyer, 'Ezekiel 18 and a Hittite Treaty of Mursilis II', *JSOT* 12 (May 1979), pp. 31-46; M.J. Gruenthaner, 'The Old Testament and Retribution in this Life', *CBQ* 4 (1942), pp. 101-10; C. Lattey, 'Vicarious Solidarity in the Old Testament', *VT* 1 (1951), pp. 267-74; Lindars, 'Ezekiel and Individual Responsibility and Retribution', pp. 452-67; May, 'Individual Responsibility', pp. 107-20; K.D. Sakenfeld, 'Ezekiel 18.25-32', *Int* 32 (1978), pp. 295-300.

41. One difficulty here is the translation of the preposition על in v. 2. The RSV, Eichrodt and Joyce translate it as 'concerning' and I prefer this. But Greenberg opts for 'on' and Zimmerli 'in'. Both Greenberg and Zimmerli claim that this word points to authorship by someone who stands outside the land of Israel. I see no reason why we cannot assume that Ezekiel was poetically ambiguous in order to allow his message to reach the widest possible audience.

42. See n. 8 above for a more detailed dicussion of the word תקהינה. Those who use the proverb are not questioning the fact that sin should be punished, but that the innocent next generation should bear the guilt of its predecessors. Greenberg, *Ezekiel, 1–20*, p. 328.

43. There is no adequate translation for the word נפש. It is the vital life force which consists of a union of body and the personality that animates it.

44. I emend חבלתו חוב to חבלת חובו with Greenberg. Greenberg, *Ezekiel, 1–20*, p. 329.

commits no robbery, gives his bread to the hungry and covers the naked with a garment, 8 does not lend at interest or take any increase, withholds his hand from iniquity, executes true justice between man and man, 9 walks in my statutes, and observes my ordinances so as to do them[45]—he is righteous, he shall surely live, says the Lord God.

10 And if he bore a violent son, one who sheds blood who did any one[46] of these things, 11 who did not do any of these things,[47] but ate upon the mountains, defiled his neighbor's wife, 12 oppressed the poor and destitute, committed robbery,[48] will not return a pledge,[49] lifted up his his eyes to idols, did an abomination, 13 loaned at interest and collected with increase—will he live?[50] He will not live; he did all these abominations, he will indeed be killed.[51] His blood will be upon himself.

14 Take note, he begot a son who saw all the sins that his father had done, and having seen,[52] he does not act likewise. 15 He did not eat on the mountains or lift up his eyes to the idols of the House of Israel; he did not defile his neighbor's wife; 16 he oppressed no one, did not take a pledge, and did not commit robbery; rather he gave his food to the hungry and

45.   Emend אמת to אתם following the LXX.

46.   Delete את with the Syriac and Vulgate. It appears to be a scribal error (cf., Lev. 4.2 and 5.13). It is possible that אח מאחד is an error generated from a text that once read אחד מאלה.

47.   This appears to be another attempt to solve the crux found in v. 10. It is unclear whether it refers to the righteous father who did no evil (Zimmerli), or to the wicked son who did no virtuous acts (Greenberg).

48.   The form גזלות only occurs here and should perhaps be emended to גזלה following the form found in vv. 7 and 16.

49.   This verb is in the future tense and could be explained by the fact that the act of not returning a pledge carries into the future until one returns it. Zimmerli suggests that perhaps one should emend to השיב inasmuch as all the surrounding verbs are perfects. The LXX appears to support such an emendation with its use of ἀπέδωκεν.

50.   It is possible that וחי should be read as an infinitive absolute (חיו) as noted by Zimmerli and the LXX. If this is true, it would be translated as, 'he surely will not live'.

51.   Some scholars emend יומת to ימות as suggested by the Syriac, Targum, Vulgate, and some Greek and Hebrew manuscripts. I follow Zimmerli and Greenberg and explain this apparent anomaly on the basis of the phrase 'his blood will be upon himself'. This phrase is used only in instances in which humans are executing justice and wish to insure that no bloodguilt adheres to them (Lev. 20.11, 12, 13 *et al.*). Thus it is likely that the latter phrase led the writer to use the standard judicial formula rather than the expected ימות.

52.   It is possible to emend ויראה to וירא which would translate, 'and he feared', thus the LXX and Vulgate. I follow Zimmerli who notes that the root ראה occurs over 75 times in Ezekiel while the root ירא occurs only four times. Also the same type of usage occurs in v. 28 as Greenberg correctly notes.

clothed the naked with a garment; 17 he restrained his hand from iniquity,[53] he did not take advanced or accrued interest;[54] he executed my rulings and followed my statutes—he will not die because of his father's guilt;[55] he will surely live.

18 But his father, because he practiced extortion, committed robbery,[56] and did what was not good among his people, he indeed died because of his iniquity.

19 Yet you say, 'Why didn't the son suffer because of his father's guilt?' But the son acted justly and righteously; he heeded all my statutes and executed them; surely he will live! 20 The person who sins, he will die; a son will not suffer because of the father's guilt, nor will a father suffer because of the son's guilt. The righteousness of the righteous man will redound to him and the wickedness of the wicked man[57] will redound to him.

21 But if the wicked person turns back from all his sins that he did and heeds all my statutes and does what is just and right, he will surely live, he will not die. 22 None of the transgressions that he did will be remembered against him; because of the righteousness that he did he will live. 23 Do I take any pleasure in the death[58] of the wicked person, declares the Lord YHWH, but rather that he turn back from his ways and live?

24 And when a righteous person turns back from his righteousness and does what is unjust, just like the abominations that the wicked person did, will he do so and live?[59] None of his righteous acts that he did will be remembered; on account of the treachery that he committed and his sin that

---

53.   I emend מעני to מעול. Logically this makes more sense. This reading gains additional support from v. 8 and from the LXX which reads καὶ ἀπὸ ἀδικίας. Greenberg suggests that the word for מעני may have arisen by attraction to the preceeding 'hungry and naked'.

54.   This is a translation borrowed from the new JPSV translation. *TANAKH: A New Translation of the Holy Scriptures* (Philadelphia: The Jewish Publication Society, 1985), p. 917.

55.   The word עון could refer to the sin, the guilt that follows from the sin, or the punishment that follows from the sin and its accompanying guilt. It is precisely a passage like this in which the preposition ב occurs that might substantiate Koch's claim that people are caught in their own powerful auras or spheres of influence which they generate by their actions. Koch, 'Doctrine of Retribution', pp. 57-87. But it is certainly not the only way to understand the use of the preposition in this verse. One could simply read it as indicating instrumentality and translate as 'by means of', 'for the sake of', or 'because of'. GKC §119 o and p.

56.   Following the LXX, Targum, Syriac and vv. 7 and 16 I emend נזל אח to גזלה.

57.   Restoring the ה as indicated by the *qere*.

58.   Emend מות to במוה following numerous manuscripts and v. 32.

59.   It is possible that the words וחי יעשה are a gloss. It is not found in the LXX and seems somewhat awkward here.

he did, for them he will die. 25 And you say, 'The way of the Lord is not equitable'. Listen up, House of Israel, Is my way not equitable? Is it not your ways that are not equitable? 26 When a righteous person turns back from his righteousness and does what is unjust and dies for it,[60] because of his unjust behavior that he committed he will die. 27 And when the wicked person turns back from his wickedness that he had committed and he acts justly and rightly, he will save his person; 28 having seen[61] and turned back from all his transgressions that he did, he will surely live, he will not die. 29 The House of Israel say, 'The way of the Lord is not equitable'. Are my ways not equitable[62], O House of Israel? Are not your ways inequitable?[63]

30 Therefore I will judge you each person according to his ways, O House of Israel, declares the Lord YHWH. Turn back and face about[64] from all your transgressions, and do not let it become a stumbling block of guilt to you. 31 Throw away all your transgressions that you committed against me,[65] and make for yourselves a new heart and a new spirit; why should you die, O House of Israel? 32 For I do not take pleasure in the death of the dead person, declares the Lord YHWH; so face about and live.

This chapter has received a good deal of scholarly attention; there is a wide divergence of opinion over its interpretation. It seems best to begin with the questions surrounding the provenance, date and intended audience of Ezekiel 18.

The question of provenance is the easiest to answer. Chapter 18 was almost certainly composed in Babylonia. Babylonia is the most likely origin for this oracle regardless of whether one advocates that this oracle is wholly composed by Ezekiel, by later redactors who transmitted Ezekiel's oracles, or was partially authored by Ezekiel and partially authored by a later editor or redactor. There is strong internal literary evidence to suggest that the original prophecies of Ezekiel were all produced in Babylonia after 593 BCE (Ezek. 1.2) and thus it is likely that most of the later editorial work on the book of Ezekiel took place in Babylonia as well.

The question of dating is a bit more difficult inasmuch as this question

---

60. The pronoun is plural and might have been generated by the language used in v. 24. It may be a later gloss.

61. The text may be corrupt here. The word ויראה is not found in the LXX and may have come from v. 14.

62. Perhaps this should be in the singular like v. 25.

63. The noun is plural and the verb is singular.

64. Greenberg, *Ezekiel 1–20*, pp. 249 and 334.

65. Emend בם to בי following the LXX (εἰς ἐμέ) and Zimmerli.

forces one to wrestle with the relationship that exists between Ezekiel 18 and two other passages, Jer. 31.29-30 and Ezek. 33.10-20. Jer. 31.29-30 is extremely terse and is located in a collection of oracles that are loosely bound together. Thus there is little evidence to argue with any surety whether Jer. 31.29-30 was composed earlier, or later, than Ezekiel 18. One should not assume that the short form of Jer. 31.29-30 automatically indicates that it is older than the more expansive text of Ezekiel 18. It could just as easily be an extract from the longer passage in Ezekiel 18. It is equally conceivable that both texts could have been produced during the same period, and could have developed out from a common written or oral source.[66]

The more complicated question is the one that surrounds the relationship between Ezekiel 18 and 33.10-20. Again, there is no conclusive proof that ch. 18 is an expansion of 33.10-20 or that 33.10-20 has excerpted part of ch. 18. But there is some circumstantial evidence to suggest that ch. 18 was written earlier than the passage found in 33.10-20. If this evidence holds up, it might also help clarify the question of the date of Ezekiel 18.

The following factors indicate the priority of ch. 18 over 33.10-20. (1) The list of offenses in vv. 5-17, and particularly the offense of 'eating on the mountains' (vv. 6, 11 and 15), strongly suggests a date before the final destruction of Jerusalem.[67] (2) The fact that in Ezekiel 18 the people are still clinging to their self-righteousness, while in Ezek. 33.10-20 the nation is filled with despair and hopelessness due to their awareness of their guilt, suggests that Ezekiel 18 was written before and Ezek. 33.10-20 after the destruction of Jerusalem.[68] (3) There are literary arguments that point to the unity of ch. 18 and that indicate that 33.10-20 assumes the existence of the fuller argument that is now found in ch. 18. For example, the phrase 'The way of the Lord is inequitable' which occurs in Ezek. 33.17, 20 does not make sense as a rebuttal to a group of depressed people who have admitted their guilt (Ezek. 33.10). But this same phrase occurs in Ezek. 18.25, 29 and it makes perfect

---

66. For more extensive discussion surrounding the date and provenance of Jer. 31.29-30, see above.

67. Greenberg, *Ezekiel 1–20*, p. 342. Although the list of these offences support a pre-exilic date they do not prove that it is addressed only to those still in the land.

68. 'Our transgressions and our sins are upon us, and we waste away because of them; how then shall we live?', Ezek. 33.11.

sense in this context.[69] In Ezekiel 18 the people's refusal to accept responsibility for their current state leads them to accuse God of acting inequitably (Ezek. 18.2, 19). The available evidence indicates that Ezek. 18.1-32 should be viewed as a single coherent oracle and that this whole chapter was probably composed earlier than Ezek. 33.10-20.[70]

The evidence just discussed tends to support Greenberg's thesis that Ezekiel 18 belongs to the period between 593[71] and 587 BCE and that the text in 33.10-20 was composed sometime after the fall of Jerusalem in 587 BCE. One other piece of evidence that has no bearing on the question of the relationship between ch. 18 and 33.10-20, but does support a pre-fall date for ch. 18, is the plea in Ezek. 18.31. In this verse the prophet orders his audience to 'make for yourselves a new heart'. It should be recognized that, in other places, Ezekiel seems to have abandoned any hope that the people could repent and be obedient unless God intervened and gave them a new heart (11.19 and 36.26). It is most likely that as the situation worsened, Ezekiel gave up on the possibilty that Israel would, or even could, repent (Ezek. 16 and 20), and thus ch. 18 would come from a period before things had reached such a nadir.[72]

In terms of the audience it was meant to address, Eichrodt argues that it must be addressed to those in exile, because the nature of the list of

69. Greenberg, *Ezekiel, 1–20*, p. 338. He also cites several other pieces of literary evidence in favor of the unity of ch. 18 and its priority over 33.10-20. Graffy argues that 18.21-32 is later than 33.10-20. He claims that 18.23 is out of place and awkward and makes more sense in relation to the question posed in 33.10. He notes that this is Zimmerli's observation. Graffy, *A Prophet Confronts his People*, p. 58-59, 74. But Zimmerli tells us explicitly that 18.1-20 only makes sense when it is combined with the call to repentance found in vv. 21-32. 'Considerations of subject matter lead to the same result. This shows that in the call to repentance, which is anticipated in 33.10-11 and which is set at the end in 18.30b, the scope of the oracle is to be found. Without such a connection with this aim vv. 1-20 remain an academic explanation.' Zimmerli, *Ezekiel 1*, p. 374.

70. For a more extensive argument supporting the unity of ch. 18, see Matties, *Ezekiel 18*, pp. 27-60.

71. The earliest oracles in Ezekiel date from 593 BCE (Ezek. 1.2).

72. Obviously not all would agree to a date before 587. Thus Zimmerli in reference to the people's proverb in v. 2 makes the following comment: 'Chronologically the saying quoted points rather to the situation after the greater collapse of 587 BC'. Zimmerli, *Ezekiel 1*, p. 377. I do not find this highly compelling inasmuch as the events of 597 were no doubt devastating enough to bring a proverb like this one into common parlance.

offenses 'is independent of any tie with the soil of Palestine or the Temple of Jerusalem'.[73] But this argument is quite weak inasmuch as 'eating on the mountains' is an offence that seems to imply certain ties to the idea of a centralized form of temple worship in Jerusalem.[74] Furthermore, the offence of approaching a woman during her menstrual flow (v. 6) and of shedding blood (v. 10) are offences that pollute the land of Israel (Num. 35.33). It is this pollution that eventually causes the divine glory to abandon Jerusalem. In fact, in opposition to Eichrodt, if one wished to insist that this oracle was addressed only to one community, it would be easier to argue that it was addressed to those still in the land of Israel. Note the use of על־אדמת ישראל in v. 2[75] and the occurrence of the word בישראל in v. 3. But rather than pursue this line of reasoning, it seems most correct to presume that the text is addressed to both the exiles in Babylon and the community that remained in Jerusalem. Thus, he uses the rather broad appellation בית ישראל (vv. 25, 29, 30, 31).

Having discussed the questions of date, authorship and provenance, it is now time to examine the structure and theological content of Ezekiel 18. As indicated above, there is sufficient evidence to support the view that the chapter should be understood as a single coherent oracle that is composed of two major sub-units, 1-20 and 21-32. The following factors support the view that Ezekiel 18 is a single coherent unit and refute those who argue that only vv. 1-20 are original and that vv. 21-32 are a late addition.[76] (1) The question posed by the proverb in v. 2 is not explicitly challenged and refuted until vv. 25 and 29. (2) The oracle lacks direction unless one accepts the call to repentance in vv. 30-32 as an authentic part of the original oracle. Simply to force the people to acknowledge their guilt, without then motivating them to turn back toward God, seems rather strange. (3) The second half of Ezekiel's argument found in vv. 21-32 is already adumbrated in v. 20b.

---

73. Eichrodt, *Ezekiel*, pp. 238-39.

74. As Greenberg astutely observes, the list of offenses in vv. 5-17 includes 'eating on the mountains' which is 'an offense peculiar to those living in the homeland, and shows...a prefall orientation'. Greenberg, *Ezekiel 1–20*, p. 343.

75. See the discussion in n. 41 above on the various translations of the preposition על in v. 2.

76. For the argument in favor of seeing vv. 21-32 as a late addition that is unrelated to the content of vv. 1-20, see Graffy, *A Prophet Confronts his People*, pp. 58-59.

Verse 20 functions rhetorically as a hinge between the two parts of the chapter... It is thought that v. 20 belongs structurally to the first half of the chapter, but if its function as a hinge between the two halves is recognized, then it stands independently, mirroring aspects of both. Verse 20a mirrors v. 4 and the argument of vv. 5-19. Verse 20b mirrors the argument of vv. 21-32.[77]

This is not to say that no new elements are introduced in 21-32, but to suggest that the new twist in the argument is both a logical extension of, and the natural conclusion to, the original argument.

If the chapter is to be understood as a unit then the next question is, what are its theological implications? A cursory reading of Ezekiel 18 tends to support what I have called the evolutionary approach to the idea of divine retribution.[78] Ezek. 18.1-20 seems to refute the doctrine that sin can be transferred across generations. Verses 21-32 appear to go even further, advocating that even within a single generation, neither previous merits nor debits carry any power. A person is judged as an autonomous individual exclusively by his or her current state of behavior. Furthermore, this idea appears to be new, in that it expresses a paradigm of divine retribution that is not widely recognized or accepted by Ezekiel's contemporaries (Ezek. 18.2, 19; 33.10).[79]

There are two major objections that can be raised against this reading of Ezekiel 18. How can one square this reading of Ezekiel 18 with other passages within the book of Ezekiel that affirm corporate notions of punishment? There are passages within Ezekiel that affirm that sometimes the innocent suffer along with the guilty of the community (Ezek. 9.5-6; 20.23-26; 21.8-9; 24.21), or that recognize that the guilty might escape the more severe forms of punishment (Ezek. 14.22; 33.21-29). Furthermore, when one understands Ezekiel 18 in this radically

---

77.   Matties, *Ezekiel 18*, p. 43.

78.   It should be noted that the evolutionary approach to Ezek. 18 is quite ancient. In the Babylonian Talmud we find the following statement attributed to R. Jose bar Hanina: 'Moses said, "Visiting the iniquity of fathers upon the sons", but Ezekiel came and annulled it: "It is the person who sins that shall die"' (*b. Mak.* 24a).

79.   Even Klaus Koch who denies the very existence of divine retribution still advocates that Ezek. 18 signals a new development within ancient Israel's conception of the relationship between sin and punishment. In reference to Ezek. 18, he states, 'What is new is...the individual limitation of the correspondence between act and destiny. This limitation cannot be found in Israel at any earlier period.' K. Koch, *The Prophets: The Babylonian and Persian Periods* (Philadelphia: Fortress, 1984), II, p. 107.

individualistic way, it is difficult to account for the corporate elements that pervade the general spirit of the oracle itself. Ezekiel is, after all, addressing the community called the House of Israel (vv. 25, 29, 30, 31). In order to elucidate the theology of the oracle more fully we must make sense of both the individualistic and the corporate language it employs, and explore how these two types of language interact with each other.

As stated above, the oracle can be broken into two major blocks, vv. 1-20 and 21-32, which in turn can be further subdivided. My analysis of the chapter will proceed in the following fashion: (1) review of the sub-structure of vv. 1-20; (2) review of the sub-structure of 21-32; (3) explore the relationship between the two halves of the oracle; (4) examine the theological implications of the passage with special attention to the interaction between individualistic and corporate language; (5) finally, address the issue of the relationship between the theology of Ezekiel 18 and the theology of various other oracles in the book of Ezekiel.

Ezekiel 18 is a disputation speech in which Ezekiel objects to the people's use of a proverb that implies the inequity of divine justice. As in Jer. 31.29-30, the proverb found in v. 2 implies that the people believe that God is wrongly punishing them for the sins of their fathers. Like the children in the proverb, they perceive themselves as completely innocent. Ezekiel first offers a theological counter thesis found in v. 4 and then proceeds to substantiate his case by means of a hypothetical case study. This case study consists of three generations of a single family. The first generation, the grandfather, is spoken about in vv. 5-9. He is described as a righteous man, who keeps various positive commandments and does not fail to avoid behavior that is illicit. In turn, he is judged to be righteous and is properly rewarded. This man then gives birth to another man who acts in a wicked manner (vv. 10-13). Indeed, he will die for his behavior. This wicked man who was the son of a righteous man in time gives birth to a son. Having witnessed his father's evil behavior, this son took heed and acted righteously (vv. 14-18). This son will not die on account of his father's behavior. Contrary to what the people expect (v. 19), the sinfulness of the middle generation is not transferred to the son, nor to the grandfather (v. 20).

On analogy to Jer. 31.29-30, when one speaks about the theology of Ezekiel 18, one can mean either the theology that the prophet intended to espouse, or the implications that flow from the language he used. This is not to imply that one can completely separate the idiom from the message, but to argue that sometimes an author will employ certain types of language, or use a particular idiom in order to facilitate his argument. In such instances one must be careful not to let the idiom obscure the primary intention of the argument. The author of Ezekiel 18 utilized language that originally functioned within the legal realm and reapplied it to the theological realm. Ezekiel 18 creatively employs various legal forms and ideas such as the lists of sins and virtues,[80] the judgment formulae which declare one's state and one's recompense,[81] and most importantly the hypothetical construct of the relationship between the three different generations. Verses 1-20 are a theological construction that is spun out from the legislation found in Deut. 24.16. The influence of Deut. 24.16 is so far-reaching that it controls the shape of this oracle and at times leads the author away from the true focus of the oracle. For example, the case of the initial innocent generation discussed in Ezek. 18.5-9 is irrelevant to the argument that Ezekiel is making to his audience. This audience is concerned only with generations two and three in which an innocent generation follows on the heels of a guilty one. Both the proverb in v. 2 and the rhetorical question in v. 19 indicate that this is the way in which the people understand their own predicament. The primary reason for the existence of the first case is because the legislation in Deut. 24.16 is written in an emphatic and inclusive way.[82] Deut. 24.16 begins with the phrase 'the fathers shall not be put to death for the children'. Thus Ezekiel creates a hypothetical drama to explore the theology found in the first two clauses of Deut. 24.16 (the fathers will not be put to death for the children, nor will the

---

80.   The nature of the list is very general. It includes cultic as well as moral issues. Some scholars attempt to derive it from a specific context such as the Decalogue, Deut. 24 (Fishbane), or temple entrance liturgy (Zimmerli). I think that it is fruitful to compare this list to other lists of proper and improper behavior, but there is no clear evidence of literary dependence on an earlier list. For a more extensive discussion of the many scholarly attempts to find the exact *Sitz im Leben* of lists such as this one, see the following: Gammie, *Holiness in Israel*, p. 51; Matties, *Ezekiel 18*, pp. 86-105; M. Weinfeld, 'Instructions for Temple Visitors in the Bible and in Ancient Egypt', *Scripta Hierosolymitana* 28 (1982), pp. 224-50; Zimmerli, *Ezekiel 1*, pp. 374-77.

81.   Matties, *Ezekiel 18*, pp. 65-78.

82.   Greenberg suggests that this supererogatory clause in Deut. 24.16 is 'a rhetorical device for emphasizing the dissociation of generations from each other's guilt'. Greenberg, *Ezekiel, 1–20*, p. 333.

children be put to death for the fathers), by constructing a tri-generational scheme with a wicked middle generation. Although he speaks about the first generation, his interest is not at all focused on the question of a vertical transference of sin from the wicked middle generation back to their fathers. In fact, nowhere in the Hebrew Bible is there an instance in which guilt works backward.

A similar argument can be made about the individualized language found in vv. 1-20. It is highly improbable that this language was employed in order to proclaim a new theology of retribution in which God judged each person as an autonomous entity. The focus all along is on generations of people, not on individuals. It should be remembered that Ezekiel 18 is addressed to the collectivity known as the 'House of Israel' (vv. 25, 29, 30, 31) and it often uses plural forms of address (vv. 2, 3, 19, 25, 29, 30, 31, 32).

> Neither the singular used in the legally styled descriptions of the righteous and wicked in vv. 5-17 nor the selection of behaviors implies a shift in focus from national community to individual souls.[83]

Ezekiel's reference to individuals, rather than to whole generations, can also be attributed to his reliance on Deut. 24.16 which not only controls the layout of Ezekiel 18, but much of its terminology as well.[84] Ezekiel is taking his language from the human legal realm and reapplying this language to the theological problem of divine retribution. But in doing so, he is leaving much of the legal terminology intact. Deut. 24.16 ends by stating that 'each man will be put to death for his own sin', and thus, like most criminal legislation, is oriented toward the individual Israelite. Although Ezekiel 18, like Jer. 31.29-30, changes the *hophal* form of מות reserved for judicial execution to the *qal* form (vv. 4, 18, 20, 21, 24, 26, 28, 31),[85] he continues to maintain the individualistic language.[86] There are good reasons why he constructed his hypothetical case with individuals, rather than with whole generations. Working with individuals would have the effect of simplifying his point and also of making his

---

83. Greenberg, *Ezekiel, 1-20*, p. 341.

84. Greenberg nicely demonstrates that v. 20 is a direct inversion of Deut. 24.16 and that such an inversion is the way the Bible marks direct literary references. Greenberg, *Ezekiel, 1-20*, p. 333.

85. The one exception in 18.13 might be explained by the presence of the formula 'his blood is upon his own head'. Greenberg, 'Some Postulates', pp. 29-30 and *Ezekiel, 1-20*, p. 331.

86. See the discussion in Chapter 6 on Deut. 24.16.

audience fully aware that God was addressing each person in his audience as an individual. Furthermore, as in the case of Jer. 31.29-30, it would create a relationship between the human legal realm and the divine legal realm and thus allow Ezekiel to draw an analogy between the two realms.

That Ezekiel 18 employs a legal idiom that tends to prefer individualistic language should not be allowed to obscure the fundamental argument that Ezekiel is making in 18.1-20. His primary goal is to force this generation to admit that they are suffering for their own misdeeds and not for the misdeeds of their ancestors. It is their failure to admit their guilt that leads them to view God's behavior as unjust and inscrutable. If God's actions are inequitable and inscrutable, there is nothing that the people can do about their situation. To overcome their general malaise, they must be re-empowered. Thus it is essential for them to stop blaming past generations for their predicament and to accept personal responsibility for their current state.

By demonstrating that guilt does not transfer across generations, Ezekiel is trying to persuade the current generation to admit its guilt and take responsibility for the current state of affairs. But at this point in his sermon Ezekiel faces a difficulty. His audience has little incentive to admit their guilt. Rather than empowering the people, such an admission of guilt may, in fact, have the opposite effect. If this generation is being justly punished, then what hope is there for restoration? And if there is no future to look forward to, then there is no incentive to admit one's guilt. Faced with this type of despair, the prophet responded with a brilliant and insightful theological twist that would help enable them to admit their guilt. He announced that righteousness and wickedness are temporal states, and that one could move from righteousness to wickedness or, more importantly, from wickedness to righteousness. If one knows that one can repent and start anew, then it is easier to admit one's guilt. Thus the repentance motif is a carrot that is held out to the people to help them admit that they are guilty and deserving of the punishment that they have received.

The second half of the oracle accomplishes its task in the following way. Verse 21, picking up on the last words in v. 20 about the wicked person who has his wickedness redound upon him, begins by discussing the case of a wicked person who repents of his past actions. It announces that a sinner who repents will live by his righteousness. In fact, his wicked deeds will no longer be reckoned against him (v. 22).

After all, God is more interested in repentance than in punishment (v. 23). Similarly, a righteous person may turn toward evil and doing thus, forfeit all the previous merits that he had earned (v. 24). Although both cases are mentioned it should be noted that the emphasis in vv. 21-29 is on the case of the wicked one who repents and is restored. Not only are more verses directed toward this scenario, but this section begins (vv. 21-23) and ends (vv. 27-28) with this case. This case is emphasized because Ezekiel is addressing a sinful audience that he hopes to motivate to repent. Verses 25 and 29 are important in that they reveal that the two halves of the oracle are closely inter-connected. These two verses show that the people continue to cling to their claim that they are innocent sufferers (v. 2). They appear ready to indict God on charges of unfairness rather than confess their own guilt.[87] By showing both the rigidity of the people's position and the flexibility of God's position, Ezekiel is hoping to move the people to confess and repent. It is not God's way that is unjust, but the people's ways. According to their punishment scheme, not only does punishment transfer across generations, but there appears to be no room for repentance and restoration. Ezekiel challenges and refutes the people's theory of divine retribution by demonstrating that God offers the wicked a chance. God's ways are discernable and just, and furthermore, they leave room for repentance and restoration (vv. 25-29). Thus the motifs of responsibility and repentance are woven together and the repentance motif is utilized both to get the people to admit their guilt and then to motivate them to repent and start anew.[88] Having established not only the guilt of

87.   Here I reject Fishbane's reading that the phrase 'the Lord acts inequitably' found in vv. 25 and 29 signals the fact that the people 'contended that the old proverb of "sour grapes" was more just, for it guaranteed punishment for sins'. Fishbane, *Biblical Interpretation*, pp. 338-39. The issue is not, as Fishbane argues, about the injustice of repentance, but about the injustice of punishing an innocent generation. The audience is not claiming that it is right that the son suffer for the sin of the father, but that this is the way in which the world operates as they have experienced it in their own lives. The phrase about God's arbitrary behavior in vv. 25 and 29 refer back to v. 2 and not to v. 19. Greenberg, *Ezekiel, 1–20*, p. 332.

88.   Here I disagree with Joyce who claims that 'vv. 25 and 29 are concerned essentially not with the possibility of repentance, but rather with the question of whose sins are being being punished in the present disaster'. Joyce, *Divine Initiative*, p. 52. It is true that these verses are urging the nation to accept personal reponsibility for its predicament, but they are employing the idea of repentance as an incentive. Admitting one's guilt is easier if one knows in advance that one can be forgiven and start anew.

this generation but also its ability to repent, Ezekiel calls upon his contemporaries to repent and live (vv. 30-32).

The language used in Ezek. 18.21-32 is an interesting mixture of individualistic legal language that speaks about the individual righteous or wicked persons and their ability to change their disposition and destiny, combined with a strong emphasis upon the fate of the community as a whole. It is evident that the individualistic language used in these verses comes from the terminology in the last clause of Deut. 24.16: 'Every person will be put to death for his own sin'. Verse 20, which is the bridge between the two halves of the oracle, begins by citing Deut. 24.16 in a slightly emended form. The second half of ch. 18 thus continues using the language of Deut. 24.16, which is in the singular, like much of the casuistic legal language found in the Hebrew Bible. Building on the idea that only the guilty one will die for his or her sin, vv. 21-29 explore the possibility of repentance and backsliding. Ezekiel uses the legal language of Deut. 24.16, but redefines what it means for an individual to be in a sinful or non-sinful state. It is the action of the present, rather than of the past, that determines one's spiritual condition.

The fact that Ezekiel 18 is constructed out of individualistic legal language that has been set into a theological context that is pervaded by corporate concerns raises the following question: how should one make sense of both the individualistic and the corporate concerns expressed in Ezekiel 18? To interpret this passage correctly, one must understand both the original context of the legal terminology that Ezekiel employs and the way in which it operates in its new application. This issue is at the heart of the various arguments that surround Ezekiel 18. One's reading of the relationship between the theology of Ezekiel 18 and the theology of various other passages both within Ezekiel and in the biblical corpus in general hinges on exactly how one understands the individualistic language in this passage.

There appear to be three basic ways in which one can attack this complex set of issues. The first line of attack argues that the individualistic language should be seen as an attempt to alter radically the traditional corporate understanding of divine retribution. An excellent example of this type of reading can be found in the following comment by Fishbane:

By narrowing the scope of individual responsibility to each and every separate action, so that repentance for a past transgression can lead to divine acceptance, the prophet has sharpened the issue of individual responsibility in order to spur the Israelites to the realization that they need not wallow (or hide) in notions of inherited guilt. Each person is responsible for his legal-religious life.[89]

Although Fishbane's view has many merits, it also has certain weaknesses. In particular, it exacerbates the tension between Ezekiel 18 and other passages within the book of Ezekiel that appear to accept corporate notions of divine retribution. Fishbane acknowledges these tensions and offers little hope of ever fully understanding them.[90] But one wonders whether he is creating more of a tension than suggested by the text. In his treatment of the passage he argues for a very strong understanding of the analogy, bordering on identity, between the legal realm and the theological realm.

By juxtaposing Deut. 24.16 and the cases of civil law with his rejection of the proverb, he implies an exegetical analogy: all cases, theological and civil, are alike. There is thus no double standard of justice, individual responsibility being the juridical fact for all transgressions.[91]

By drawing such a close analogy between these two cases, Fishbane increases the individualistic emphasis of Ezekiel 18. But it remains highly dubious that Ezekiel intended to make such an exact analogy. As noted by Joyce, there is not really a precise correspondence between the legal and the theological cases.

---

89. Fishbane, *Biblical Interpretation*, p. 338.

90. 'The remarkable inconsistencies in Ezekiel's oracles raise in an unavoidable way the question of historical authenticity: Could one person have spoken such contradictories? Who, we may ask, is the true Ezekiel? Is he champion of repentance and individual responsibility, or is he the theologian of historical fate and doom? Or is he all these things and perhaps more, speaking the divine word as it came to him at different times and with different emphases? Admittedly, before this theological tangle our modern sensibilities bristle and beg for some consistency—or at least enough factual information to allow for a resolution of the inconsistencies on the basis of social-historical diversity. To some, of course, this need for consistency may seem an unfair criterion by which to judge divine oracles. But if this is so, one must either take the evidence as it stands—together with the radical (and somewhat anarchic) theological implications which are hidden in such a position—or acknowledge that we cannot identify a clear continuity in the thought and ideology of the prophet Ezekiel.' Fishbane, 'Sin and Judgment in the Prophecies of Ezekiel', p. 145.

91. Fishbane, *Biblical Interpretation*, p. 339.

Thus, whilst it would seem to be universally true of legal practice that a man who commits a crime is held responsible, regardless of his former righteousness (cf. vv. 24, 26), the statement that when a wicked man repents his past transgressions will not be held against him (vv. 21-22, 27-28) is more surprising! Despite the legal terminology, it is clear that here we are dealing with a statement about how YHWH himself acts.[92]

It seems that Fishbane's attempt to understand the exegetical relationship between Deut. 24.16 and Ezekiel 18 has led him to overlook the unique ways in which Ezekiel 18 employs Deut. 24.16. By focusing exclusively on the individualistic language, Fishbane has missed the major point of the oracle.

It is unthinkable that Ezekiel is 'narrowing the scope of individual responsibility to each and every separate action'. Ezekiel is not dealing with the question of divine acceptance, which is dependent on the current status of an individual's actions, as Fishbane states. Rather, Ezekiel is seeking to reconstitute a devastated congregation in exile.[93]

The second approach to this problem is to play down the significance of the individualistic language and explain it as primarily an accidental by-product caused by the fact that Ezekiel built his oracle from legal language. The following comment by Joyce illustrates this position:

We conclude, then, that throughout the chapter the unit of responsibility envisaged by Ezekiel is the nation as a whole. In vv. 1-20 it is the present generation of Israel whom the prophet shows to be responsible for the disaster of defeat and exile and in vv. 21ff. it is that same community whom he exhorts to 'turn, and live'. Although the distinction between legal and theological discourse is less rigorously maintained in Ezek. 18.21ff. than in the first part of the chapter, it is again the case that the citing of individuals is due to the legal convention of dealing with particular cases.[94]

It should be noted that Joyce's approach is quite nuanced. He acknowledges that there are individualistic elements in ch. 18 as well as elsewhere in Ezekiel, but he understands these 'to be subordinate to a more collective primary theme, namely the imminent onset of the thorough judgment of the nation'.[95]

While such an interpretive maneuver is effective at mitigating the tension between Ezekiel 18 and other passages that stress corporate

92. Joyce, *Divine Initiative*, p. 54.
93. Matties, *Ezekiel 18*, p. 142.
94. Joyce, *Divine Initiative*, pp. 54-55.
95. Joyce, *Divine Initiative*, p. 76.

aspects of punishment, inasmuch as the tension is more imagined than real, this position also has its weaknesses. Although Joyce does reckon with the existence of the individualistic language, he seems to understate its importance. Note the following comment made by Joyce in the midst of his discussion of the formula 'he is righteous, he will certainly live':

> However, whilst the positive declarations of Ezekiel 18 may quite possibly have their origin in some such 'liturgy of entrance', it is important to recognize that (whatever the specific source of the phrases) this language has now been reapplied to the discussion of a crisis which was inevitably communal and national. To assume that the positive declarations of Ezek. 18.9, 17 may be taken as evidence of an individualistic concern on the part of Ezekiel is to fail to take seriously the reapplication of language which they represent.[96]

Joyce is correct in his assertion that this individualistic legal language has been re-applied to a new context which is pervaded by the theme of communal disaster. But he is overstating his argument when he claims that one cannot take the individualistic language as evidence for a concern with the individual. The primary focus may in fact be communal, but that does not preclude a strong concern for the individual. Just as the general context qualifies the individualistic language and indicates that it is being used in the service of a communal sermon, the individualistic language qualifies the communal elements in certain ways. Joyce's reading of the re-application of various forms of individualistic legal terminology seems to assume that such language is simply vestigial, left over from the borrowed legal forms, and serves little or no purpose in its present context. But Joyce's contention is dubious. If Ezekiel had no intention of speaking about individuals, why did he not change the legal language? Conventions may be strong, but there is evidence that the prophet could change them to fit his purpose. Thus, as discussed earlier, he changed the juridical use of the *hophal* of מות to the *qal*. That Ezekiel maintains this individualistic language strongly suggests that it serves a larger purpose than Joyce proposes. Such language signals an important emphasis upon the individual. It indicates that God addresses the nation through the individuals who make up this nation. Such individualistic language may not indicate an attempt to assert the total moral autonomy of each individual, but it seems very likely that Ezekiel employs it as an attempt to arouse the individuals who compose the larger nation to accept responsibility for the current state of the nation and to realize that

96. Joyce, *Divine Initiative*, p. 47.

each of them has the ability to change his or her ways and again become righteous.

The third position is advocated by Matties, and it falls somewhere between Fishbane's and Joyce's positions. Matties puts forward the intriguing idea that Ezekiel's use of individualistic language in combination with the corporate motifs is part of an attempt to reconstruct the future through a form of social imagination.

> There is no self apart from the moral community, just as there is no community apart from moral selves. The part and the whole are not separable...Ezekiel seeks to reconstruct the 'house of Israel' using the old traditions, but is calling for commitment to a new orientation within the old traditions. In dialogue with the past, Ezekiel seeks to imagine a new reality. That is the function of his individual-community motif. It is not to place religion on a new foundation of individualism, but to create a new interdependence that will create a community of character again.[97]

Matties' reading of Ezekiel 18 manages to strike a balance between the corporate and the individualistic elements in the passage. Furthermore, this type of interpretation, like that offered by Joyce, helps to explain the apparent tension between the individualistic stress of this passage and other passages within Ezekiel that continue to affirm the corporate nature of divine retribution. Rather than viewing Ezekiel 18 as a doctrinal statement that must be in contradiction with other passages that are also doctrinal statements, one comes to recognize that Israelite theology consists of a series of non-systematic episodes that are produced under the influence of various situations. Ezekiel 18 is an attempt to provide encouragement to those who have lost their hope by trying to imagine new ways in which God operates. But it is important to see that Ezekiel 18 is only one form of social imagination about the way in which God acts. It is by no means clear that it is meant to nullify all the other instances in which God is imagined as one who punishes corporately.

In general, I find Matties' reading the most compelling because it makes sense out of both the individualistic and the corporate elements as well as elucidating the relationship between Ezekiel 18's theology and various other theological ideas found elsewhere in Ezekiel. But, while favoring Matties' approach, I recognize that Fishbane's interpretation of the passage does justice to an aspect or level of the text that both Matties and Joyce seem to gloss over. Matties' argument does not

97. Matties, *Ezekiel 18*, pp. 149-50.

acknowledge that, although this passage may never have intended to make a doctrinal change, at some level it does in fact do so. That is, the passage clearly challenges the notion of transferring retribution from a guilty to an innocent generation.[98] This view of divine retribution is opposed to the notion commonly found in the ancient Near East and in the Hebrew Bible, that innocent progeny may suffer for the sins of their ancestors (Num. 14.18; 2 Sam. 12.14).[99] Furthermore, Ezekiel 18 implies that divine punishment is not only totally individualized and thus

---

98. Although at first glance Ezek. 18 seems like an all-out attack on the concept of trans-generational retribution, a closer examination reveals that the complaint in 18.2 does not imply that trans-generational retribution is inherently unjust in all instances. Ezek. 18 does not address the problem of two or three guilty generations who follow each other in a serial order. If a second or third generation was as guilty as its ancestors were, one could argue that ancient Israelites, including those alive in Ezekiel's time, might not object to the idea that a punishment should fall especially hard on the last generation. After all, it had time to learn from previous generations' mistakes and it carried its own guilt as well as its predecessors. There is no evidence that those using the proverb in Ezek. 18.2, nor Ezekiel's response to them is an attempt to reject trans-generational retribution even in instances when all generations are guilty. The proverb and the argument that Ezekiel uses to refute it are focused specifically on the question of an innocent generation that is apparently being punished for something that earlier generations committed. The notion, that a guilty generation may be punished for its own errors and for those that its predecessors committed, is strongly implied in several places in the Hebrew Bible (Exod. 32.34; Lev. 26.39; Jer. 3.25; 16.10-13). For further comment on this idea, see Chapter 2. On the way in which the rabbis elaborated upon it, see Chapter 2, n. 35 above.

99. Note the 'Plague Prayer of Mursilis' in which we find the following: 'It is only too true, however, that the father's sin falls upon the son. So, my father's sin has fallen upon me'. *ANET*, p. 395. Or the 'Instructions for Temple Officials' which state, 'If then, on the other hand, anyone arouses the anger of a god, does the god take revenge on him alone? Does he not take revenge on his wife, his children, his descendants, his kin, his slaves, and his slave-girls, his cattle (and) sheep with his crop and will utterly destroy him'. *ANET*, p. 208. The biblical evidence is not as clear-cut, inasmuch as it is possible that passages such as Exod. 20.5, Num. 14.18 and Deut. 5.9 never intended to endorse trans-generational retribution in cases where the children were innocent. See above for further discussion of these passages. Regardless, there are narrative instances in the Hebrew Bible that describe cases in which sin is transferred across generations to an innocent party (2 Sam. 12.14). It should be noted that Ezek. 20.23 affirms the concept of trans-generational retribution regardless of the innocence or guilt of the later generation. Even as late as Jn 9.2 we find the principle of trans-generational retribution assumed by most people, and it is not clear whether Jesus is here presented as denying its validity in general, or only in this specific case.

does not spread across a single generation from guilty to innocent people, but also implies that each individual is unaffected by his or her past deeds. Albeit, this is not the major thrust of the oracle, but at some level these ideas are present. Clearly these ideas conflict with other, more corporate ideas of retribution found in the book of Ezekiel[100] and in the Hebrew Bible.

Several important questions arise from the above-mentioned observations. First of all, one must ask what led Ezekiel[101] in ch. 18 to reject the standard view of divine retribution found throughout the Hebrew Bible and also found within other places in the book of Ezekiel? Why does he argue against trans-generational retribution when the contemporary generation is innocent, and against any form of intra-generational merit or debit?

It is possible to argue that the theology of Ezekiel 18 is in tension with other aspects of the book because later tradents produced this particular chapter and interpolated their ideas into an older text. But this explanation is used too readily on any text that appears to be awkward or

---

100. There are passages in Ezekiel such as 9.5-6 and 21.8-9 that affirm intra-generational punishment. (By this I mean cases in which the innocent may suffer along with their guilty contemporaries.) Ezek. 14.12-23 is a passage that is germane to this discussion, but unfortunately of little help because it is a *crux interpretum*. It is unclear whether Ezek. 14.12-20 is a rejection of intra-generational retribution, because it deals with a person and his children who are currently alive, or trans-generational retribution, because it is about the fact that merit cannot be transferred between a father and his children. I am inclined to view it as the former rather than the latter. But the passage contains additional problems because vv. 21-23 state that in the case of Jerusalem guilty survivors will escape punishment, thus showing that reality does not follow Ezekiel's theological schema which he proposes in ch. 14. Greenberg argues that vv. 21-23 should not be read as a post-exilic attempt to square prophecy with reality because such an inconsistency is normal in prophetic speech (Jer. 44.27-28). Although it is difficult to know if vv. 21-23 are a late exilic addition, I concur with Greenberg that when vv. 21-23 inform us that some survive, it is not to affirm their innocence, but their guilt. Greenberg, *Ezekiel, 1–20*, pp. 256-63. Whether one accepts Greenberg's wholistic reading, or views vv. 21-23 as a late addition, it is clear that the principal of strict and exact retribution laid out in 14.12-20 is violated in vv. 21-23.

101. Even if we say that this is a post-exilic addition written by someone other than Ezekiel, we are still left with the difficulty of explaining why someone who witnessed the destruction of Jerusalem would argue that the punishment was completely exact. It is hard to believe that anyone witnessing such a catastrophe would claim that all were equally guilty, that no one suffered innocently, and that no guilty people escaped punishment (Ezek. 9.6; 14.22; 21.8-9).

difficult. I find little evidence to sustain this line of argument in Ezekiel 18. Even in cases in which there is compelling evidence of late editorial activity, scholars are still obligated to take the final form of the text seriously and not simply to sidestep the hermeneutical task by dissolving the text into various strata. The most fruitful way to explain the anomalous view of divine retribution found in Ezekiel 18 is to challenge the idea that a prophet must espouse a consistent theological viewpoint over the course of his career. There are understandable reasons for which a prophet might contradict himself. These include the fact that prophets are prone to speak in exaggerated and metaphorical ways, frequently describing situations in terms of sharp contrasts. The prophetic corpus is filled with oracles of hope and of doom that employ contrasting images such as light and darkness, salvation and ruin, peace and war, and faithfulness versus betrayal. Although such images are quite poetic and thus speak to our imagination, they rarely, if ever, are true to the complexities of life.[102] One should also be aware that the prophets were not systematic theologians and that they tailored their oracles to specific situations and therefore their messages were bound to vary from situation to situation. And finally one might ponder the question of whether teaching people about the way in which God operates in the world inherently involves the use of contradiction.[103]

I am arguing that Ezekiel found himself with an audience of obstinately self-righteous people and therefore was compelled to force his audience to view differently the way that God operates in relation to humans. This model of divine retribution and forgiveness is constructed to fit the needs of the moment.

> Using the concept of individual responsibility, Ezekiel has broken through the conventional theory of a divine retribution prolonged through succeeding generations. He does so by insisting that the justice of God in dealing with the nation cannot be less than the justice that is recognized in matters of

---

102. An excellent discussion of the various ways in which prophets make use of rhetorical devices is to be found in Miller, *Sin and Judgment*. Also see M.H. Lichtenstein, 'The Poetry of Poetic Justice: A Comparative Study in Biblical Imagery', *JANESCU* 5 (1973), pp. 255-65.

103. Note the way in which Maimonides, in his introduction to *The Guide of the Perplexed*, explains that certain types of contradictions are necessary in order to teach obscure philosophical and/or theological matters. M. Maimonides, *The Guide of the Perplexed* (trans. S. Pines; Chicago: University of Chicago Press, 1969), pp. 17-20.

the individual. He thus stands in the great prophetic tradition, in which *the attributes of God are brought to clearer expression in the process of coping with a particular situation.*[104]

Ezekiel's argument in ch. 18 does not automatically preclude the possibility that on other days, faced with a different audience and a new situation, Ezekiel might have presented another model of divine retribution and forgiveness.[105] Theologians often affirm two premises that are in contradiction with each other, and they label this affirmation of contradictory notions with the rather benign term paradox.[106]

Having reviewed the theology of the passage we have come to see that the issue is clouded because there are various levels on which one can read the text. Each of the three interpreters discussed is reading a different level of the text. Fishbane is reading the text as an inner-biblical exegesis that is aimed at re-writing the theology of divine retribution. Joyce is reading the text as a speech that is directed at the community, which for various reasons has preserved certain forms of individualistic language. Matties is reading the text as a form of social imagination which is intended to help the individual re-create the community of the future. Although I believe that Matties' reading is the most comprehensive, in that it reckons with both the individualistic and communal elements in the text, I do acknowledge, with Fishbane, that the text does in fact challenge certain corporate ideas of divine retribution. But this challenge should not be read as an unconditional rejection of the older corporate conceptions of divine retribution, or as an attempt to replace these older ideas with a new individualism. This prophetic challenge is not a doctrinal statement, but a form of theological exploration. As such, its stress on the individual and its challenge to the ideas of trans- and intra-generational retribution do not signal a fading of the importance of the community as a whole. Furthermore, rather than replacing the older corporate ideas, this text serves to qualify them. It gives us new ways in which one can understand how it is that God might deal with people.

104. Lindars, 'Ezekiel and Individual Responsibility', p. 464. Emphasis is mine.
105. 1 Sam. 15 contains a similar problem in that it both affirms that God changes his mind (vv. 11 and 35) and also denies it (v. 29).
106. A classic example of the way a religion might openly affirm two mutually exclusive theories about the way in which the world operates is: 'Everything is foreseen [by God], yet freewill is granted; the world is ruled with grace, and yet all is according to the number of [man's] deeds (*m. Ab.* 3.19).

> The seeming unrealism of this view of a collective guilt compounded of innumerable individual guilts, each to be requited, is nevertheless thoroughly understandable as a serious effort by the prophet to combine the predominant collective guilt theory with a sharp re-emphasis and heightening of an equally ancient belief in individual responsibility. It is not that Ezekiel first introduces 'individualism' but rather that he reasserts individual guilt in company with collective guilt as two ways of seeing the same truth.[107]

My analysis of Ezekiel 18 may be summarized as follows.

1. Ezekiel 18 is primarily an attempt to get the whole generation to admit its guilt (vv. 1-20) and to offer this same generation the power to free themselves from their guilt through repentance (vv. 21-32).

2. The individualistic language found in Ezekiel 18 comes from Deut. 24.16. This individualistic language should not be understood as either the sole focus of the oracle or as totally irrelevant. Such language should be seen as an attempt to appeal to and motivate the individual members who together make up the community of Israel.

3. Although the focus of Ezekiel's oracle is to speak words of hope and encouragement to a people who are currently in despair, rather than to make a doctrinal statement about retribution, nevertheless, it should be recognized that this oracle presents a new and different view of divine retribution. It rejects the notion of trans-generational retribution when the current generation is innocent; it abolishes the idea that a generation could live off its previous merits, or is completely doomed because of its earlier misdeeds; it implies that God judges each individual autonomously, and only on the basis of his or her current disposition.

4. Such theological innovations should be seen as *ad hoc* creations that were not necessarily intended to systematically reject the more usual corporate conceptions of divine retribution. It is very dubious to highlight such an *ad hoc* speech and thus to interpret it as signaling a general shift in Ezekiel's understanding of divine retribution.

5. Ezekiel is not a systematic theologian and thus it is possible for him to have advocated different theological positions on divine retribution at different moments in his prophetic career. At this level, it seems to me that one should just acknowledge that Ezekiel is not systematic; rather he is driven by pastoral necessity.

6. Although Ezekiel 18 is challenging certain ideas of individualized

---

107. N.K. Gottwald, *All the Kingdoms of the Earth* (New York: Harper & Row, 1964), p. 309.

retribution, this passage is not signaling an evolution from older corporate concerns to newer individualistic concerns. Because the theology of divine retribution found in Ezekiel 18 is not a systematic doctrinal statement about how God always operates, one should not read it as an utter rejection of the older, more corporate model of divine retribution. Rather, one should see it as providing a new vision that attempts to challenge and qualify the older corporate ideas. Ultimately, the two conceptions function in a complementary, rather than in a contradictory, fashion.

Chapter 8

THEOLOGICAL CONCLUSIONS

This study has attempted to present a more sympathetic understanding
of various corporate ideas found within the Hebrew Bible as well as a
more nuanced reading of the tension between these corporate ideas and
various passages that emphasize the individual. By doing this, I have
often challenged certain persistent tendencies found within the scholarship on this topic. Although recent scholarship has been more cautious
and nuanced than earlier scholarship in its attempt to grapple with the
both the corporate and the individualized elements within the Hebrew
Bible, even the most recent scholarship is not completely immune from
making certain dubious assertions about the texts examined in this
project.[1] If, as argued throughout this book, corporate ideas are so
prevalent in the Hebrew Bible, why has there been a persistent predilec-
tion to treat them as unusual deviations, or as primitive concepts that
eventually became outmoded?

There is evidence to suggest that the persistent tendency to denigrate
various corporate ideas found in the Hebrew Bible stems from a larger
Enlightenment bias that places greater value upon moral systems that
emphasize the individual over against those that value the community.
This proclivity to stress the atomistic autonomy of the individual has
resulted in the disparagement of other societies, be they earlier or contemporary, that focus less on the rights of the individual and more on

---

1. Note the following comment made in a recent book on the concept of holiness
in the Hebrew Bible: 'Ezekiel 18 should be ranked among those passages of the Old
Testament that receive special attention in a course on biblical ethics'. Gammie,
Holiness in Israel, p. 50. One wonders why Ezek. 18 should receive such an important
place in a class on biblical ethics. The obvious answer is that interpreters who place a
great deal of importance on passages that stress individualism do so precisely because
they believe such passages are indicative of a new and more progressive view of
divine retribution.

the individual's responsibilities to society.[2] Additionally, it has led to a failure to recognize the importance that collective ideas continue to exert even today.[3]

A growing number of recent thinkers have begun to question the success of the modern attempt to construct an individualistic society and have started to re-appropriate older corporate ideas and called for a return to a more communitarian approach to life.[4] The focus of these critiques is the contention that the failure to produce a modern rational approach to ethical issues is a sign that the modern stress upon the individual has severe limitations. Scholars such as Alasdair MacIntyre have argued quite convincingly that this fundamental shift of focus toward the rights of the individual that occurred during the Enlightenment is the direct cause of the current crisis in moral theory. In particular, he demonstrates that many specific terms and ideas utilized by modern philosophers to construct an individualistic moral system have been removed from the larger communal contexts within which they originally functioned. Focusing upon the notion of virtue, he notes that this term has become meaningless because it has been detached from the larger philosophic tradition that helped define it. Once this has occurred, it becomes impossible to mediate between the various competing moral claims made by different groups of people.[5] Furthermore,

2. Note Daube's statement about Abraham's plea for communal merit in Gen. 18: 'The substitution for communal responsibility of communal merit, instead of individual responsibility, is a sign of a certain backwardness in regard to legal methods'. Daube, *Studies in Biblical Law*, p. 160.

3. Even today certain collective ideas, such as social responsibility for the wrongs perpetrated by the larger collective groups to which one belongs, remain important. It is precisely this mentality that resides behind notions such as war reparations or affirmative action programs. For more on the philosophical background behind the modern notions of collective responsibility, see S. Knapp, 'Collective Memory and the Actual Past', *Representations* 26 (Spring 1989), pp. 123-49.

4. Many recent critics have begun to question various aspects of enlightenment thought. The most important philosopher in this area is A. MacIntyre, *After Virtue* (Notre Dame: University of Notre Dame, 2nd edn, 1984). MacIntyre's argument has spilled into various theological discussions, especially those surrounding moral theory and narrative theology. See S. Hauerwas, *A Community of Character* (Notre Dame: University of Notre Dame, 1981), *idem, Naming the Silences* (Grand Rapids: Eerdmans, 1990), and the excellent collection of articles *Why Narrative: Readings in Narrative Theology* (ed. S. Hauerwas and L.G. Jones; Grand Rapids: Eerdmans, 1989).

5. MacIntyre focuses his critique by comparing two recent attempts to use

the problem is exacerbated by our failure to acknowledge that these moral differences cannot be resolved within the current framework.

It is not just that we live too much by a variety and multiplicity of frag-
mented concepts; it is that these are used at one and the same time to
express rival and incompatible social ideals and policies and to furnish us
with a pluralist political rhetoric whose function is to conceal the depth of
our conflicts.[6]

The only way to resolve the modern moral impasse, according to MacIntyre, is to restore the ties between the vocabulary employed within so much modern moral argumentation and the larger philosophic traditions that created and developed this terminology. The concept of virtue only holds meaning as part of a larger tradition that is community oriented. Not only are individual concepts such as virtue part of a larger philosophic tradition, but even the larger systems are themselves part of an ongoing intellectual endeavor. Thus all forms of knowledge are only useful when they are set within a larger narrative framework.[7] And narrative frameworks are created by communities, not by autonomous individuals.

For the story of my life is always embedded in the story of those
communities from which I derive my identity. I am born with a past; and to
try to cut myself off from the past, in the individualist mode, is to deform
my present relationship. The possesion of an historical identity and the
possession of a social identity coincide.[8]

It should be noted that MacIntyre's constructive proposals have received some very heavy criticism. The major difficulty is that people today often have membership in more than one community; thus, allowing a community to define various moral terms may not solve the

Enlightenment ideas in constructing a modern moral theory: R. Nozick, *Anarchy,
State and Utopia* (Oxford: Basil Blackwell, 1974), and J. Rawls, *A Theory of Justice*
(Oxford: Clarendon Press, 1972). He demonstrates quite nicely that these two posi-
tions are both utterly incompatible and that in the current debate one cannot rationally
decide between rights based upon entitlement (Nozick) versus rights based upon need
(Rawls). MacIntyre, *After Virtue*, pp. 244-55. On the way that the idea of absolute
rights has impeded political discourse in America, see M.A. Glendon, *Rights Talk*
(New York: Free Press, 1991).

6. MacIntyre, *After Virtue*, p. 253.

7. Alasdair MacIntyre, 'Epistemological Crises, Dramatic Narrative, and the
Philosophy of Science', *Monist* 60 (October 1977), pp. 453-72.

8. MacIntyre, *After Virtue*, p. 221.

problem of whether a certain community's norms are superior or inferior to another community's norms.[9] In spite of these problems, MacIntyre's critique of Enlightenment moral discourse and his insight that communities mediate the ways in which we think about morality are ideas that have great relevance to this study. By highlighting the various passages in the Bible that focus on more individualized types of retribution, many biblical scholars and theologians are simply following the modern tendency to view justice as primarily a concern of the individual. Behind this rampant focus upon individuals and their rights is the whole notion of a social contract into which autonomous individuals enter voluntarily. This type of thinking excludes 'any account of human community in which the notion of desert in relation to contribution to the common tasks of that community in pursuing shared goods could provide the basis for judgments about virtue and injustice'.[10] This individualistic bias not only distorts the past, but in so doing it obscures our ability to imagine new and different philosophical and theological options that might be made available for the future. 'An adequate sense of tradition manifests itself in a grasp of those future possibilities which the past has made available to the present.'[11] Thus my contention that there has been a systematic distortion in certain streams of biblical scholarship is not of purely historical interest. This distortion has blinded various critics to the fact that the Bible may provide a critique of certain modern assumptions, and furthermore that it may contain ideas that could be used to erect a more rational and coherent intellectual approach to various ethical problems than those options currently in circulation.

In order to expose both the effects of this Enlightenment bias on biblical scholarship and the way in which it has suppressed certain important biblical moral ideas, it will be necessary to compare the moral theology of those passages that stress individual retribution to those that take a more corporate view of retribution. Engaging in this task will require a shift in methodology. In the earlier chapters of this volume, the primary strategy was to clarify the inner-Israelite understanding of

---

9. He has responded to some of this criticism in the postscript to the second edition of *After Virtue*. He has also continued his line of argument in *Whose Justice? Which Rationality?* (Notre Dame: University of Notre Dame Press, 1988). Still many of the same difficulties remain. See F.I. Gamwell, *The Divine Good* (San Francisco: Harper Collins, 1990), pp. 61-84.

10. MacIntyre, *After Virtue*, p. 251.

11. MacIntyre, *After Virtue*, p. 223.

retribution. This task involved elucidating the theological assumptions that animate many of the corporate ideas within Israelite religion, as well as coming to terms with certain textual tendencies that highlight the importance of the individual. This process required careful internal analysis, in order to grasp what many scholars would call the grammar, or conceptual language, of the religious system.[12] This particular method, often referred to as the cultural-linguistic model, is excellent at revealing the internal dynamics of a worldview. Its effectiveness is enhanced precisely because it brackets out evaluative judgments that all too often interfere with a balanced and fair understanding of other peoples' belief systems. But such an approach has its limitations, especially when one is engaged in making evaluative judgments. At some point one may be impelled to compare various religious systems to each other, or be led to compare certain sets of ideas to other sets of ideas found in the same religion. To bracket out these types of questions totally, questions about whether corporate religious notions are rationally or morally as coherent or perceptive as individualistic ideas, is to fail to take these religious ideas seriously.[13]

In order to make some type of evaluation about the theological usefulness of these two sets of ideas, one must test them against certain criteria. To facilitate this task, I have opted to utilize various ideas and methods generated by David Tracy. Tracy suggests that one can test the coherence and validity of a theological system by the three following criteria: it should be appropriate to the tradition to which it claims to speak; it must be true to our common human experience; and it should be logically coherent.[14] With these criteria in mind I will analyze the

12. C. Geertz, 'Religion as a Cultural System', in *The Interpretation of Cultures* (New York: Basic Books, 1973), pp. 87-125. Originally published in M. Banton (ed.), *Anthropological Approaches to the Study of Religion* (London: Tavistock, 1966), pp. 1-46. George Lindbeck, *The Nature of Doctrine* (Philadelphia: Westminster Press, 1984), pp. 112-38.

13. This is one critique levelled at Lindbeck's ideas. See P. Griffiths, 'An Apology for Apologetics', *Faith and Philosophy* 5 (October 1988), pp. 399-420, and D. Tracy, 'The Uneasy Alliance Reconceived: Catholic Theological Method, Modernity, and Postmodernity', *TS* 50 (September 1989), pp. 548-70.

14. These criteria are a rather simplified form of Tracy's argument. Tracy notes that the relationship between common human experience and tradition needs to be articulated through a method of correlation. Furthermore, he notes that tradition must be clarified through historical and hermeneutical enquiry into its classic texts. Finally, it should be noted that my criterion of logical coherence is a simplified form of

theology of divine retribution found in Ezekiel 18, a theology that emphasizes the importance of the individual, and ask whether it is in fact superior to the more standard corporate notions of divine retribution found within the Hebrew Bible.[15] In doing this, it should be noted that it is not my intention to prove that the theology of Ezekiel 18 is inferior to the older corporate notions of divine retribution and thus should be dismissed. Rather, it is my contention that both sets of ideas are important and essential to a proper understanding of the relationship between the individual and the community in ancient Israel. But inasmuch as it is apparent that a good deal of the discussion of various retributional ideas found in the Hebrew Bible has taken place within an Enlightenment framework that tends to favor passages that stress individual over corporate forms of divine retribution, it seems fair to ask if this tendency to view individualized forms of retribution as morally and theologically superior to corporate notions is warranted.

I have argued that Ezekiel 18 announces that God rewards or punishes individuals for their own deeds or misdeeds (Ezek. 18.1-20) and furthermore, that individuals are unconnected to their earlier actions (Ezek. 18.21-32). The only essential factor in God's interaction with Israel is the current spiritual state of each individual to whom Ezekiel is speaking. The first difficulty that one notices with this theology of retribution is that it does not accord with our common human experience. This point is eloquently made by Klaus Koch in his discussion of Ezekiel 18:

> It may seem right and just that each individual alone should bear the fruits of what he does; but none the less, general human experience tells us that children also have to suffer when their parents suffer. The ties between the generations, and collective liability, cannot be entirely abrogated, even in a nation. (We only have to remember, for example, the intensive discussion that went on after 1945 about the collective guilt of all Germans; or today's anxiety about the burdens laid on future generations by our present treatment of the environment.) If we take this everyday experience into account, does not Ezekiel go too far?[16]

Tracy's notion that one must ultimately test the truth-status of the cognitive claims that one asserts. See D. Tracy, *Blessed Rage for Order* (New York: Seabury, 1978), pp. 43-87.

15. Although the discussion will focus primarily on Ezek. 18, many of the same points could be made about the other passages that also indicate a tendency to focus retribution upon the individual.

16. Koch, *The Prophets*, II, p. 108.

Here Koch is only mentioning the intense connection between various individuals in different generations. It seems that the theological difficulty is exacerbated when one goes further, as Ezekiel does in ch.18, and advocates that a person's past deeds will have no effect on his or her current state. This is not to criticize Ezekiel 18 for trying to help the nation to see that there is room for repentance, but to argue that if one takes this theology to its extreme, it becomes unreal.

There are additional theological difficulties with the theology of Ezekiel 18 that fall under the category of appropriateness to the tradition. The idea that the consequences of one's actions can linger and have great effects later in time is very common within the Hebrew Bible and is even spoken of in the book of Ezekiel (Num. 14.26-35; Deut. 4.31; 23.4-7; 25.17-19; 2 Kgs 21.10-15; Ezek. 16.60; 20.23). If one reads Ezekiel 18 as an intentional rejection of this corporate theology, one is forced to acknowledge that the portrait of God in these other passages is primitive and incorrect. If one places too much emphasis on the theology found in Ezekiel 18, one is forced to treat the more prevalent corporate ideas as holdovers from an earlier period. Such a view, as I have argued throughout this book, is quite inaccurate.

But the greatest flaw in the thinking of those who highlight passages like Ezekiel 18 and denigrate the importance of older corporate ideas falls under the rubric of logical coherence. It is presumed that the individualistic theology of Ezekiel 18 is theologically more perceptive than the older corporate theology because it is closer to our own modern notions of justice.[17] But are these individualistic notions in fact theologically more perceptive than those ideas that undergird the older corporate ideas of retribution? While it is true that Ezekiel 18 may be closer to the modern outlook on justice, that does not automatically mean that its message is more theologically profound or perceptive.

The biblical tradition stresses two major aspects of God: justice and mercy. The Bible gives attention to both, but clearly, divine mercy

17. Thus note the language that von Rad employs in his discussion of this text: 'Ezekiel thus disputes the popular thesis of a yawning gulf between act and effect—indeed, in the way in which he speaks of the individual and his life, and not of the generations or of any still wider settings, he shows himself to be even more radical and modern than his querulous contemporaries'. Von Rad, *Old Testament Theology*, I, p. 393.

ultimately triumphs.[18] If this were not so, it is unlikely that humanity would continue to exist (Gen. 8.21; Pss. 51.3; 130.3; Ezek. 20.44). Theologians and biblical scholars who celebrate Ezekiel 18 do so precisely because they believe it proclaims both God's justice and his mercy. According to Ezekiel 18, God is just, inasmuch as he only punishes the guilty and never the innocent; he is merciful inasmuch as he allows even the guilty to repent of their evil behavior. It is the fact that one is judged only in relation to one's current state that makes this text so appealing to modern readers who favor autonomy and individualism.

But before declaring that this theology is obviously an advance over older corporate ideas, let us analyze theologically a biblical text that espouses the traditional mode of divine retribution. The most obvious passage for comparison is Genesis 18, which narrates the fate of Sodom and Gomorrah.[19] When comparing Ezekiel 18 to Genesis 18, one quickly notices that these two passages share many elements and that both contain arguments about divine justice versus divine mercy. But there are differences as well. In Genesis 18 Abraham appears to appeal to God's sense of justice (v. 25), but he in fact is arguing for mercy. He wants a whole city to survive on the merit of a few righteous men.[20] And God accepts Abraham's reasoning as correct in principle, although Abraham fails to produce enough righteous men to merit saving the wicked inhabitants of these two cities. In Ezekiel 18 God looks as though he is being merciful by judging individuals only by their current state. But upon closer scrutiny, one notices that he is judging them by a very strict standard of justice.

> In Ezekiel chap. 18 and 33.1-20 the appeal is to the justice rather than the mercy of God; he judges each strictly in accord with his ways, remembering neither past goodness nor wickedness (18.29; 33.20). Not

18. It should be mentioned that the attributes of God mentioned in Exod. 34.6-7 emphasize mercy over justice.

19. For further discussion of this passages see the following: Blenkinsopp, 'Abraham and the Righteous of Sodom', pp. 119-32; Daube, *Studies in Biblical Law*, pp. 154-60; M. Roshwald, 'A Dialogue Between Man and God', *Scottish Journal of Theology* 42 (1989), pp. 145-65; von Rad, *Old Testament Theology*, II, pp. 394-95.

20. Gen. 18 is germane to our point on both levels. Not only does it stress the triumph of divine mercy over divine justice, but it also ties the concept of divine mercy to the idea that we benefit, as well as suffer, from other peoples' actions. Divine mercy is dependent on the idea of human relationality.

remembering the evil a man has done is not an act of grace, but a principle of measured justice, for God also remembers not the good that a man has done when he turns wicked. This is the law for divine judgement.[21]

It is easy to understand that Ezekiel felt compelled to advocate a strict standard of justice in order to force the people to admit their guilt and to allow them the possibility to repent. Nevertheless, I think that the theology of divine mercy found in Genesis 18, and stated very eloquently in Pss. 25.6-11, 51.3-16, 103.8-14 and 130.3, is a theology that is at least as coherent and perceptive as the theology of exact justice that Ezekiel 18 proclaims. It should be noted that it is this theology of divine mercy, predicated on corporate relationality, that stands behind notions such as God's promise after the flood (Gen. 8.21), Israel's election especially as it relates to the promise to the patriarchs (Deut. 9.4-5), and God's willingness to restore Israel after the exile (Deut. 4.29-31; Jer. 31.31-34; Ezek. 36.22-32). Additionally, the corporate view of divine retribution takes into account the fact that we humans inevitably commit sins and thus depend on not being judged according to our ways (Job 4.12-21; 7.17-21; 1 Kgs 8.46-53; Pss. 51.3-16; 103.8-14 and 130.3). Finally, this theology is consonant with our common human experience, that informs us of exactly how interconnected each one of us is with his or her own past deeds, as well as with the past deeds of those who live with us.

Thus it appears that those who claim that Ezekiel 18 speaks about a more just view of God than do the older corporate ideas may in fact be correct. But a God who is so rigorously just may be less theologically profound than a God who is not always equitable, but errs on the side of mercy (Jon. 4 and Mt. 20.1-16).

If Ezekiel 18 is not theologically superior to the older corporate ideas, then one can ask why the theology of exact justice found in Ezekiel 18 continues to enjoy so much popularity. The only plausible explanation is that although moderns are not opposed to the idea of benefitting from the merits of one's ancestors, or from one's own earlier righteous deeds, the thought of suffering for other peoples' misdeeds is so distasteful that we reject any theology that advocates such a linkage. And we do this, even though this theology of mercy which stresses human relationality is truer to the reality we experience than the standard of strict justice we discover in Ezekiel 18.

The biblical writers were aware that our individuality can only be

---

21. May, 'Individual Responsibility and Retribution', p. 117.

understood in relation to the various collectivities in which we participate and that being human means that we are linked to other people through the consequences of their actions. But this does not mean that the Bible ignores the importance of the individual. In fact, as I have argued throughout this study, the Bible has a very nuanced theology of the relationship between the individual and the community. Rather than playing off the more individualistic passages within the Bible against those that espouse a more corporate view, one can see the way in which these elements qualify and complement each other. Inasmuch as the biblical view of the relationship between the individual and the community takes account of both poles, but places more emphasis upon the community and the individual's responsibility to that community, it can provide a much needed corrective to current ethical thinking that seems to treat society as nothing more than a collection of unrelated individuals who just happen to live together. A more nuanced theology that takes greater account of one's personal responsibilities toward the larger community will be necessary in the attempt to solve many modern issues, inasmuch as they are global issues (economics, environmental protection, the drug problem, energy planning, disease control and eradication, arms control etc.) Acknowledging our responsibility to the larger communities in which we live will not only facilitate solving global issues, but it will create a greater sense of meaning, inasmuch as it will allow individuals to realize that we all share a common narrative. Indeed, it is time that we accepted the fact that we are our 'brothers' keepers'.

Conclusions

1. Many scholars have both downplayed the importance of texts that contain corporate ideas of retribution and highlighted those passages that advocate a more individualized form of divine retribution. Sometimes this has even been described as a chronological development that demonstrates a growth from a less developed to a more developed theology. In this last section I have attempted to explore and call into question the bias that appears to undergird this type of assessment. The proposition that Ezekiel 18 and other passages that question the corporate model of divine recompense are a major theological advance in Israel's understanding of divine retribution is dubious. There is evidence to suggest that the standard of justice found in Ezekiel 18, although highly appealing to our sense of fairness, may in fact be theologically

problematic. It fails to stand up to our common human experience and it assumes that inasmuch as the more corporate view is sometimes inequitable, it is therefore theologically inferior to a more individualized form of divine retribution. Such a view fails to take account of the fact that, while corporate ideas are sometimes less than equitable, they may allow for a greater leeway when it comes to divine forgiveness.

2. Scholars who praise the individualized tendencies within Ezekiel 18 and denigrate corporate ideas seem to be invoking a modern preference for individualism. Recently, certain critics have begun to question the philosophical basis behind the modern stress on the individual. There is a growing body of evidence to suggest that the corporate ideas contained within the Hebrew Bible may provide certain key elements to new theological constructs that would take greater account of the importance of the way in which the individual has communal responsibilities. Such a theology is very necessary at a time when it is becoming apparent that many contemporary problems are communal and even global in nature.

3. Rather than viewing Ezekiel 18 as a superior theology that has come to displace the older corporate ideas, one can affirm the importance of both sets of ideas and come to understand how they qualify and thus complement each other. Such a theology affirms the importance of God's relationship to society and to the individuals who compose that society. This type of theology can empower people inasmuch as they can now see that their actions as individuals are part of a larger narrative framework that belongs to the community as a whole. Not only does this give a greater significance to each individual's personal actions, but it helps guide individuals in the choices they make. They come to realize that they must act not only for their own benefit, but for the greater good of the community in which they function as an individual and from which they derive their life-narrative.

Appendix

RETRIBUTIONAL CHART

Passage	Subject	Type*	Object
Gen. 3	God	Trans	Humanity
Gen. 6	God	Uni	Humanity
Gen. 9	Noah[1]	Trans	Canaan's sons
Gen. 18–19	God	Uni	Sodom
Exod. 7	God	Uni	Egypt[2]
Exod. 20.5	God	Trans	Haters of God
Exod. 32.10	God	Uni	Israel
Exod. 32	God	Uni+Trans[3]	Israel
Lev. 10.6	God	Uni	Israel
Num. 11	God	Uni	Israel
Num. 14.12	God	Uni	Israel
Num. 13	God	Uni	Israel
Num. 16.21	God	Uni	Israel
Num. 17.9	God	Uni	Israel
Num. 25	God	Uni	Israel
Num. 32.14	God	Uni	Israel
Deut. 1.37	God	Uni	Moses
Deut. 3.36	God	Uni	Moses
Deut. 4.21	God	Uni	Moses
Deut. 13.16	People[4]	Uni	Israel's idolaters

* Trans is short for transgenerational and indicates that punishment extends across several generations. Uni is short for uni-generational and means that punishment is limited to a single generation but may spread across that generation to other innocent people. I sometimes refer to Trans as Inter and Uni as Intra.

1. Inasmuch as Noah uses a curse, one might speak of God as participating in this act.

2. Exod. 9.20 indicates that some Egyptians are innocent.

3. Uni because of Exod. 32.20 in which they must drink the water; 32.28 in which they kill 3000 people; 32.35 in which God sent a plague on the people; 33.3 in which God refuses to journey with them; 33.5 in which they must remove their ornaments. Trans because of 32.34.

4. The nation destroys the whole city by divine imperative.

Passage	Subject	Type	Object
Deut. 20.17	People[5]	Uni	7 nations
Deut. 23.4	People	Trans	Ammon+Moab
Josh. 7	People[6]	Uni	Achan's family
Josh. 22.20	God	Uni	Israel
1 Sam. 2.31	God	Trans	Eli's family[7]
1 Sam. 6.19	God	Uni	Men of Beth-Shemesh
1 Sam. 15	People[8]	Uni	Amalek
2 Sam. 12	God	Trans	David's child[9]
2 Sam. 21	Gibeon[10]	Trans	Saul's sons
2 Sam. 24	God	Uni	Israel
1 Kgs 11.12	God	Trans	Solomon's son
1 Kgs 14	God	Trans	Jeroboam's family[11]
1 Kgs 15.29	Baasha[12]	Trans	Jeroboam's family
1 Kgs 16.34	God[13]	Trans	Hiel's sons
1 Kgs 17.18	God[14]	Trans	Widow of Zarephath
1 Kgs 21.29	God	Trans	Ahab's sons
2 Kgs 1	God[15]	Uni	Fifties
2 Kgs 5.27	God[16]	Trans	Gehazi's family
2 Kgs 9.26	Ahab	Trans	Naboth's sons
2 Kgs 20.16	God[17]	Trans	Hezekiah's sons
2 Kgs 21.9	God	Trans	All Judah[18]

5.   The nation destroys these peoples by divine command.

6.   The nation executes the culprit by divine imperative.

7.   This punishment may extend to all Israel who lost the battle at Aphek.

8.   The people destroy the Amalekites by divine command. Note Deut. 25.17.

9.   There are multiple punishments here and some are against David himself. These include uni- and trans- generational elements. 2 Sam 12.10 says the sword will never leave David's house, and v. 11 talks about events that will transpire while he is alive.

10.   This case involves multiple people. David hands over Saul's sons because God has put a famine in the land due to Saul's bloodguilt or the Gibeonites failure to bless the land (21.3).

11.   This is a complex case in which his son dies but it is not clear that this is a punishment because at least he receives a proper funeral (1 Kgs 14.13).

12.   Baasha here acts in accordance with God's word proclaimed by Ahijah in ch. 14.

13.   Partially Joshua in that he swore an oath to this effect in Josh. 6.26.

14.   It is partially Elijah whose holiness brings the woman's sin to God's attention.

15.   By Elijah's word.

16.   By Elisha's word.

17.   By means of the Babylonian king.

18.   Also note 2 Kgs 23.26ff.

BIBLIOGRAPHY

Adamiak, R., *Justice and History in the Old Testament* (Cleveland: John T. Zubal Inc., 1982).

Ahlström, G.W., *Royal Administration and National Religion in Ancient Palestine* (Studies in the History of the Ancient Near East, 1; Leiden: Brill, 1982).

Anderson, G.A., *Sacrifices and Offerings in Ancient Israel* (Atlanta: Scholars Press, 1987).

Barr, J., *The Semantics of Biblical Language* (Oxford: Oxford University Press, 1961; repr.; London: SCM Press, 1987).

Barton, J., 'Natural Law and Poetic Justice in the Old Testament', *JTS* NS 30 (April 1979), pp. 1-14.

Begg, C.T., 'The Function of Josh 7,1-8,29 in the Deuteronomistic History', *Bib* 67 (1986), pp. 320-33.

Ben Zvi, E., 'Who Wrote the Speech of Rabshakeh and When?', *JBL* 109 (Spring 1990), pp. 79-92.

Bin-Nun, S.R., 'Formulas from Royal Records of Israel and of Judah', *VT* 18 (October 1968), pp. 414-32.

Blenkinsopp, J., *Gibeon and Israel* (Cambridge: Cambridge University Press, 1972).

—*Prophecy and Canon* (Notre Dame: University of Notre Dame Press, 1977).

—'Abraham and the Righteous of Sodom', *JJS* 33 (Spring 1982), pp. 119-32.

Boadt, L., *Jeremiah 26–52, Habakkuk, Zephaniah, Nahum* (Old Testament Message, 10; Wilmington, DE: Michael Glazier, 1982).

Boling, R.G., *Joshua* (AB; Garden City, NY: Doubleday, 1982).

Bright, J., *Jeremiah* (AB; Garden City, NY: Doubleday, 1965).

—*A History of Israel* (Philadelphia: Westminster Press, 3rd edn, 1981).

Brock, S.P., 'An Unrecognized Occurence of the Month Name Ziw (2 Sam. XXI 9)', *VT* 23 (January 1973), pp. 100-103.

Brueggemann, W., *Jeremiah 26–52* (International Theological Commentary; Grand Rapids: Eerdmans, 1991).

Buber, M., *Moses* (London: East & West Library, 1946).

Callaway, J.A., 'New Evidence on the Conquest of "AI"', *JBL* 87 (September 1968), pp. 312-20.

Carmichael, C.M., *The Laws of Deuteronomy* (Ithaca, NY: Cornell University Press), 1974.

—*Law and Narrative in the Bible* (Ithaca, NY: Cornell University Press, 1985).

Carroll, R.P., *The Book of Jeremiah* (OTL; Philadelphia: Westminster Press, 1986).

Causse, A., *Du groupe ethnique à la communauté religieuse: Le problem sociologique de la religion d'Israël* (Paris: Alcan, 1937).

Cazelles, H., 'David's Monarchy and the Gibeonite Claim', *PEQ* 87 (1955), pp. 165-75.

Childs, B.S., *Isaiah and the Assyrian Crisis* (London: SCM Press, 1967).

—*Introduction to the Old Testament as Scripture* (Philadelphia: Fortress Press, 1979).

Clements, R.E., *Abraham and David* (SBT, Second Series 5; Naperville, IL: Allenson, 1967).

—*Jeremiah* (Atlanta: John Knox, 1988).

Coats, G.W., *Rebellion in the Wilderness* (Nashville: Abingdon Press, 1968).

—'The Wilderness Itinerary', *CBQ* 34 (1972), pp. 135-52.

—'The Yahwist as Theologian? A Critical Reflection', *JSOT* 3 (July 1977), pp. 28-32.

Collins, J.J., 'Apocalyptic Eschatology as the Transcendence of Death', *CBQ* 36 (January 1974), pp. 21-43.

—'The Mythology of Holy War in Daniel and the Qumran War Scroll: A Point of Transition in Jewish Apocalyptic', *VT* 25 (July 1975), pp. 596-612.

Cooke, G.A., *The Book of Ezekiel* (ICC; Edinburgh: T. & T. Clark, 1936).

Craigie, P.C., *The Problem of War in the Old Testament* (Grand Rapids: Eerdmans, 1978).

Cross, F.M., *Canaanite Myth and Hebrew Epic* (Cambridge, MA: Harvard University Press, 1973).

Crenshaw, J.L. (ed.), *Theodicy in the Old Testament* (Philadelphia: Fortress Press, 1983).

—'Popular Questioning of the Justice of God in Ancient Israel', *ZAW* 82 (1970), pp. 380-95.

Damrosch, D., *The Narrrative Covenant* (San Francisco: Harper & Row, 1987).

Daube, D., *Studies in Biblical Law* (Cambridge: Cambridge University Press, 1947).

Day, J., *Molech: A God of Human Sacrifice in the Old Testament* (University of Cambridge Oriental Publications, 41; Cambridge: Cambridge University Press, 1989).

Dearman, A. (ed.), *Studies in the Mesha Inscription and Moab* (Archaeology and Biblical Studies, 2; Atlanta: Scholars Press, 1989).

Dentan, R.C., 'The Literary Affinities of Exodus 34,6f.', *VT* 13 (January 1963), pp. 34-51.

Dozeman, T.B., 'Inner-Biblical Interpretation of YHWH's Gracious and Compassionate Character', *JBL* 108 (Summer 1989), pp. 207-23.

Driver, S.R., *Notes on the Hebrew Text of the Books of Samuel* (Oxford: Clarendon Press, 1890).

Durkheim, E., *The Elementary Forms of Religious Life* (trans. J. Swain; New York: The Free Press, 1915).

Dus, J., 'Gibeon—eine Kultstätte des ŠMŠ und die Stadt des benjaminitischen Schicksals', *VT* 10 (1960), pp. 353-74.

Eichrodt, W., *Theology of the Old Testament* (trans. J.A. Baker; 2 vols.; Philadelphia: Westminster, 1961, 1967).

—*Ezekiel* (OTL; Philadelphia: Westminster Press, 1970).

Eilberg-Schwartz, H., *The Savage in Judaism* (Bloomington: Indiana University Press, 1990).

Ellis, E.E., 'Biblical Interpretation in the New Testament Church', in M.J. Mulder (ed.), *Mikra* (Assen: Van Gorcum, 1988), pp. 717-20.

Erlandsson, S., 'The Wrath of YHWH', *TynBul* 23 (1972), pp. 111-16.

Evans-Pritchard, E.E., *Nuer Religion* (New York: Oxford University Press, 1956).
Fahlgren, K., *Ṣedaka, nahestehende und entgegengesetzte Begriffe im Alten Testament* (Uppsala: Almqvist & Wiskell, 1932).
Fensham, F.C., 'The Treaty between Israel and the Gibeonites', *BA* 27 (September 1964), pp. 96-100.
Finkelstein, J.J., *The Ox that Gored* (Transactions of the American Philosophical Society; Philadelphia: Independence Square, 1981).
Fishbane, M., *Biblical Interpretation in Ancient Israel* (Oxford: Clarendon Press, 1985).
—'Sin and Judgment in the Prophecies of Ezekiel', *Int* 38 (April 1984), pp. 131-50.
Fretz, M., 'Herem in the Old Testament: A Critical Reading', in W. Swartley (ed.), *Essays on War and Peace: Bible and Early Church* (Elkhart: Institute of Mennonite Studies, 1986), pp. 7-44.
Friedman, R.E., *The Exile and Biblical Narrative* (HSM, 22; Atlanta: Scholars Press, 1981).
—'From Egypt to Egypt: Dtr 1 and Dtr 2', in Halpern and Levenson (eds.), *Traditions in Transformation*, pp. 167-92.
—*Who Wrote the Bible?* (New York: Summit, 1987).
Gammie, J.G., 'The Theology of Retribution in the Book of Deuteronomy', *CBQ* 32 (1970), pp. 1-12.
—*Holiness in Israel* (Overtures to Biblical Theology; Philadelphia: Fortress Press, 1989).
Gamwell, F.I., *The Divine Good* (San Francisco: Harper Collins, 1990).
Garstang, J., *Joshua Judges* (London: Constable, 1931).
Geertz, C., 'Religion as a Cultural System', in *The Interpretation of Cultures* (New York: Basic Books, 1973). Originally published in M. Banton (ed.), *Anthropological Approaches to the Study of Religion* (London: Tavistock, 1966), pp. 1-46.
Geyer, J.B., 'Ezekiel 18 and a Hittite Treaty of Mursilis II', *JSOT* 12 (May 1979), pp. 31-46.
Gladson, J.A., 'Retributive Paradoxes in Proverbs 10–29' (PhD dissertation, Vanderbilt University, 1978).
Glendon, M.A., *Rights Talk* (New York: Free Press, 1991).
Glück, J.J., 'Merab or Michal', *ZAW* 77 (1965), pp. 72-81.
Gnuse, R., *Heilsgeschichte as a Model for Biblical Theology: The Debate concerning the Uniqueness and Significance of Israel's Worldview* (College Theology Society Studies in Religion, 4; Lanham, MD: University Press of America, 1989).
Gordis, R., 'A Cruel God or None—Is there no other Choice?', *Judaism* 33 (1972), pp. 277-84.
Gordon, R.P., *I & II Samuel* (Library of Biblical Interpretation; Grand Rapids: Zondervan, 1988).
Gottwald, N.K., *All the Kingdoms of the Earth* (New York: Harper & Row, 1964).
—*The Tribes of YHWH* (Maryknoll, NY: Orbis Books, 1979).
Graffy, A., *A Prophet Confronts his People* (AnBib, 104; Rome: Pontifical Biblical Institute, 1984).
Gray, J., 'The Wrath of God in Canaanite and Hebrew Literature', *Journal of the Manchester University Egyptian and Oriental Society* 25 (1947–53), pp. 9-19.
—*I & II Kings* (OTL; Philadelphia: Westminster Press, 1963).

Greenberg, M., 'Herem', in *EncJud*, VIII, cols. 344-49.
—'Some Postulates of Biblical Criminal Law', in M. Haran (ed.), *Yehezkel Kaufmann Jubilee Volume* (Jerusalem: Magnes Press, 1960), pp. 5-8. Reprinted in J. Goldin (ed.), *The Jewish Expression* (New Haven: Yale University Press, 1976), pp. 18-37.
—*Ezekiel, 1–20* (AB; Garden City, NY: Doubleday, 1983).
—'More Reflections on Biblical Criminal Law', *Scripta Hierosolymitana* 31 (1986), pp. 1-17.
Greenspoon, L.J., 'The Origin of the Idea of Resurrection', in Halpern and Levenson (eds.), *Traditions in Transformation*, pp. 247-321.
Griffiths, P., 'An Apology for Apologetics', *Faith and Philosophy* 5 (October 1988), pp. 399-420.
Gruenthaner, M.J., 'The Old Testament and Retribution in this Life', *CBQ* 4 (1942), pp. 101-10.
Gunkel, H., 'What is Left of the Old Testament', in *What Remains of the Old Testament* (trans. A.K. Dallas; New York: Macmillan, 1928).
Haldar, A., 'The Notion of Desert in Sumero-Accadian and West Semitic Religions', *UUÅ* (1950), p. 3.
Halpern, B., *The First Historians* (San Francisco: Harper & Row, 1988).
—'Jerusalem and the Lineages in the Seventh Century BCE: Kinship and the Rise of Individual Moral Liability', in B. Halpern and D. Hobson (eds.), *Law and Ideology in Monarchic Israel* (JSOTSup, 124, Sheffield: JSOT Press, 1991).
Halpern, B., and J.D. Levenson (eds.), *Traditions in Transformation* (Winona Lake, IN: Eisenbrauns, 1981).
Haney, H.M., *The Wrath of God in the Former Prophets* (New York: Vantage, 1960).
Hauerwas, S., *A Community of Character* (Notre Dame: University of Notre Dame Press, 1981).
—*Naming the Silences* (Grand Rapids: Eerdmans, 1990).
Hauerwas, S., and L.G. Jones (eds.), *Why Narrative: Readings in Narrative Theology* (Grand Rapids: Eerdmans, 1989).
Hayes, J.H., and J.M. Miller (eds.), *Israelite and Judean History* (OTL; Philadelphia: Westminster Press, 1977).
Heider, G., *The Cult of Molech* (JSOTSup, 43; Sheffield: JSOT Press, 1985).
Heller, J., 'Die schweigende Sonne', *Communio Viatorum* 9 (1966), pp. 73-79.
Hengel, M., *Crucifixion* (Philadelphia: Fortress Press, 1977).
Hertzberg, H.W., *I & II Samuel* (OTL; London: SCM Press, 1964).
Heschel, A.J., *The Prophets* (New York: Harper & Row, 1962), II.
Hoffner, H.A., Jr, 'Second Millennium Antecedents to the Hebrew Term *'ÔBB'*, *JBL* 86 (December 1967), pp. 385-401.
Holladay, W.L., 'A Fresh Look at "Source B" and "Source C"' in Jeremiah', in L.G. Perdue and B.W. Kovacs (eds.), *A Prophet to the Nations* (Winona Lake, IN: Eisenbrauns, 1984), pp. 213-28.
—*Jeremiah 2* (Hermeneia; Minneapolis: Fortress Press, 1989).
Jackson, B.S., *Theft in Early Jewish Law* (Oxford: Clarendon Press, 1972).
—*Essays in Jewish and Comparative Legal History* (SJLA, 10; Leiden: Brill, 1975).
Jacobs, L., *Religion and the Individual* (Cambridge: Cambridge University Press, 1992).

Johnson, A.R., *The Vitality of the Individual in the Thought of Ancient Israel* (Cardiff: University of Wales Press Board, 1949).

—*The One and the Many in the Israelite Conception of God* (Cardiff: University of Wales Press Board, 2nd edn, 1961).

Johnson, E., 'אָנֵף', in *TDOT*, I, pp. 348-60.

Jones, G.H., '"Holy War" or "YHWH War"?', *VT* 25 (July 1975), pp. 642-58.

Joyce, P., 'The Individual and the Community', in J. Rogerson (ed.), *Beginning Old Testament Study* (Philadelphia: Westminster Press, 1982), pp. 75-89.

—*Divine Initiative and Human Response in Ezekiel* (JSOTSup, 51; Sheffield: JSOT Press, 1989).

Kadushin, M., *The Theology of Seder Eliahu* (New York: Bloch, 1932).

Kaminsky, J., Review of R. Gnuse, *Heilsgeschichte as a Model for Biblical Theology: The Debate Concerning the Uniqueness and Significance of Israel's Worldview*, *JR* 71 (April 1991), pp. 255-56.

Kang, S.M., *Divine War in the Old Testament and in the Ancient Near East* (BZAW, 177; Berlin: de Gruyter, 1989).

Kapelrud, A.S., 'God as Destroyer in the Preaching of Amos and in the Ancient Near East', *JBL* 71 (1952), pp. 33-38.

—'King and Fertility: A Discussion of II Sam. 21:1-14', *Norsk Teologisk Tidsskrift* 56 (1955), pp. 113-22.

Kaufmann, Y., *The Religion of Israel* (trans. M. Greenberg; Chicago: University of Chicago Press, 1960; New York: Schocken Books, 1972).

Kimbrough, S.T., Jr, *Israelite Religion in Sociological Perspective* (Studies in Oriental Religions, 4; Wiesbaden: Otto Harrassowitz, 1978).

Klein, R.W., *Textual Criticism of the Old Testament* (Philadelphia: Fortress Press, 1974).

—*Ezekiel: The Prophet and his Message* (Studies on Personalities of the Old Testament; Columbia: University of South Carolina Press, 1988).

Knapp, S., 'Collective Memory and the Actual Past', *Representations* 26 (Spring 1989), pp. 123-49.

Knoppers, G.N., *Two Nations under God: The Deuteronomistic History of Solomon and the Dual Monarchies* (2 vols.; HSM, 52-53; Atlanta: Scholars Press, 1993, 1994).

Knox, B., 'The Oldest Dead White European Males', *The New Republic* (25 May 1992), pp. 27-35.

Koch, K., 'Gibt es ein Vergeltungsdogma im Alten Testament?', *ZTK* 52 (1955), pp. 1-42. This article was later translated (by T.H. Trapp) and partially reprinted as 'Is there a Doctrine of Retribution in the Old Testament?', in J.L. Crenshaw (ed.), *Theodicy in the Old Testament* (Philadelphia: Fortress Press, 1983), pp. 57-87.

—'Der Spruch "Sein Blut bleibe auf seinem Haupt" und die israelitische Auffassung vom vergossenen Blut', *VT* 12 (1962), pp. 396-416.

—*The Growth of the Biblical Tradition* (trans. S.M. Cupitt; New York: Charles Scribner's Sons, 1969).

—*Um das Prinzip der Vergeltung in Religion und Recht des Alten Testaments* (Darmstadt: Wissenschaftliche Buchgesellschaft, 1972).

—*The Prophets: The Babylonian and Persian Periods* (2 vols.; Philadelphia: Fortress Press, 1983, 1984).

Kosmala, H., 'His Blood on us and on our Children', *ASTI* 7 (1970), pp. 94-126.

Lattey, C., 'Vicarious Solidarity in the Old Testament', *VT* 1 (October 1951), pp. 267-74.

Levenson, J.D., 'Who Inserted the Book of the Torah?', *HTR* 68 (July 1975), pp. 203-33.

—*Theology of the Program of Restoration of Ezekiel 40–48* (HSM, 10; Atlanta: Scholars Press, 1976).

—'The Davidic Covenant and its Modern Interpreters', *CBQ* 41 (1979), pp. 205-19.

—'From Temple to Synagogue: 1 Kings 8', in Halpern and Levenson (eds.), *Traditions in Transformation*, pp. 143-66.

—'The Temple and the World', *JR* 64 (July 1984), pp. 275-98.

—'The Last Four Verses in Kings', *JBL* 103 (September 1984), pp. 353-61.

—*Sinai and Zion* (New Voices in Biblical Studies; Minneapolis: Winston, 1985).

—*Creation and the Persistence of Evil* (San Francisco: Harper & Row, 1988).

—'Cataclysm, Survival, and Regeneration in the Hebrew Bible', in D. Landes (ed.), *Confronting Omnicide: Jewish Reflections on Weapons of Mass Destruction* (Northvale, NJ: Jason Aronson, 1991), pp. 49-56.

—*The Death and Resurrection of the Beloved Son* (New Haven: Yale Unievrsity Press, 1993).

Levine, B.A., *In the Presence of the Lord* (SJLA, 5; Leiden: Brill, 1974).

Levinson, B.M., 'Calum M. Carmichael's Approach to the Laws of Deuteronomy', *HTR* 83 (July 1990), pp. 227-57.

—'The Human Voice in Divine Revelation: The Problem of Authority in Biblical Law', in M.A. Williams, C. Cox and M.S. Jaffee (eds.), *Innovation in Religious Traditions* (Berlin: de Gruyter, 1992), pp. 35-71.

Lewis, B., *History Remembered, Recovered, Invented* (Princeton: Princeton University Press, 1975; repr., New York: Simon & Schuster, 1987).

Lichtenstein, M.H., 'The Poetry of Poetic Justice: A Comparative Study in Biblical Imagery', *JANESCU* 5 (1973), pp. 255-65.

Lindars, B., 'Ezekiel and Individual Responsibility', *VT* 15 (October 1965), pp. 452-67.

Lindbeck, G., *The Nature of Doctrine* (Philadelphia: Westminster Press, 1984).

Lindblom, J., *Prophecy in Ancient Israel* (Philadelphia: Fortress Press, 1962).

Lindström, F., *God and the Origin of Evil* (ConBOT, 21; Lund: Gleerup, 1983).

Lohfink, N., 'Der Bundesschluss im Land Moab', *BZ* 6 (1962), pp. 32-56.

—'חָרַם', in *TDOT*, V, pp. 180-99.

Ludwig, T.M., 'The Shape of Hope: Jeremiah's Book of Consolation', *CTM* 39 (September 1968), pp. 526-41.

Lukes, S., 'Some Problems about Rationality', in B. Wilson (ed.), *Rationality* (Oxford: Basil Blackwell, 1974), pp. 194-213.

MacIntyre, A., 'Epistemological Crises, Dramatic Narrative, and the Philosophy of Science', *Monist* 60 (October 1977), pp. 453-72.

—*After Virtue* (Notre Dame: University of Notre Dame Press, 2nd edn, 1984).

—*Whose Justice? Which Rationality?* (Notre Dame Press: University of Notre Dame Press, 1988).

Mackenzie, M.M., *Plato on Punishment* (Berkeley: University of California Press, 1981).

Maimonides, M., *The Guide of the Perplexed* (trans. S. Pines; Chicago: University of Chicago Press, 1969).

Malamat, A., 'Doctrines of Causality in Hittite and Biblical Historiography: A Parallel', *VT* 5 (1955), pp. 1-12.

—'The Ban in Mari and in the Bible', in *Proceedings of the Ninth Meeting of 'Die Ou-Testamentiese Werkgemeenskap in Suid-Afrika'* (Stellenbosch: University of Stellenbosch Press, 1966), pp. 40-49.

Marmorstein, A., *The Doctrine of Merits in Old Rabbinical Literature* (New York: Ktav, 1968 [1920]).

Matties, G., *Ezekiel 18 and the Rhetoric of Moral Discourse* (SBLDS, 126; Atlanta: Scholars Press, 1990).

May, H.G., 'Individual Responsibility and Retribution', *HUCA* 32 (1961), pp. 107-20.

Mayes, A.D.H., *Deuteronomy* (NCB; Grand Rapids: Eerdmans, 1981).

McCarter, P.K., *II Samuel* (AB; New York: Doubleday, 1984).

McCarthy, D.J., 'The Wrath of YHWH and the Structural Unity of the Deuteronomistic History', in *Institution and Narrative* (AnBib, 108; Rome: Biblical Institute Press, 1985). Originally published in J.L. Crenshaw and J.T. Willis (eds.), *Essays in Old Testament Ethics: J.Philip Hyatt, In Memoriam* (New York: Ktav, 1974), pp. 97-110.

Meeks, W., *The Moral World of the First Christians* (Philadelphia: Westminster Press, 1986).

Melinek, A., 'The Doctrine of Reward and Punishment in Biblical and Early Rabbinic Writings', in H.J. Zimmels, J. Rabbinowitz and I. Feinstein (eds.), *Essays Presented to Chief Rabbi Israel Brodie on the Occasion of his Seventieth Birthday* (London: Soncino, 1967), pp. 275-90.

Mendenhall, G.E., 'The Census Lists of Numbers 1 and 26', *JBL* 77 (1958), pp. 52-66.

—'The Relation of the Individual to Political Society in Ancient Israel', in J.M. Meyers (ed.), *Biblical Studies in Memory of H.C. Alleman* (Locust Valley, NY: J.J. Augustin, 1960), pp. 89-108.

—*The Tenth Generation* (Baltimore: The Johns Hopkins University Press, 1973).

Meyers, C., 'The Roots of Restriction: Women in Early Israel', *BA* 41 (1978), pp. 91-103.

Milgrom, J., *Cult and Conscience* (SJLA, 18; Leiden: Brill, 1976).

—'The Paradox of the Red Cow', *VT* 31 (January 1981), pp. 62-72.

—*Studies in Cultic Theology and Terminology* (SJLA, 36; Leiden: Brill, 1983).

—*Numbers* (The JPS Torah Commentary; Philadelphia: The Jewish Publication Society, 1990).

—*Leviticus 1–16* (AB; New York: Doubleday, 1991).

Miller, P.D., *The Divine Warrior in Early Israel* (HSM, 5; Cambridge, MA: Harvard University Press, 1973).

—*Sin and Judgment in the Prophets* (SBLMS; Chico, CA: Scholars Press, 1982).

Muffs, Y., 'Reflections on Prophetic Prayer in the Bible', *Eretz-Israel* 14 (1978), pp. 48-54 [Heb.].

—'Who Will Stand in the Breach?: A Study of Prophetic Intercession', in *Love and Joy* (New York: Jewish Theological Seminary of America, 1992).

Nelson, R.D., *The Double Redaction of the Deuteronomistic History* (JSOTSup, 18; Sheffield: JSOT Press, 1981).

Neusner, J., *The Idea of Purity in Ancient Judaism* (SJLA, 1; Leiden: Brill, 1973).

Newman, L.I., *The Hasidic Anthology* (New York: Charles Scribner's Sons, 1934).

Nicholson, E.W., *Deuteronomy and Tradition* (Oxford: Basil Blackwell, 1967).

—*Preaching to the Exiles* (Oxford: Basil Blackwell, 1970).

—*God and his People* (Oxford: Clarendon Press, 1986).

Niditch, S., *War in the Hebrew Bible* (New York: Oxford University Press, 1993).

Noth, M., *Das Buch Josua* (HAT; Tübingen: Mohr, 1953).

—*Numbers: A Commentary* (trans. J.S. Bowden; OTL; Philadelphia: Westminster Press, 1968).

—*A History of the Pentateuchal Traditions* (trans. B. Anderson; Englewood-Cliffs, NJ: Prentice–Hall, 1972).

—*The Deuteronomistic History* (JSOTSup, 15; Sheffield: JSOT Press, 1981).

Nozick, R., *Anarchy, State and Utopia* (Oxford: Basil Blackwell, 1974).

O'Brien, M.A., *The Deuteronomistic History Hypothesis: A Reassassment* (OBO, 92; Göttingen: Vandenhoeck & Ruprecht, 1989).

Olson, D.T., *The Death of the Old and the Birth of the New* (Chico, CA: Scholars Press, 1985).

Otto, R., *The Idea of the Holy* (repr.; trans. J.W. Harvey; London: Oxford University Press, 1980 [1923]).

Patai, R., 'The Control of Rain in Ancient Palestine', *HUCA* 14 (1939), pp. 267-68.

Pax, E., 'Studien zum Vergeltungsproblem der Psalmen', *SBFLA* 11 (1960), pp. 56-112.

Pedersen, J., *Israel: Its Life and Culture* (4 vols.; London: Oxford University Press, 1926, 1940).

Phillips, A., *Ancient Israel's Criminal Law: A New Approach to the Decalogue* (Oxford: Basil Blackwell, 1970).

Porter, J.R., 'The Interpretation of 2 Samuel VI and Psalm CXXII', *JTS* NS 5 (1954), pp. 161-73.

—'The Legal Aspects of the Concept of "Corporate Personality" in the Old Testament', *VT* 15 (1965), pp. 361-80.

Provan, I.W., *Hezekiah and the Books of Kings* (BZAW, 172; Berlin: de Gruyter, 1988).

Rad, G. von, *Old Testament Theology* (trans. D.M.G. Stalker; 2 vols.; New York: Harper & Row, 1962, 1965).

—*Deuteronomy* (trans. D. Barton; OTL; Philadelphia: Westminster Press, 1966).

—*Holy War in Ancient Israel* (trans. M.J. Dawn; Grand Rapids: Eerdmans, 1991).

Raitt, T.M., *A Theology of Exile* (Philadelphia: Fortress Press, 1977).

Rankin, O.S., *Israel's Wisdom Literature* (New York: Schocken Books, 1969).

Rawls, J., *A Theory of Justice* (Oxford: Clarendon Press, 1972).

Rendtorff, R., 'The "Yahwist" as Theologian? The Dilemma of Pentateuchal Criticism', *JSOT* 3 (July 1977), pp. 2-10.

Reventlow, H.G., 'Sein Blut komme über sein Haupt', *VT* 10 (1960), pp. 311-27.

Riemann, P.A., 'Desert and Return to Desert in the Pre-Exilic Prophets' (PhD dissertation, Harvard University, 1964).

Ringgren, H., *Israelite Religion* (trans. D.E. Green; Philadelphia: Fortress Press, 1966).

Robinson, H.W., *The Christian Doctrine of Man* (Edinburgh: T. & T. Clark, 1911).

—'The Hebrew Conception of Corporate Personality', in *Corporate Personality in Ancient Israel* (Philadelphia: Fortress Press, rev. edn, 1980), pp. 25-44.

200   *Corporate Responsibility in the Hebrew Bible*

Originally published in P. Volz, F. Stummer and J. Hempel (eds.), *Werden und Wesen des Alten Testaments: Vorträge gehalten auf der Internationalen Tagung alttestamentlicher Forscher zu Göttingen vom 4.-10. September 1935* (BZAW, 66; Berlin: Töpelmann, 1936), pp. 49-62.

Rogerson, J.W., 'The Hebrew Conception of Corporate Personality: A Re-Examination', *JTS* NS 21 (April 1970), pp. 1-16.

—'The Old Testament View of Nature: Some Preliminary Questions', *OTS* 20 (Leiden: Brill, 1977), pp. 67-84.

Roshwald, M., 'A Dialogue between Man and God', *SJT* 42 (1989), pp. 145-65.

Rowley, H.H., *The Faith of Israel* (London: SCM Press, 1956).

Russell, D.S., *The Method and Message of Jewish Apocalyptic 200 BC–AD 100* (Philadelphia: Fortress Press, 1964).

Sakenfeld, K.D., *The Meaning of Ḥesed in the Hebrew Bible* (HSM, 17; Missoula, MT: Scholars Press, 1978).

—'Ezekiel 18:25-32', *Int* 32 (July 1978), pp. 295-300.

Scharbert, J., 'Formgeschichte und Exegese von Ex 34,6f. und seiner Parallelen', *Bib* 38 (1957), pp. 130-50.

Schechter, S., *Aspects of Rabbinic Theology* (New York: Schocken Books, 1961 [1909]).

Schoneveld, J., 'Jeremiah 31:29,30', *VT* 13 (July 1963), pp. 339-41.

Schwager, R., *Must there be Scapegoats?* (trans. M. Assad; San Francisco: Harper & Row, 1987).

Seitz, C.R., *Theology in Conflict* (BZAW, 176; Berlin: de Gruyter, 1989).

Sherlock, C., 'The Meaning of ḤRM in the Old Testament', *Colloquium* 14 (1982), pp. 13-24.

Smend, R., *YHWH War and Tribal Confederation* (trans. M.G. Rogers; Nashville: Abingdon Press, 1970).

Smith, H.P., *The Books of Samuel* (ICC; New York: Charles Scribner's Sons, 1904).

Smith, J.Z., *Map is not Territory* (SJLA, 23; Leiden: Brill, 1978).

Smith, M., 'A Note on Burning Babies', *JAOS* 95 (1975), pp. 477-79.

—*Palestinian Parties and Politics that Shaped the Old Testament* (London: SCM Press, 2nd edn, 1987).

Snaith, N.H., review of A.R. Johnson, *The One and the Many in the Israelite Conception of God*, *JTS* 44 (1943), pp. 81-84.

Soggin, J.A., *Joshua* (OTL; Philadelphia: Westminster Press, 1972).

—*Introduction to the Old Testament* (trans. J. Bowden; Louisville: Westminster/John Knox, 3rd edn, 1989).

Stager, L., 'The Archaeology of the Family in Ancient Israel', *BASOR* 260 (Fall 1985), pp. 1-35.

Stern, P.D., *The Biblical Ḥerem* (BJS, 211; Atlanta: Scholars Press, 1991).

Sutcliffe, E.F., *Providence and Suffering in the Old and New Testaments* (London: Nelson, 1953).

Talmon, S., 'The "Desert Motif" in the Bible and Qumran Literature', in A. Altmann (ed.), *Biblical Motifs, Origins and Transformations* (Cambridge, MA: Harvard University Press, 1966).

Ten, C.L., *Crime, Guilt, and Punishment* (Oxford: Clarendon Press, 1987).

Thiselton, A., 'The Supposed Power of Words in Biblical Writings', *JTS* NS 25 (October 1974), pp. 283-99.

Toorn, K., van der, *Sin and Sanction in Israel and Mesopotamia* (Studia Semitica Neerlandica; Assen: Van Gorcum, 1985).

Towner, W.S., *How God Deals with Evil* (Philadelphia: Westminster Press, 1976).

Tracy, D., *Blessed Rage for Order* (New York: Seabury, 1978).

—'The Uneasy Alliance Reconceived: Catholic Theological Method, Modernity, and Postmodernity', *TS* 50 (September 1989), pp. 548-70.

Tunyogi, A.C., *The Rebellions of Israel* (Richmond, VA: John Knox, 1969).

—'The Rebellions of Israel', *JBL* 81 (1982), pp. 385-90.

Tur-Sinai, N.H., 'The Ark of God at Beit Shemesh (1 Sam. 6) and Pereṣ 'Uzzah (2 Sam. VI; 1 Chron. XIII)', *VT* 1 (October 1951), pp. 275-86.

Urbach, E.E., *The Sages* (trans. I. Abrahams; Cambridge, MA: Harvard University Press, 1987).

VanderKam, J.C., 'Davidic Complicity in the Deaths of Abner and Eshbaal', *JBL* 99 (December 1980), pp. 521-39.

Vaux, R. de, *Ancient Israel: Its Life and Institutions* (New York: McGraw-Hill, 1965).

—*The Early History of Israel* (trans. D. Smith; Philadelphia: Westminster Press, 1978).

Volz, P., *Das Dämonische in YHWH* (Sammlung gemeinverständlicher Vorträge und Schriften aus dem Gebiet der Theologie und Religionsgeschichte, 110; Tübingen: Mohr [Paul Siebeck], 1924).

Vries, S.J. de, 'The Origin of the Murmuring Tradition', *JBL* 87 (1968), pp. 51-58.

Weinfeld, M., 'The Period of the Conquest and the Judges as Seen by the Earlier and Later Sources', *VT* 17 (1967), pp. 93-113.

—*Deuteronomy and the Deuteronomic School* (New York: Oxford University Press, 1971).

—'Pentateuch', in *EncJud*, XIII, cols. 232-63.

—'The Worship of Molech and of the Queen of Heaven and its Background', *UF* 4 (1972), pp. 133-54.

—'Instructions for Temple Visitors in the Bible and in Ancient Egypt', in *Scripta Hierosolymitana* 28 (1982), pp. 224-50.

—*Deuteronomy 1-11* (AB; New York: Doubleday, 1991).

Weippert, M., '"Heiliger Krieg" in Israel und Assyrien: Kritische Anmerkungen zu Gerhard von Rads Konzept des "heiligen Krieges im alten Israel"', *ZAW* 84 (1972), pp. 460-93.

Wenham, G.J., 'The Deuteronomic Theology of the Book of Joshua', *JBL* 90 (1971), pp. 140-48.

Westermann, C., *The Living Psalms* (trans. J.R. Porter; Grand Rapids: Eerdmans, 1989).

Whitelam, K.W., *The Just King* (JSOTSup, 12; Sheffield: JSOT Press, 1979).

Wolff, H.W., *Hosea* (trans. G. Stansell; Hermeneia; Philadelphia: Fortress Press, 1974).

Yerushalmi, Y.H., *Zakhor: Jewish History and Jewish Memory* (New York: Schocken Books, 1989).

Zevit, Z., 'Archaeological and Literary Stratigraphy in Joshua 7-8', *BASOR* 251 (Summer 1983), pp. 23-35.

Zimmerli, W., *Ezekiel 1* (trans. R.E. Clements; Hermeneia; Philadelphia: Fortress Press, 1979).

INDEXES

INDEX OF REFERENCES

HEBREW BIBLE

INDEX OF AUTHORS

JOURNAL FOR THE STUDY OF THE OLD TESTAMENT

Supplement Series